"If you read your company's HR strategy, would you be able to tell which company it was written for? Does it demonstrate a deep understanding of how talent can be deployed to drive real competitive advantage for your company? Are you focused on the war for talent or on winning the war with talent? This terrific new book challenges many of the prevailing assumptions in organizations and provides a road map for HR and operating leaders to work together in a new way to drive strategic success. It merits a place at the top of your reading list."

—Lucien Alziari, Senior Vice President,
Human Resources, Avon Products

"What struck me about this book was not the workforce so much, or even strategic talent—which I really agree with—but its observations on the profound impact that line managers have on the creation of firm culture and the attraction, growth, and development of strategic talent. HR is important. But if you are going to build great organizations, you need to do it with great leaders. Great leaders attract great talent. They grow great talent and retain great talent. Clearly, we hold leadership accountable for financial material, information, and time as resources. But we must also hold them accountable for the workforces they manage. They shape culture, they shape talent. Unless they do it well, they are not the leaders we need for the future."

—Jürgen Brokatzky-Geiger,
Head of Human Resources, Novartis

"*The Differentiated Workforce* is a book for everyone to read. It provides the necessary insight and path forward to apply the principles of talent leadership in any and all types of organizations. It truly captures the essence of how strategic talent leadership can be the differentiator, and one can assume these ideas will be emphasized by positive organizational outcomes. Everyone who reads this book can only be enlightened by its importance and application. Truly a book for our time. A masterpiece in the world of human capital leadership."

—Lawrence B. Costello, Managing Director, The Lawrence
Bradford Group, LLC, and former Senior Vice President,
Human Resources, American Standard Companies

At the end of this book, the reader will understand why traditional approaches to aligning people with the firm strategy or valuing jobs in organizations do not work. In fact, the way these relationships are structured at many companies is precisely the problem. Overall, this book will show companies how to leverage their people to create a sustainable competitive advantage that is not easily copied by their competitors. CEOs, line managers, and HR professionals will think differently about how to organize their human assets after reading this book. And employees could use this book to help them identify companies that can leverage their strength and capabilities in the best possible way."

—Boris Groysberg, Associate Professor of Business
Administration, Harvard Business School

"In my almost twenty-five years of professional life, I have read many books—some out of choice and some to keep up-to-date. Very few have the clarity and simplicity of *The Differentiated Workforce* with a thought-action fusion that has such profound implications for business in leveraging its talent in a strategic way. For once, I can gift a book to my colleague business leaders without worrying about the return on their time spent reading it!

This book is likely to be the Global Positioning System of HR strategy. Irrespective of where you are today in your HR strategy, you can find an appropriate route to your intended outcome, if you follow the framework of action it suggests. If this book cannot offer a platform for line and HR managers to effectively play their part in aligning their firm capabilities to their strategy, then perhaps no book will be able to do so."

—Dr. Santrupt B. Misra, Director, Group H.R. & I.T.,
Aditya Birla Management Corporation Ltd.

"This book is all about talent . . . strategic talent. It addresses the need to assess, invest in, reinvest in, or divest the talent that really makes a difference—the talent that has a profound impact on the creation of a company's customer and economic value. These issues are clearly articulated in *The Differentiated Workforce*, and a practical road map for how to leverage strategic talent is provided. The roles of HR and hire managers—too often blurred—are brought into sharp focus. This is a must-read."

—Craig Eric Schneier, PhD, Executive
Vice President, Human Resources, Public Affairs
and Communications, Biogen Idec

"Paraphrasing Jim Collins, every manager's number-one problem is talent, but hiring A players is not the solution; hiring the *right* A players is. These authors are the best researchers and writers I know of who truly get it—that HR can no longer be nonaccountable administrators, measuring cost-to-hire and time-to-fill. Those measures get you a lot of C players hired quickly and cheaply!

Following *The HR Scorecard* and *The Workforce Scorecard*, *The Differentiated Workforce* hits the bull's-eye. As the consultant who brought talent differentiation methods to some of the companies mentioned in the book—GE, Honeywell, and the American Heart Association—I'm impressed with how the authors have added what sometimes is a missing link: they provide the conceptual framework and practical examples to be sure that the A players you hire are the *right* A players."

—Brad Smart, President, Smart & Associates, Inc.,
and author of *Topgrading: How Leading Companies
Win by Hiring, Coaching and Keeping the Best People*

"*The Differentiated Workforce* not only drives home the importance of investing in talent but also, most importantly, the competitive advantage that can be gained from disproportionately investing in key players in key positions. An excellent read for senior HR leaders."

—Charles G. Tharp, PhD, President,
National Academy of Human Resources

"Business strategy is interesting. Execution, business performance, and value creation is everything. *The Differentiated Workforce* principles provide a road map and a compelling case to rethink how you manage and develop top talent, define the top value-creating roles in your business, and how you must disproportionately invest in those roles to drive execution and success! A must-read for anyone accountable for growing a business and leading a workforce."

—Garrett Walker, Vice President, Human Resources,
IBM Software Group Sales

The
Differentiated
Workforce

The Differentiated Workforce

Transforming Talent into Strategic Impact

Brian E. Becker
Mark A. Huselid
Richard W. Beatty

Harvard Business Press
Boston, Massachusetts

Printed in the United States of America

13 12 11 10 09   5 4 3 2 1

ISBN: 978-1-4221-0446-0

The paper used in this publication meets the requirements of the American National Standard for Permanence of Paper for Publications and Documents in Libraries and Archives Z39.48-1992.

CONTENTS

FOREWORD

Cash is an important asset. Even in hard times (*especially* in hard times), organizations endeavor mightily to keep the business going without impairing their capital, except as a last resort.

People are also an important asset. How many times have you heard some senior executive make the claim that "our people are our most important asset"? Yet at the first hint of approaching trouble, many organizations' initial reaction is to systematically impair the value of their labor force. For example, despite the self-evident logic of Jack Welch's observation that "in tough times you need training more, not less," the training budget is often the first casualty of any downturn.

Another frequent victim of hard times is the compensation strategy. Most firms seek to practice some version of "pay for performance" and often spend considerable time and money trying to identify and attract the best people, measure and provide feedback about performance, and give superior financial and nonfinancial rewards to the best performers. When times get tough, however, many organizations abandon whatever pay-for-performance practices are in place in favor of across-the-board budget cuts, hiring freezes, and salary increases that do not differentiate on the basis of performance.

At the other extreme, there are a relative handful of organizations that, sometimes of their own volition but more often because of union or civil service requirements, are ready to live and, if necessary, die for the sake of putting people (or at least, people with seniority) first. Unfortunately, though their intentions may be noble, the inability of these organizations to adapt their strategies to changing conditions is inevitably harmful to both the organization and its people. By far the best approach, as this book persuasively argues, is to devise a flexible workforce strategy that is linked to an organization's strategic capabilities, thus rendering it useful for strategy execution. Because it is so responsive to changing circumstances, the workforce strategy can then serve to direct resources to people, jobs, and economic opportunities in a way that maximizes value to both the organization and its members. The authors make the important point that workforce differentiation is not achieved merely by "doing HR" in an unusual way, though they do offer the reader many useful tips in this regard. Among the book's principal contributions is its description of a four-stage framework, backed by many practical examples, of how to devise a workforce strategy for any organization that is in good alignment with the talent requirements of its overall strategy.

Another important contribution of *The Differentiated Workforce* lies in its ability to clarify and simplify the essential ingredients of strategy and the role of strategy in informing organization practice. In some ways, the book reminds me of what we sought to do at Crotonville while I was at GE. By the time I left the company, we had, on average, four requests per workday from organizations seeking to visit, benchmark, or study Crotonville. I recall greeting visiting executives—including CEOs and management committee members of major corporations—by telling them:

> My task this morning is to un-impress you, and I feel confident that I will be successful. You're not going to find out today that we have secret schools from which we recruit or management theories you've never heard about. In GE all we do are the basics, but we do them well and, most important, we make sure that all our organizational practices are connected to each other, and to our strategies.

Our goal at GE was not to overly complicate things but rather, as Jack Welch was fond of saying, to "have the courage to be simple." What Becker, Huselid, and Beatty have done is to take a potentially dense subject and make it clear and comprehensible. To cite just one example: "Firms need to move away from conventional approaches to determining job importance and job worth and toward a model where job value is determined by the strategic capabilities needed to execute strategy. They then need to invest disproportionately in their most strategic positions, ensuring that they place 'A' players in 'A' positions for 'A' customers." They go on to explain, in plain language and without suggesting that the reader spend money he or she probably doesn't have, how this can be done.

However, we all know that it takes more than courage to make complicated things seem simple, so permit me to make one final observation. No small part of the appeal of *The Differentiated Workforce* is that its authors bring to their work an unusual blend of academic rigor and practical advice. Their own careers have been a highly successful blend of research-based articles in the best journals, publications that have significantly contributed to the practice of management, and consultancy to some of the world's most important and interesting corporations. This combination of insight and experience stands the authors in very good stead, and their book significantly benefits from what they have learned along the way.

Steve Kerr
Senior Advisor, Goldman Sachs

PREFACE AND ACKNOWLEDGMENTS

This book is about the central role that workforce strategy plays in the successful execution of your organization's strategy. In our experience, most firms don't really have a workforce *strategy*. They have talent initiatives and broad expressions that "people are their most important asset," and they can usually point to programs that reflect their investments in people. What's missing is the kind of focus—what we call *workforce differentiation*—in these efforts that results in clear and demonstrable strategic impact. To put it bluntly, the problem is that most of these initiatives begin with people, rather than with strategy.

This book puts strategy first using your workforce strategy to drive your organizational strategy. Putting strategy first means making choices that recognize that jobs and roles can differ dramatically in the extent to which they contribute strategically and that the workforce needs to be managed accordingly. Differentiation is not just a feature of a successful workforce strategy; it is *the* most important feature. It requires that you understand where you invest, what jobs you focus on, who is held accountable for workforce success, and how success is measured. This means that developing and executing a workforce strategy is both a business decision *and* an HR decision. As such, the ideas in this book are equally important for line managers and HR professionals.

The approach to workforce strategy described here is practical, research based, and above all, will deliver results. As academics, our research focuses on the relationships among HR, workforce issues, and firm performance. Our research has appeared in the leading academic journals and continues to be some of the most heavily cited work in the field of management. But just as important, we have tested and revised these ideas as part of our consulting and executive education activities. In short, they are "taxi tested."

For more than twenty years, we have tried to transform the way academics and managers think about human resources and workforce management. Our view is that HR—the function and the practice—should have a more significant impact on the fortunes of the organization. HR as a function should be more than an administrative cost center, and HR as a practice should be more than a collection of functional techniques.

When we think of HR transformation, we think of a *broader* role, not just a different role. While traditional roles requiring transactional efficiency, policy compliance, employee relations, and program management skills continue to have value, HR transformation means only one thing to us: the HR function, line managers, and some portion of an organization's HR professionals will be jointly responsible for strategy execution. Measured in terms of the potential impact on firm success, this is without doubt the most important HR role in the twenty-first century.

There are a lot of books, consulting practices, and even academics who use strategic, HR, and workforce in the same sentence. Too often this reminds us of what we like to call "HR alchemy." Traditional operational and administrative activities are simply given a strategic patina. By contrast, our approach is a fundamentally different way to think about the role of HR in your organization and, more broadly, the role of the workforce. As a result, the transformation is not limited to HR professionals; it includes line managers as well. To be successful, a strategic role for HR requires a responsibility for workforce strategy that is shared with line managers.

Acknowledgments

For Brian Becker and Mark Huselid, this is the third book (and the second for Dick Beatty) published by the Harvard Business Press on a continuing theme—how should organizations manage their workforce and HR functions to build a competitive advantage? The book is particularly focused on translating this theme into action. Such an undertaking is possible only with the generous advice and feedback of our colleagues, our students, and our consulting clients. Each provided the different perspectives required to make this project possible.

All of us are deeply indebted to our colleagues at Harvard Business Press, who continue to epitomize the very best and highest levels of professionalism. HBP editors Melinda Merino and Kathleen Carr exhibited remarkable patience and grace with three authors who were consistently behind schedule. Melinda and Kathleen are a constant source of encouragement, support, advice, and ideas. They are the best of the best. We are also grateful to Stephani Finks and Ethan Becker for their contributions to the cover design. Their patience and flexibility were much appreciated. We all wanted a striking design and we got it.

We also all want to acknowledge the critical support provided by our respective academic homes, the School of Management at the State University of New York at Buffalo (UB) and the School of Management and Labor Relations (SMLR) at Rutgers. This support was not only in tangible resources; perhaps more importantly, both institutions encourage scholarship that makes an impact on management practice.

Brian would especially like to thank Professor Nick Everest for his thoughtful feedback and gentle critiques of these ideas. Nick's experience as a senior HR executive and consultant sharpened his thinking and contributed immeasurably to the quality of the final product.

Also, appreciation is indeed deserved to the many students in Rutgers Global Executive Master's in Human Resources Leadership Program who have suffered under the development of these concepts and hopefully found them useful in their attempts to implement them around the globe. Dick and Mark are most grateful for their suggestions, challenges, and patience. Mark would also like to extend a special note of gratitude to the team at the American Heart Association, whose work is highlighted in chapter 7. All the AHA team, but especially Senior Vice President Bill Achenbach, Chief Operating Officer Nancy Brown, and CEO Cass Wheeler, have made a remarkable transformation in that organization, and Mark was privileged to be a part of it. Similarly, Keith Holmes, Randy MacDonald, and Garrett Walker and their team at IBM continue to lead management practice on workforce management, differentiation, and measurement, and we are grateful for their contributions.

Mark and Dick thank academic friends and colleagues at Rutgers, including Paula Caligiuri, Dave Lepak, Steve Director, David Finegold, Susan Jackson, Dave Lepak, Barbara Lee, and Randall Schuler, who make SMLR such an exceptional place to work.

We are all especially grateful to Steve Kerr for providing the foreword to this book. And as a team we would like to thank many professional friends and colleagues who have influenced the thinking and provided the sites where many of the concepts found in this book were developed or implemented. We continue to benefit immensely from a wide variety of clients and colleagues, including Lucien Alziari (Avon), Marcia Avedon (Ingersoll Rand), Laurent Bernard (Steelcase), Ron Bendersky (University of Chicago), Carlo Bertelegni (Telecom Italia Group), Gwendolyn Doden (Boehringer Ingelheim), Ray Carson (Wyeth Healthcare), Ron Cheeley (Schering-Plough), Deb Cohen (SHRM), Larry Costello (American Standard), Scott Crum (ITT Industries), Ken Disken (Lockheed Martin), John Donnelly (Citi), John Erikson (PCC), Peter Fasolo (KKR), Clayton Fitzhugh (Catholic Health East), Mark Gilstrap (American Century), Lou Forbringer (CHI), Steve Grossman (Hoffman-LaRoche), Tom Helfrich (Key Bank), Bill Joyce (Dartmouth), Steve Kirn, Rene Lewin (Wyeth), Sue Meisinger (SHRM), Hallstein Moerk (Nokia), Paul Newton-Syms (Roche Pharmaceuticals), David Nurnberger (Boehringer Ingelheim), Dan Phelan (GlaxoSmithKline), Peter Scarborough (SCHOTT Glass), Natalie Schilling (Alcoa), Craig Schneier (Biogen-Idec), Brad Smart (Smart & Associates, Inc.), Lynn Tetrault (Astra Zeneca), Herb Vallier (Catholic Health Initiatives), Peter Watts (Alpharma), and Roy White (Sony Europe).

Finally, and most significantly, we would like to thank our families for their love, support, and patience. And specifically, Dick would like to thank his grandchildren Grace and Jake for their pride in their grandfather's work whenever they visit a bookstore. Our work is dedicated to them.

CHAPTER 1

Put Strategy, Not People, First

SENIOR MANAGERS and readers of the popular business press are probably familiar with the mantra that *people* are the new source of competitive advantage. Many of these same managers can also offer a compelling rationale for the importance of winning the "war for talent"—as long as the elevator ride is a short one. But despite all the talk about a new strategic emphasis on the workforce, most companies haven't yet capitalized on the opportunity for strategic success that effective workforce management can provide.

Significant investments in attempting to win the war for talent in many organizations and new leadership development programs or an emphasis on becoming an employer of choice often have the look and feel of a strategic workforce initiative. They certainly emphasize the people aspect of the organization and focus on large segments of the workforce or, in the case of leadership initiatives, the traditionally high-value segments. Often, a parallel effort demonstrates the financial contribution of these people initiatives.

However, in our view, it is those very characteristics of breadth and generality that limit the value of workforce strategy for many organizations. While a focus on people issues often reflects a new, different emphasis for managers, what it doesn't necessarily represent is a fundamental change in perspective on the role of workforce strategy. New leadership initiatives, a focus on attracting top talent, or a demonstration of the financial contribution of HR initiatives may all be good business practices and improve operational excellence, but they don't necessarily contribute to strategic success. These initiatives are seldom based on a clear line of sight between workforce success and strategic success. The irony is that building competitive advantage requires the right workforce strategy, but that doesn't mean simply putting people first. It means putting strategy first and developing a workforce that executes that strategy.

Putting strategy first means that the message of this book is as important for senior line managers as for HR professionals. This book is about solving the strategic challenges facing senior line management. Specifically, it is about making senior managers more successful at executing their strategy. For most organizations, that success has an important talent dimension. When it comes to workforce strategy, our approach requires that line managers define success but that HR professionals deliver the solution. This requires a new perspective on workforce strategy for both.

Based on our nearly two decades of academic research and hundreds of consulting engagements and executive education classes, we are persuaded that most organizations, whether profit or nonprofit, lack a truly *strategic* workforce strategy. This book provides both the rationale and the developmental road map that any organization can use to create a workforce strategy, with an emphasis on the word *strategy*. The results will be apparent for both senior line managers and HR professionals and, most important, on the bottom line. The outcomes include:

- Strategy execution will improve and, with it, the likelihood of strategic success.

- Senior managers will follow *strategic* workforce issues as closely as they follow financial issues.

- Line managers and HR professionals will be able to distinguish strategic workforce investments from the latest best-practice fads.

- Workforce investments will be targeted where they create the highest strategic return and will be reduced or eliminated where there is no return.

- Line managers and HR professionals will not have to figure out how to implement vague slogans such as "people are our most important asset," which will be replaced with a specific, actionable *strategic human capital plan.*

- It will be clear when the HR function is providing "administrative efficiency" and when it is providing "strategy management," because what is strategic and what isn't will be clear.

- The HR function's contribution to firm performance will be obvious and measurable.

- The strategic contribution of the workforce will be obvious and measurable.

The Differentiated Workforce

We believe in the need for a fundamental change in the entire approach to workforce strategy. We call this approach a *differentiated* workforce strategy. Just as any good business strategy involves making the right choices and the right investments, the same is true of a workforce strategy. It involves more than investing on the people side of the enterprise, but involves disproportionate investments where you can expect disproportionate returns—those specific jobs and those specific people within jobs that help create strategic success. Few companies admit to using the same corporate strategies that worked in the 1950s, but many organizations seem unable to move beyond 1950s workforce strategies. They may be spending more on people, and the jargon may have changed, but few companies approach their workforce strategy with the same standards and discipline as they do their larger organizational strategy. The strategic *potential* of a workforce strategy to create new wealth has increased dramatically over the past fifty years, but the approach to workforce strategy in most organizations never realizes that potential.

As with most strategic decisions, you have to make choices about your workforce. Differentiation is not just a feature of your workforce strategy; it is *the* most important feature. It will determine where you invest, what jobs you focus on, who is held accountable for workforce success, and how success is measured.

Workforce differentiation is important for strategic success because strategy is concerned with creating competitive advantage—doing things that your customers value in new, different ways. Sustainable competitive advantage is the basis for above-average growth and profitability, relative to competitors. When competitors can easily copy a competitive advantage, those above-average profits erode more quickly. Not only does workforce differentiation have the potential to create strategic value though improved strategy execution, but it is not easily copied by competitors. Indeed, when fully implemented, the strategic focus is so well aligned with an individual firm's strategy that simple imitation has little value to a competitor. (See "A Lesson from *Moneyball*" for an example.)

Workforce differentiation *creates value via the differences in how an organization designs and manages its workforce strategy*. But what kinds of differences are important? We aren't talking about variations in specific HR or workforce practices, though they might result from a differentiated strategy. For example, choosing a particular compensation plan, sourcing channel, or development program is not necessarily a strategic decision. The choice and design of particular practices *follow* from a differentiated workforce strategy; they do not define the strategy.

Differentiation is a choice about how tightly your workforce strategy will be aligned with the talent requirements of your enterprise strategy; it can have several facets. It can occur between organizations, within parts of the same organization, and among employees in a single part of one organization. The most effective and powerful workforce strategy is differentiated along *each* of these facets. How to determine the level of differentiation in your organization is one focus of this book.

What Is Workforce Strategy?

Effective business strategies differentiate your company in ways that your customers value and your competitors cannot easily copy. But to differentiate on the outside, you also need to differentiate on the inside, and the need to differentiate extends to *how* you execute your strategy. Harvard strategy guru Michael Porter highlights this internal focus, emphasizing

A Lesson from *Moneyball*

Major league baseball provides a simple illustration of the distinction between a war *for* talent and a war *with* talent. Consider the lesson of *Moneyball*, the bestseller by Michael Lewis.[a] Every major league baseball team is playing the same "game," but the Oakland A's didn't compete in a "war for talent." Instead, the team developed a differentiated workforce strategy. Other teams treated talent like a commodity with equal value to each team. They bid up the price, and the richer teams ended up with more talent. The A's developed an entirely different strategy for winning games, one in which the team could make unique use of players that other clubs didn't value as highly. For most organizations, the strategic return should emphasize the numerator of the ROI equation (the unique economic value of each position) rather than the denominator (the market price of the position). The opportunity is to achieve *superior* organizational performance with *similar* workforce expenses. The A's turned strategic advantage upside down, attempting to remain highly competitive while investing *much less* in its workforce.

Most organizations have an advantage the A's don't enjoy. The problem for the A's is that its strategy is relatively transparent, and clubs wishing to do so can copy that strategy, as some have. By contrast, the competitive advantage a typical organization gains from a differentiated workforce strategy is much more sustainable. First, it is not easily copied because, rather than following a best practice, it is as unique as the strategic activities that serve as the basis for differentiation. Second, there is little incentive to copy the workforce strategy since it will have little value to a competitor unless the competitor has a similar system of strategic activities with which to align it. In this case, the only best practice is the *differentiation process* that is the foundation of the workforce strategy. Simply knowing the results of this process, which is the more common focus of benchmarking activities, has little strategic value to other organizations.

[a]Michael Lewis, *Moneyball* (New York: Norton, 2003). See also M. A. Huselid and B. E. Becker, "Improving HR's Analytical Literacy: Lessons from *Moneyball*," in *The Future of HR: 50 Thought Leaders Call for Change*, eds. Dave Ulrich, Mike Losey, and Sue Meisinger (New York: John Wiley and Sons, 2005), 278–284.

that strategy is about creating a *unique* set of organizational activities that bring the value proposition to the customer. Those unique activities constitute a firm's strategy execution system, and for many firms the lynchpin of that system should be the workforce strategy.

The problem is that while successful strategy execution calls for a unique set of business processes and activities, when it comes to workforce strategy, for most firms the emphasis is on best practices and "me too" fads. Often, managers are forced to defend departures from industry "best practices," even though the business logic for a more differentiated approach to workforce strategy might be compelling. Perhaps it is the modern version of the old adage, "No one ever got fired for buying IBM." However, in a *Harvard Business Review* article, Eric Bonabeau reminds us that, ". . . the homogenizing nature of best practices can destroy value for corporations, which forget that strategy is, at its heart, all about differentiation."[1] This holds for workforce strategies as well.

Like any strategy, a workforce strategy has two essential elements. The first is the strategic goal. The second is a clear statement of how a company will achieve that strategic goal. Getting the systems, initiatives, and practices right from a strategic perspective begins with getting the goals right. Every workforce strategy should answer two simple questions: How does the workforce contribute to the firm's competitive advantage? How should the workforce be managed to realize that value? In other words, both design and execution are critical.

What do we mean when we say that a workforce strategy should contribute to the firm's competitive advantage? Along with Robert Kaplan, David Norton, and Larry Bossidy, we focus on execution.[2] Some companies' strategic success depends on having the very best talent; they succeed simply because their workforce is more talented than that of their competitors. But what are the implications of a workforce strategy premised on a "war for talent"? Presumably, competition for a relatively fixed pool of talent increases as more firms pursue this competitive advantage. This demand will drive up compensation levels until fewer and fewer firms can afford a given level of talent. Ultimately, without growth in talent supply, the strategic gains of winning deteriorate into a "winner's curse," where higher compensation levels completely erode the value of the organization's hard-won competitive advantage. More fundamentally, a war-for-talent strategy violates the most basic tenet of a successful strategy; namely, it is very easy to copy.

Clearly, you shouldn't ignore talent when thinking about workforce strategy. But instead of thinking in terms of a war for talent, the emphasis should be on a war *with* talent. Talent can be a strategic asset, but like any asset, its value depends on the future returns relative to the costs of acquiring and maintaining that asset. Legal compliance, compensation systems influenced by rank and tenure, concerns for internal equity, and natural aversions to providing tough performance evaluations are just some of the pressures that lead to the perpetuation of relatively undifferentiated workforce strategies. This homogenizing influence is further reinforced by the absence of any obvious way to value and measure the success of a workforce strategy. Some firms understandably turn toward external comparisons and benchmarks to validate workforce decisions because there seems to be no good alternative. However, while benchmarking might provide accessible performance metrics, there is by definition nothing strategic about them.[3] Too many organizations underinvest in high-return (truly strategic) talent and overinvest in nonstrategic talent. The workforce strategy is not appropriately differentiated.

Strategy involves differentiation and value creation; benchmarking involves homogenization, "me too" comparisons, and cost control. But if the corporate strategy is concerned with differentiation and building unique sources of competitive advantage, does it make sense to manage the most important driver of strategy execution as an undifferentiated commodity? Traditional workforce strategies have a natural logic and the powerful appeal of the status quo, but have little to do with managing the strategic role of talent in the organization. Building competitive advantage means that your strategic talent needs to be differentiated in the same way as those unique set of "strategic activities" that truly define your strategy.

The box, "Signs You're Not Differentiating Enough," gives some indicators for determining if your own company has a largely undifferentiated workforce strategy. Not every organization with such a strategy has all these attributes, but these provide a quick diagnostic. Keep them in mind as we develop the differentiated workforce framework in the

Signs You're Not Differentiating Enough

Your organization has the wrong strategic perspective on talent:

- There is no explicit workforce strategy.

- No one can really explain how your company's workforce strategy contributes to the organization's strategic success.

- There is no clear line of sight between value of workforce practice and strategic success.

- The financial conversation with HR largely focuses on controlling its overall budget.

- HR confuses being a business partner with playing a strategic role.

- There is talk of HR "transformation," but never any time for it.

- The value of workforce practices is based on how they compare with external best-practice standards.

- Concerns about some employees feeling "left out" makes it difficult to disproportionately invest in high-value employees.

---

subsequent chapters. As you can see, this strategy involves more than the design of specific workforce practices. The symptoms are apparent when senior line managers and HR professionals discuss talent.

The Stages of Workforce Differentiation

While we believe that optimal strategic alignment and success requires a workforce differentiated along multiple facets, even differentiation on a smaller scale can provide more limited and transitory benefits. Figure 1-1 shows a four-stage framework for thinking about the relationship between differentiation and strategic success.

Your organization has the wrong approach to common workforce practices:

- Poor performance is tolerated, sometimes even in critical roles.

- Employee performance goals seldom have any obvious relationship to the company's strategy.

- Annual compensation changes are not all that different for high performers and low performers.

- Senior line managers are not held accountable for the management of strategic talent.

- Very little development rotation occurs, or else it is provided as a general development opportunity.

- Conversations between HR professionals and line managers largely focus on employee relations, costs and budgets, programs, and staffing decisions.

- When evaluating the financials of a workforce initiative, the focus is largely on the cost.

Source: Adapted from Mark A. Huselid, Brian E. Becker, and Richard W. Beatty, "'A' Players or 'A' Positions? The Strategic Logic of Workforce Management," *Harvard Business Review*, December 2005.

However, we do not intend the notion of stages to represent a journey that begins in stage 1 and culminates in stage 4. The workforce strategy for some organizations might reflect elements from several stages simultaneously. Our purpose in describing these stages of differentiation in detail is to make the choices more explicit than implicit. You will recognize your workforce strategy within the mix of these stages and be able to reflect on whether your current workforce strategy will have the desired strategic impact. This comparison allows us to highlight how the approach in stage 4—the differentiated workforce strategy—can be

FIGURE 1-1

The four stages of workforce differentiation

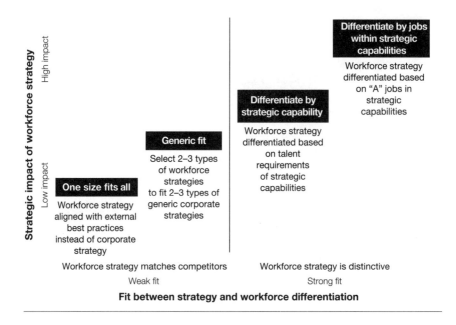

viewed against the workforce strategies we commonly find in practice. So in addition to helping you evaluate the value of your current workforce strategy, the four-stage framework will provide a useful point of reference for where your company is and where it should go.

Company Examples

Where possible, we use company examples to illustrate the difference between our approach and more common practice. The examples enliven the concepts and answer the question, how would that really work in practice? The examples are not, however, intended to validate the effectiveness of a differentiated workforce strategy, and this book is not a collection of the best practices of leading companies. Our goal is to provide the kind of thought leadership that will be considered a best practice, so if you are looking for validation based on a list of prominent companies adopting the exact approach described, you will be disappointed.

Many leading companies have adopted elements of our approach and are well on their way toward a workforce strategy entirely consistent with the one described here. From our experience, the list would include Biogen-Idec, GlaxoSmithKline, General Electric, Roche Pharmaceuticals, IBM, Wyeth, American Century Investments, Colgate-Palmolive, Sony Europe, Honeywell, Cisco, and the American Heart Association. While the specific form of workforce differentiation will no doubt vary across these companies, at its core is a common focus on disproportionately investing in strategic talent. Biogen-Idec Executive Vice President of HR Craig Schneier summarizes this approach from HR's perspective: "We win with talent. The main focus of HR must be great talent, thus advocates for any workforce criteria beyond talent must come from outside HR—the employees' boss or the employees themselves. Employee advocacy is no longer HR's job."

Our examples usually use fictitious company names to give us flexibility to illustrate our points clearly without providing the contextual background and qualifying language a named company would expect. However, the examples are based on actual companies with which we are familiar. We use them to show how their strategies illustrate different stages of workforce differentiation. Sometimes those decisions are wise; sometimes it is clear that another choice would have been more appropriate.

In this chapter, we use a company we call Auto-Aerospace Systems (AA Systems) to illustrate how the perspective on workforce strategy changes for each stage of differentiation. AA Systems is a leading supplier of products and systems to the auto and aerospace industry. The company is the product of a recent multinational merger and now operates in over thirty countries, with annual sales approaching $6 billion. AA Systems is organized into four automotive divisions (braking, electrical, electronic systems, diesels), an automotive aftermarket division, and a separate aerospace division. As a tier one supplier, AA Systems competes with companies like Siemens, Delphi, Visteon, and Bosch.

Each division of AA Systems is led by a managing director with separate profit and loss responsibilities, who in turn reports to a chief operating officer (COO) at a small corporate center. The COO is part of a top management team that includes the CEO, chief financial officer (CFO), senior vice president for planning, and senior vice president for human resources. Within each division, a vice president for HR reports directly to the managing director, with a dotted-line relationship to the corporate senior vice president. There are three corporate HR functions: compensation and benefits, health and safety, and leadership and development (including succession planning).

Low-Impact Differentiation

Although our focus in this book is on stages 3 and 4, we first provide some background information by describing the differentiation at stages 1 and 2.

Stage 1: One Size Fits All

Stage 1 is called "one size fits all" because at its core it is a best-practice workforce strategy. The fundamental implication of this approach is that the workforce contributes to strategic success similarly in every organization, so the best way to improve strategic performance is to identify HR best practices in the industry and then adopt them as quickly as possible. In principle, a best-practices approach to workforce strategy suggests very little differentiation: you are simply mimicking the perceived industry leaders. As a result, there is no basis for a sustainable competitive advantage because workforce differentiation disappears as more firms approach the best-practice standard. Said another way, you can't standardize your way to greatness.

In practice, there is often an *early mover* advantage. The first firms adopting best practices can gain a competitive advantage, which erodes surprisingly slowly. Our research suggests that even at stage 1, there is emergent differentiation in what we call *high-performance work systems* (HPWS). Workforce management systems have a number of component parts, including equity concerns, efficiency, employee relations, legal compliance, labor relations, health and safety, and workforce performance. The distinguishing feature of an HPWS is the focus on delivering workforce performance. Other dimensions of workforce management may or may not be given equal priority, but there is no compromise on performance.

In an HPWS, each element of the HR *system* is focused on delivering superior performance. For example, while cycle time and costs for new hires might be tracked, a hiring and selection function that fails to deliver outstanding workforce performance is never acceptable. Whatever form the selection process takes, a high-performance focus requires that the process is effective at delivering the kind of performance the organization requires. Similarly, compensation and rewards policies would have significant links between pay and performance. Pay practices that give top performers increases similar to those of low performers are not tolerated. In short, the design of each element of the HR system poses potential trade-offs between performance and nonperformance considerations. A high-performance system more often than not resolves those choices in favor of the performance dimension.

The relationship between HPWS and firm performance is one of the most well-documented in academic research. Our work is based on data collected from more than three thousand firms over more than ten years. We measured the extent to which firms use validated selection practices, invest in training and development, regularly and effectively measure employee performance, and link pay and rewards to performance. We then linked this data with measures of operational (productivity) and financial (profitability and shareholder value) performance so that we could study the impact of current HR management systems on future firm performance. There was nothing particularly new or exotic about any of the practices we studied, even when we began this program of research nearly twenty years ago. All these practices had substantial support in the academic literature as drivers of workforce performance, and we suspect that few HR professionals would have disagreed.

What was new about our research was the notion that when you considered all these decisions as a system, rather than as a set of individual practices, the system would have a financially significant impact on firm performance. After more than a decade of research and five national surveys, our results were remarkably similar. Firms with *high-performance* HR systems were more successful on every measure of financial performance, including market value, return on assets, and employee productivity (sales per employee). For example, firms with a 35 percent higher value on our HPWS measure had a 10 percent to 15 percent higher market value to book value, after controlling for the effects of differences in industry, growth rates, R&D investments, employment, and unionization.

Figure 1-2 shows how the returns to a high-performance work system might compound over time. It tracks the ratio of market value to book value of two groups of firms from the early 1990s through 2004. The first set of firms (high) was above average on the HPWS measure, and the second set (low) was below average. Beginning from a relatively small difference in market value to book value in 1991, the difference grew to more than 35 percent in thirteen years. What's important in this simple comparison is not so much the difference in firm performance in any particular year, but the higher sustained performance by firms using high-performance work systems.

FIGURE 1-2

Firms with above-average HPWS scores significantly outperformed low HPWS firms (1991–2004)

These differences are both economically and statistically significant: high HPWS firms averaged $90,566 greater sales per employee and $348,817 greater market value per employee from 1991–2004.

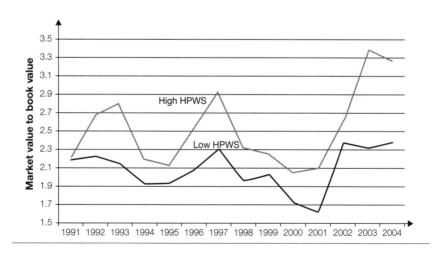

Our earlier research illustrates two important points about a differentiated workforce strategy. First, differentiation matters, even in its simplest form. The pattern of the results tells us, perhaps unsurprisingly, that organizations vary in their emphasis on performance when designing their overall HR systems. We suspect that if you reflect on your own workforce management system, there is more than one element that in some way compromises workforce performance. But when organizations do emphasize workforce performance in designing HR systems, when they differentiate on that basis, there are significant financial returns.

In the early 1990s, the notion that a firm's HR system could significantly contribute to a firm's financial success, other than through cost control, was met with considerable skepticism. Today, however, the idea that HR and workforce strategy more generally has the *potential* to drive firm performance is no longer controversial. Senior management, consultants, and academics recognize that the value of traditional sources of competitive advantage has eroded, and by implication, there is an increasingly important role for intangibles in general and human capital in particular. More than a decade of academic research demonstrates these effects in a wide range of national and international firms.

The second point is that differentiation matters because the differences are remarkably persistent. In theory, a best practice should result in very little differentiation among firms, because most firms will want to adopt such a practice. As more and more firms adopt the same workforce strategy, all firms will improve what Michael Porter calls "operational excellence," but their similarity precludes any sustained competitive advantage. Achieving the best practice simply represents the price of admission. Ignoring that practice, however, can leave an organization at a competitive disadvantage.

While we might have expected to find considerable differentiation in the 1990s before the support for high-performance work systems had been well established, much differentiation continues more than a decade later. Jeffrey Pfeffer and Robert I. Sutton documented the barriers to knowledge diffusion more broadly in *The Knowing-Doing Gap*.[4] This slow diffusion is by no means limited to management issues, however. Leading health care research takes seventeen years before it is widely adopted, while financial innovations can take more than twenty years to be implemented at the retail level.[5]

The lesson here is not so much the reasons for the slow diffusion of high-performance HR systems, but rather that slow diffusion continues to represent a significant opportunity. HR professionals and line managers must recognize this opportunity and not wait for the safety and comfort of simply following a practice widely adopted by their competitors. You wouldn't deny the benefits of a diversified investment portfolio, simply because the majority of individual investors might not be diversified. Similarly, the validity of a workforce strategy depends on the business case for that strategy, not on the number of other firms that have adopted the same approach.

The Limits of Stage 1 at AA Systems

AA Systems, a global competitor, prides itself on identifying and implementing the best practices from around the world. Leading gurus routinely share their thinking with senior executives, and senior HR professionals regularly visit companies that exemplify best practices in a wide range of countries. If you examined any of AA Systems' workforce practices individually, you would conclude that they represented the current thinking in HR and workforce management. But what is the strategic impact of these decisions?

AA Systems implemented best practices in compensation and focused these policies disproportionately on what it considered to be its most important workforce segment. These corporate assets (managing directors and direct reports), however, were determined by their position in the organizational hierarchy rather than by their strategic role. Positions below this level, but strategically important, were excluded, and all positions within this level, even those less strategically important, were included. Therefore, while AA Systems developed a very sophisticated bonus system to align pay and performance, it applied the same bonus system equally for all senior managers. It was focused on people, not strategy. The results were counterproductive. Managers in units with no strategic role earned 200 percent bonuses and happily wheeled into the parking lot with their new BMWs and Mercedes.

Managers in units identified as the future growth engines of the company, who often struggled to build their business, got no bonuses, and even ended up with their bonus bank in the red.

The company applied a similar one-size-fits-all approach to severance agreements. Acquisitions were the source of much of AA Systems' growth, and the loss of experienced managers in these acquired assets was a significant risk. Therefore, AA Systems developed a generous policy of severance payments in return for noncompete agreements. Once again, it didn't differentiate among managers who were really in strategic roles and those that weren't. AA Systems overspent to secure noncompete agreements from many managers who did not represent a competitive loss if they were to leave. AA Systems no doubt benefited from its best-practice workforce system, but it left a lot of value on the table.

Stage 2: Generic Fit

Why should an organization differentiate its workforce strategy and, perhaps more important, *how* should it differentiate its strategy? A best-practice approach (stage 1) to workforce strategy is often the first one that HR professionals and line managers begin to think about in a strategic HR transformation. But, as we saw, a best-practice approach to workforce strategy is fundamentally not a differentiating approach and thus makes a limited contribution to building *sustainable* competitive advantage. Limited differentiation is a direct result of the tenuous fit between the general approach of a best practice and the unique requirements of a particular organization's strategy.

Stages 2 through 4 move beyond best practice and begin to create a tighter fit between the workforce strategy and the firm's business strategy. Despite the fact that adopting a *high-performance* work system continues to offer meaningful improvements in firm performance, limiting the focus of your workforce strategy to a best-practice approach represents significant missed opportunities. First, the returns to the HPWS approach will likely fall in the coming years as more firms continue to adopt it. Second, and more important, even when a best-practice approach yields a positive return, failing to implement higher level stages of workforce differentiation means failing to create the sources of *sustainable* competitive advantage that will generate important financial returns in the long run. The unrealized gains from more systematic differentiation are still available.

Truly differentiating your workforce strategy requires that you begin in the same way that you differentiate your corporate strategy. It means fitting the differentiation of your workforce strategy to the level of differentiation in your corporate or business strategy. We call stage 2 "generic fit" or "generic business strategy meets generic workforce strategy" because it describes a simple alignment between the two. There is more than one best-practice or high-performance work system. In theory, there would be an appropriate workforce strategy for each corporate strategy.

Richard Beatty and Craig Schneier describe three different workforce strategies designed to fit with the three strategic choices proposed by Treacy and Wiersema—operational excellence, product leadership, and customer intimacy.[6] Beatty and Schneier have developed a set of workforce attributes appropriate for each of the three strategies, focusing largely on the workforce mind-sets required to produce the strategically appropriate behaviors. For example, the core workforce mind-set for a product innovation strategy includes higher tolerance for risk taking and long-term focus. The desirable strategic workforce behaviors include problem solving and a high degree of creative behavior.

At stage 2, a company begins the process of workforce differentiation, but only scratches the surface. We don't disagree with the proposed link between these workforce attributes and strategic foci; we just don't think this level of differentiation makes much progress toward developing the workforce as a source of competitive advantage. First, it's as easy to imitate as stage 1. Stage 2 differentiation doesn't leave much doubt about how to proceed (or how to imitate). For organizations with the same corporate strategy (like customer intimacy), it's one size fits all.

Second, stage 2 doesn't provide the systems-level fit with strategy that realizes the full strategic potential of a differentiated workforce. If you have started down the path of differentiation with stage 2, it is a little like driving to California from New York and choosing to stop in Columbus. You are certainly headed in the right direction, but you also have a long road ahead of you. Recall Eric Bonabeau's caution that strategic homogeneity destroys value. Realizing the full strategic potential of a workforce strategy means fully exploiting the opportunities for differentiation. But differentiate how?

The quote often attributed to Thomas Edison, "vision without execution is hallucination," is especially true of strategic vision. We believe that strategies fail less for the quality of their vision and more for the quality of their execution. A workforce strategy contributes to strategic success only when it enhances an organization's ability to execute. The magnitude of the contribution is directly proportional to the fit between the workforce strategy and the activities that execute the firm's strategy. Increasing the differentiation of the workforce strategy is how an organization increases the fit between that strategy and the execution of its business strategy. Stages 1 and 2 provide only a loose fit between the two strategies. The link between the two may not be a hallucination, but as senior HR executives who have tried to explain HR's strategic significance to top management know, the line of sight is blurred at best.

Stage 2 Limits at AA Systems

AA Systems exemplifies how an organization without a well-developed workforce strategy can simultaneously have several stages of differentiation in its de facto strategy. It shows the difficulty in categorizing a workforce strategy based on a larger corporate strategy. AA Systems did not fit neatly into any of the three Treacy-Wiersema strategy types. Its customers, worldwide leaders in the auto and aerospace industries, relentlessly pressured AA Systems to cut costs. As a result, there was a strong emphasis on operational excellence, and much of the performance management system was increasingly focused on efficiency, accountability, quality, and results to reinforce the appropriate mindset for operational excellence. At the same time, profitable growth was possible only through significant attention to product development. The success of the product development strategy turned on the quality of cross-functional collaboration. The workforce strategy also reflected this focus. AA Systems invested heavily in development programs designed to improve the systems-thinking competencies of the workforce. More important, it hired three hundred new systems engineers to upgrade and support the entire systems capability.

On both the operational excellence and production innovation dimensions, AA Systems implicitly differentiated its workforce strategy on the mind-set required to support those larger strategic emphases. This reflected more strategic focus than just an effort to implement the latest best practices. But, had AA Systems done all it could to drive strategic success through its workforce strategy? How should the workforce system reconcile the competing implications of a focus on operational excellence and customer intimacy? A more differentiated workforce strategy would have helped to resolve those questions.

High-Impact Differentiation

While differentiation at stages 1 and 2 may provide a positive strategic return, our focus in this book is on stages 3 and 4. Extending the idea of workforce differentiation follows directly from the requirements of business strategy and provides a clear line of sight between the workforce strategy and measures of strategic success. Improving the fit between the workforce strategy and the activities that drive strategic success is the first and only design benchmark. The focus is not on what workforce strategies look like in other firms; it's on what the strategy in your organization requires. The only best practice is the process by which you create a differentiated workforce strategy. There is no right or wrong result, only a right or wrong approach to developing that strategy.

Just as strategic differentiation reduces external homogeneity, internal homogeneity should also become much less important. Successful strategy execution requires that the workforce strategy make a disproportionate investment in certain jobs and employees. Talent is important, but being able to recognize and manage *strategic talent* is more important. The fact that the workforce strategy disproportionately focuses on certain jobs and employees is not necessarily a departure for some organizations. What will be new, however, is the *basis* for that differentiation. A successful workforce strategy requires that the basis for differentiation among jobs and employees follows directly from the strategic role of those jobs, and that the *degree* of differentiation is sufficient to execute the firm's strategy. While there is no amount of differentiation that can be described as a best practice, most organizations need to add more differentiation to their current workforce strategy.

Stage 3: Differentiate by Strategic Capability

The whole notion of competing on intangibles, the strategic value of human capital, and the war for talent often creates excitement and interest among executives for new approaches to managing the workforce, based on the considerable promise of gains in financial performance. But the line of sight between workforce strategy and strategic success is typically so indirect that figuring out how to get from here to there is difficult. As a result, we believe that focusing on how the workforce drives strategy execution and making that link concrete and actionable is the best way to put these ideas into practice.

First, we have to shorten the line of sight. There are few instances when a selection system, a performance management system, or leadership development program has a direct impact on the firm's bottom line, making it hard to see how those decisions translate into strategic success. The more likely and plausible explanation is that the entire HR system and workforce strategy can together deliver performance at key points in the strategic value chain, which ultimately drives firm performance. The workforce strategy seldom has a *direct* influence on firm performance, but instead operates indirectly through its impact on strategy execution. Ask ten different managers how talent drives shareholder value, and you might get ten different answers. Ask the same ten managers how talent drives one dimension of the customer value proposition or the product innovation process, and you will get much more agreement. Focusing on those intermediate points in the strategy execution process makes the line of sight between workforce strategy and ultimate strategic success much clearer.

Strategic capabilities are key points in the strategic value chain. In stage 3, the line of sight is clear because the fit of the workforce strategy is linked to the strategic value chain itself, where the emphasis is on execution. Stage 1 has no direct link with strategy. Stage 2 at best attempts to tie workforce strategy to two or three generic strategy types. In stage 3, however, the basis for differentiation is the underlying strategic *capabilities* that are key to successful strategy execution.

What do we mean by a strategic capability, a term that others have used, often with different meanings? Instead of increasing the level of abstraction, we are trying to be as concrete as possible. We use the term *strategic capability* to describe those business processes absolutely essential to executing a firm's strategy. Ask yourself what your company does in the execution of its strategy that is the basis of competitive advantage. The answer is your strategic capability, or capabilities. They don't just keep you in business; they give your business the potential to earn above-average profits year after year.

Capabilities typically combine both organizational systems and talent. Examples might include the R&D process in Big Pharma, but more specifically the capability to develop commercially viable applications. The logistics and distribution capability at Wal-Mart is a classic example. In contrast, some organizations grow largely through acquisitions. In these firms, merger and acquisition capability and, in particular, the ability to effectively identify candidates with similar cultures or integrate acquisitions with different cultures are the key to strategic success. For the Oakland A's, the analytical system and the people implementing that system off the field provide a source of competitive advantage, not necessarily the players on the field.

At stage 3, strategy is about making choices. In the case of the workforce strategy, a disproportionate focus is on investments in those parts of the business most important to the successful execution of the firm's strategy. These are areas where you can expect the greatest return from your workforce investment. The essence of stage 3 is that strategic capabilities give a clear logic for understanding workforce strategy's impact. Once the focus is on driving performance in a strategic capability, the conversation between senior HR professionals and senior line managers will change. Now, for example, they understand that the strategic impact of the workforce strategy is its influence on the process of commercializing R&D or profitability from new acquisitions. The conversation is no longer focused on vague allusions to "managing critical talent by becoming the employer of choice."

Missed Stage 3 Opportunities at AA Systems

Having a strategy with a disproportionate focus on one segment of the workforce is fairly common. The problem is the focus of that workforce strategy. It has nothing to do with the strategic capabilities in the organization. In those cases, differentiating incorrectly is just as bad or worse than failing to differentiate. AA Systems is a good example. The company's corporate center was relatively small, and the CEO was very accessible. The CFO, who was particularly assertive, proclaimed the strategic importance of his finance unit at every opportunity. He argued that not only did his department require above-market compensation to avoid losing key talent, but that all his staff required considerable development opportunities to ensure a long talent pipeline. Without a compelling strategic logic to identify where those investments *should* go, personal influence and traditional levers of power carried the day. Sound familiar? AA Systems made a disproportionate investment in a capability. It just wasn't a strategic capability. Corporate finance was necessary, but it was not a source of competitive advantage for AA Systems.

Had AA Systems used our approach, it would have first realized that one of its most important strategic capabilities was the product introduction process, not corporate finance. Indeed, at one level it recognized the importance of product introduction with a stage 2 strategy that focused on a systems mind-set. Its management didn't think of the product introduction process, however, as a strategic capability and what it meant for the entire workforce strategy. We suggested a simple litmus test to begin thinking about how to identify a strategic capability: What does our company do in the execution of our strategy that is the basis of our competitive advantage? For AA Systems, product introduction was one answer, because its core strategy required that it modify and adapt products to new product lines for existing customers.

With a better understanding of which business processes are strategic capabilities, a company can see the basis for appropriately differentiating the workforce strategy more clearly. What AA Systems should have done was focus and direct its workforce strategy toward improving the execution of the product introduction process, not the corporate finance unit. The resources invested in above-market pay levels, development opportunities, and succession planning in the finance unit would have been focused first on those activities vital to executing AA Systems' strategy. Since this wasn't done, the product introduction process continued to struggle, it couldn't deliver the value proposition required by its customers, and AA Systems' financial results were disappointing.

Stage 4: Differentiate by Jobs Within Strategic Capabilities

Differentiating the workforce strategy ultimately means investing disproportionately in certain employees and groups of employees, based on their strategic roles. But it isn't the people that you are investing in—it's your organization's strategy. In the simplest form, at stage 2, some jobs and employees are more important for one strategy than another. For example, at AA Systems, system engineers played a strategic role in the newly recognized product introduction focus. But the real opportunities for differentiation were realized only at stages 3 and 4. While both stages of differentiation begin with a focus on your organization's strategic capabilities, stage 4 continues to differentiate at the level of the job. At stage 3, your firm might differentiate its workforce strategy across several capabilities, as well as between the strategic capabilities and nonstrategic capabilities. But the focus of the workforce strategy is on the capability as a whole. So, at AA Systems, stage 3 was represented by a focus on all jobs in the product introduction process. In stage 4, however, you drill down one more level—to the job.

In stage 4, the focus is not on just a strategic capability, but on those jobs within that capability that have a disproportionate impact on the success of the capability. We refer to these jobs as "A" jobs because of their strategic significance. (Chapter 3 is devoted to identifying these jobs, as opposed to "B" and "C" jobs, and how each would be managed in a differentiated workforce strategy.) There are two reasons to differentiate at the level of the job. First, the job is where workforce strategy and business strategy intersect, where talent is translated into strategic impact. Second, a focus on strategic jobs provides a clear, unambiguous strategic alignment for a workforce strategy. Once the organization understands its strategic capabilities, focusing on jobs offers a concrete, actionable direction for the workforce strategy. "A" jobs are strategic assets, but managing those jobs strategically doesn't require new competencies as much as a new perspective. Employee performance, retention of high performers, removing low performers, strategic sourcing, compensation policies, and managerial accountability for "A" job performance all have a clear, straightforward, but strategic focus. The design of workforce and HR systems to drive that performance and measures of success is much more obvious and acceptable because the line of sight to the organization's strategic success is clear.

At stage 4, jobs and the employees in those jobs are managed differently, even when they have similar levels of education and training. For example, computer programmers in a software development capability are managed differently from programmers working an IT support function within the same company. Relationship managers in one business unit in a bank have "A" jobs because they determine the success of a key growth area, while relationship managers in another lending unit are not in "A" jobs because the business is expected to be flat or declining. Similar job titles all represent talent, but only one represents *strategic* talent.

Again, this approach puts strategy, not people, first. Talent has strategic value only when it drives the execution of your strategy. Increasingly differentiating what talent you will focus on is the foundation of a successful workforce strategy. Paul Newton-Syms, senior human resources vice president at Roche Pharmaceuticals, points out, "In significantly upgrading our workforce, we identified our strategic positions first and then addressed the talent issues." Sony Europe has adopted a similar perspective; Roy White, senior human resource vice president, observes, "We must significantly change our workforce to meet the significant competitive challenges Sony faces. To do this we must identify the strategic positions first and then assess the talent in those positions."

What Might Have Been: Stage 4 at AA Systems

Recognizing the strategic centrality of its product introduction process allowed AA Systems to differentiate its workforce at stage 3. But it could have differentiated further. AA Systems came to realize too late that its problems with product development were directly related to the performance of a handful of key engineering positions. This was where the talent and strategic role intersected to translate new design concepts into actual products and, as important, adapt existing products to key customers' new product lines. The disproportionate investments in compensation and development opportunities that had been focused on the finance department were not available to the genuinely strategic jobs. Not surprisingly, performance was lackluster, turnover among key engineering positions was high, and the talent bench strength was nearly nonexistent.

Not only would appropriately differentiating the workforce strategy at the level of stage 4 have increased the focus and investment on certain engineers, it would have avoided the misdirected investment in finance. Disproportionate investment doesn't necessarily mean higher overall investments in the workforce. It means a strategically informed investment in the workforce. Moreover, in the case of AA Systems, it would not include all engineers, only the "A" jobs in the strategic capabilities. So, for example, mechanical engineers largely tasked with finding cost savings for noncore products would not be considered to have "A" jobs.

Focus and Organization of This Book

Our perspective on a differentiated workforce turns conventional wisdom on its head. To the extent that talent is a source of competitive advantage in your business, it's not the people that are the strategic asset, but rather your organization's ability to manage that talent strategically. It's not a war *for* talent, but a war *with* talent. Competitive advantage and strategic success demands that you offer something different for your customers. Whatever the basis of that strategic differentiation, it must be matched with a similar workforce differentiation.

This book is our third on the strategic impact of a firm's human resources and the human resources function. We continue several of the key themes from the earlier books. In *The HR Scorecard*, we laid the foundation for HR's strategic contribution. First, we demonstrated that the HR function and a firm's human resources more generally can have a meaningful effect on the bottom line, not just through expense management. Second, we developed a process that builds on the Balanced Scorecard framework of Kaplan and Norton and can be used to manage and measure that strategic impact. In *The Workforce Scorecard*, we broadened the analysis from HR to line managers, emphasizing the joint responsibility of line managers and HR professionals for workforce success and, by implication, strategic success. Although the second book was an extension of our Scorecard focus, we introduced the notion of workforce differentiation, "A" jobs and "A" players, to this perspective.

The focus of this book is a clearer statement of how an organization's underlying workforce strategy should be designed and managed so the strategic impact of the workforce will be fully realized. Getting the measures right is the last step in the design and execution of a successful workforce strategy. Despite the tremendous attention in recent years to measuring the financial contribution of HR and talent, there is much less attention to getting the underlying workforce strategy right. Measures are the last step but only have value if they are tracking a coherent and well-developed workforce strategy.

In this chapter, we have explained what we mean by a differentiated workforce strategy and how an increased level of differentiation will foster the strategic success of your organization. In the subsequent chapters, we go through each step for developing such a strategy. We follow a top-down approach, beginning with the business case for focusing the workforce strategy on strategic capabilities. We provide numerous examples of how to make this decision in your own company. With that strategic anchor in place, we begin to move from strategic outcome to strategic driver. We discuss how to determine the number of potential "A" jobs in a particular strategy, the role of the "A" players, and how to differentiate those jobs and employees. Based on that foundation, we describe the important role of the workforce philosophy and culture and the new relationship between line managers and HR professionals. Finally, we move into the HR function and focus on the architecture of the HR system required to drive the differentiated workforce strategy and the appropriate scorecards for both the workforce and the HR function.

The following chapters are organized around these questions:

- *Chapter 2: Link Strategic Capabilities to Workforce Strategy.*
  Why are strategic capabilities the point of differentiation? How does an organization determine which of its capabilities are truly

strategic? How does the workforce contribute to the success of those capabilities?

- *Chapter 3: Identify Strategic Positions.* How do we identify "A" and non-"A" jobs and what does it mean to manage them differentially? What is an "A," "B," and "C" player? What role does each have in a differentiated workforce strategy?

- *Chapter 4: Establish Leadership Accountability for Workforce Success: The Line Manager's HR Role.* What is the role of line managers in ensuring strategic success through workforce management? How can we design and implement a Strategic Human Capital Plan to ensure that we consistently place "A" players in "A" positions for "A" customers?

- *Chapter 5: Design an HR Architecture for the Differentiated Workforce.* How does the HR system need to be differentiated in order to fit the workforce strategy? How do we develop a workforce philosophy and a culture of strategy execution? What does a differentiated workforce strategy mean for the organization structure of the HR function?

- *Chapter 6: Develop Strategic Workforce Measures.* How does an organization develop the appropriate performance measures to track both the strategic contribution of the workforce and the HR function? How do you have workforce measures that are strategically meaningful to senior line managers, but also a set of HR measures that give a strategic focus to the functional activities of HR professionals?

- *Chapter 7: Make It Happen in Practice: Creating a Differentiated Workforce at the American Heart Association.* Based on a unique, comprehensive example from the AHA, we show how to identify and implement the key lessons learned in designing and developing a differentiated workforce.

CHAPTER 2

Link Strategic Capabilities to Workforce Strategy

I N THIS CHAPTER, we focus on the rationale for two key threshold decisions in this process: Why link the workforce strategy to strategic capabilities? How much should you *differentiate* your workforce strategy? First, we provide the business case for the importance of strategic capabilities. In short, workforce or talent strategies don't matter strategically in their own right. They matter only when they make a difference in strategy execution. Their link to one or more strategic capabilities provides that rationale. Second, we describe several approaches to determining the strategic capabilities in your organization. The goal is to implement the strategic focus and benefits of your workforce strategy. Finally, we show how the structure of a differentiated workforce strategy follows from a focus on capabilities. We discuss the design, implementation, and performance measures for this approach to workforce strategy in subsequent chapters.

As we noted in the last chapter, the first step in this process requires a new perspective on workforce strategy, namely, putting strategy first. The decision to depart from the more traditional approach to workforce strategy can have any number of motivations. See the boxes for the two ends of the motivational continuum. In "Realizing Global Aspirations," a very successful company wants to rise to the level of global leadership.

Realizing Global Aspirations

Boehringer Ingelheim, Germany's largest pharmaceutical firm, aspires to become an industry leader worldwide. Its new direction in workforce strategy is not motivated by a near miss with financial disaster, but instead by aspirations to move from good to great. Boehringer quickly realized it lacked the strategic talent to execute its strategy. Its historical workforce strategy was a blend of best practices drawn from around the world and primarily emphasized long-term employment and workforce engagement.

Boehringer had been putting people first, but now it realized it needed to put strategy first. The goal was to achieve stage 4 differentiation. First, it identified several strategic capabilities including drug discovery and development and prescription medicine marketing. Second, it identified the positions ("A" jobs) within those capabilities that were critical to delivering the customer value proposition. Third, it aligned both the workforce system and managerial accountability to deliver this talent. Fourth, it supported the new workforce strategy with disproportionate investments in strategic talent.

"Out of the Abyss" gives a new perspective on workforce strategy as a matter of survival. Both companies, however, have restructured their workforce strategies to be consistent with the principles we discuss.

Aligning the Workforce Strategy

A *differentiated* workforce strategy represents a unique approach to workforce management for most organizations. As with any strategy, choices have to be made about what is strategic and what isn't. Therefore, the first step in developing a workforce strategy is determining what part of the workforce makes a strategic contribution and what part doesn't. We hope all jobs are important; otherwise we wouldn't continue to fund them. But not all jobs are strategic. Making this

Out of the Abyss

Adopting a new perspective on workforce strategy is not always an easy decision. However, the consequences of not putting strategy first can be even more unpleasant. At a leading office products manufacturer, this was a hard, but valuable lesson. The company was just recovering from a perilous financial position and a relentless round of retrenchment at all levels of the workforce. No one wanted to live through that again. Something had to be done. The manufacturer realized that it had to completely transform its workforce strategy. According to the senior vice president for HR:

> We start focusing on the customer—the real customer, the only customer—the people and users who buy our products. We stop talking about internal customers, line managers as customers, and employees as customers and start focusing on the external customer. We will stop being internally focused and siloed and start being a concerted integrated HR team whose *sole* responsibility is to assure that customers and investors are extraordinarily well served.

> In order to do that we are going to link our HR strategy directly to the company strategy. And measure ourselves in terms of adding value to the stakeholders. Our *one main* deliverable is a top-notch workforce that is designed to meet *the company's* strategy. Our primary responsibility becomes the advocacy and delivery of strategic talent.

distinction requires a top-down analysis and follows directly from the nature and human capital content of the firm's *strategic capabilities*. By strategic capability, we mean those business processes that execute the firm's strategy and are the source of any competitive advantage, which is similar to Harvard strategy guru Michael Porter's notion that an effective strategy "means performing *different* activities from rivals or performing similar activities in *different ways*."[1] The choice then of which part of the workforce is strategic is directly related to which part of the workforce is essential to the success of those strategic activities.

Michael Porter also makes the point that a focus on strategic activities introduces a "greater level of specificity" to strategic thinking than the more familiar generic strategies of cost leadership, differentiation, and focus.[2] There is more than one way to execute these generic strategies, and those differences will increasingly become unique to individual firms. According to Porter, "[C]ompetitive strategy . . . means deliberately choosing a different set of activities to deliver a unique mix of value."[3] Those "sets of activities" are similar to what we call *strategic capabilities*, which has two implications for the design and focus of workforce strategy. First, the workforce strategy should be aligned directly to the human capital requirements of the strategic capabilities. Second, just as those capabilities are unique or differentiated relative to competitors, the workforce strategy should be differentiated accordingly. Strategic capabilities are the basis for what is, in fact, strategic about a firm's approach to workforce management. Focusing on those capabilities is what puts strategy into a workforce strategy.

While there is no best practice for how much to differentiate, "not at all" would typically be the exception, not the rule. In other words, it isn't a question of *whether* your organization should take a strategic approach to your workforce, but *how much* of your workforce strategy will really be strategic. In particular, the degree to which you differentiate your workforce strategy is directly related to the number of strategic jobs in your organization. In some cases, there may be only one strategic capability and job within that capability. In other organizations, there may be several strategic capabilities and jobs within each. The first step in making this decision, however, is to understand your organization's strategic capabilities.

Clarifying the Strategic Impact of Workforce Strategy

For the past fifteen years, there has been much interest in the strategic role of the workforce and the HR function. But quite often, there have been more questions generated than answers, or more accurately, the answers didn't really fit the questions. Senior line managers and senior HR professionals agree on the central question: how can the HR function and the workforce contribute to firm performance? The answers, unfortunately, tend to focus on how particular workforce decisions such as compensation and staffing levels or particular development programs can be made more strategic. Too often, this means equating the immediate financial impact, typically the cost, with strategic impact. Naturally, any or all of these decisions *could* be strategic, but only in the same sense that a broken watch has the correct time twice a day.

Unfortunately, with workforce decisions, the costs are clear and immediate, while the benefits are vague, ill defined, and in the future. Making that investment calculus clear, not just in terms of the magnitude of the impact but where it is located, is one focus of this chapter. Our approach won't necessarily change the cost of improvements in workforce strategy execution, although they may be reallocated. It also won't change the time frame; as with most investments, the benefits occur well after the costs are incurred. What our approach does, however, is to make clear what is and is not a *strategic* benefit. We begin with the assumption that workforce strategy is *only* about improving the execution of a particular business strategy. That means placing *strategy* at the center of any decisions on how you will design your workforce strategy and defining the strategic benefits in terms of its contribution to the execution of your business strategy.

Compare our approach with what, in many firms, represents a strategic workforce initiative. Perhaps it is a high-profile leadership development program, maybe even one focused on a reasonably narrow set of jobs. Both line managers and HR professionals are often understandably concerned about the value of the program. The reason for the angst is that any strategic benefits simply aren't clear. The program decision is guided more by a general concern to undertake some kind of talent initiative than a clear understanding of how the decision will drive strategy execution. With our approach, you don't begin with the talent, you begin with the strategy. Put another way, when thinking about a workforce strategy, *you don't begin with the workforce!* In fact, you begin with those processes that execute your strategy. That's where the strategic problems facing your organization are located.

The question is: how will you execute your strategy effectively? Once the processes or capabilities that are the foundation of your competitive advantage are clear, the rationale for the talent initiative and its potential benefits and their measures are much easier to recognize. Thinking strategically about the workforce means moving away from a traditional functional or program focus on workforce issues. The strategic workforce concern is not a particular initiative or HR function, but rather the cumulative effect of all these decisions—the workforce system—that determines the successful execution of a strategic capability.

Identifying Your Strategic Capabilities

The idea of a strategic capability has been around in one form or another for more than twenty years. Its premise is the notion that competitive advantage is based in part on a firm's unique ability to execute one or more business processes that drive its strategy. We use the term *capability* because it is an organizational asset that combines talent, information, technology, and routines. We aren't proposing a new perspective on strategic capabilities, but instead use the location of a capability as the focus for a workforce strategy. To do so, the concept of a strategic capability must be concrete and actionable. HR professionals and line managers need to be able to recognize the capability in their organization in a way that makes sense for their particular business. We cannot tell you, for example, that there are six strategic capabilities that every firm requires for success and then tell you how to measure and manage them. On the contrary, we believe that capabilities vary considerably across firms, and they are executed differently. This difference in execution is one of the bases for differentiating the workforce strategy and potential strategic advantage.

For example, we don't argue that speed, innovation, and flexibility are essential strategic capabilities. While these might be desirable organizational attributes and even represent the results of a well-executed strategic capability, this approach is not very helpful when it comes to developing a workforce strategy. It is neither concrete nor actionable. First, these attributes are seldom managed directly, especially when the line of sight between workforce decisions and concepts such as speed and innovation is indirect at best. Second, any "best of" list will necessarily imply that all organizations should compete on the same capabilities. That makes it difficult to rely on capabilities as a source of differentiation when you and your competitors are all adopting the same approach.

Consider the example of product innovation. Certainly, the ability to deliver new products, services, and solutions to customers and new applications of existing products can be fundamental to many customer value propositions. But the particular nature of that innovation and the way it is executed and delivered to the customer can be unique to a particular business. *At this next level, the level of strategy execution in your particular company, innovation is the basis of competitive advantage.* The workforce strategy needs to focus on this level. So, as we'll see, BankCo, a major regional bank, is focusing strategically on the mid-level commercial credit market. Innovation for this bank has nothing to do with new products or services. To the extent that innovation plays a role in the bank's strategy, it's about relationship managers delivering innovative solutions within the bank's relatively standard portfolio of products. Therefore, one element of the bank's workforce strategy focuses disproportionately on the position of relationship manager in the commercial credit business. One measure of strategic impact for the workforce is how commercial credit customers evaluate the bank's ability to provide innovative solutions to its customers.

Where to Begin

A list of strategic capabilities that guaranteed your organization strategic success would be convenient. From our own experience, we could probably list at least thirty strategic capabilities that apply to at least one firm in one industry. Imagine a list that included capabilities like alliance management, real estate acquisition, and fashion buying. You would naturally look for the capabilities that seem to be more appropriate for your company. You might be drawn to processes that are common in any company, such as service or product innovation. What do you do next? You carefully analyze exactly what role that capability played in your firm's strategy. Maybe such a list would get you started, but if you reflect on how to use this list, we think you would find yourself returning to the unique elements of your strategy as the basis for your decision making. Therefore, that's where we recommend you begin.

For the purposes of aligning your workforce strategy, there are several approaches to identifying your organization's strategic capabilities. Remember, identification is not an end in itself; it is simply a process that allows you to refocus your workforce strategy. This book is not about strategic planning and determining which capabilities your organization *ought* to use as a basis for building competitive advantage. If you adopt our perspective on workforce strategy, however, you may be forced to consider some of those issues. Instead, we begin from the assumption that your organization has a competitive strategy in place, either explicitly or implicitly. The question of where and how it competes has been decided, if not necessarily well articulated, but there has been little systematic discussion about how that strategy is executed. The process of identifying your organization's strategic capabilities is one of discovering and articulating them within an existing strategy, so they can serve as a strategic anchor for the workforce strategy.

There is no single approach that works best in every organization. Some organizations with relatively simple value propositions are able to articulate their strategic capabilities quite easily. When asked to think about the business processes that drive strategy execution and are the bases of their competitive advantage, they are able to do so. This is particularly true in service-based organizations, especially nonprofits, where the line of sight between the workforce and strategic success is clear and short.

As you think about possible candidates for strategic capabilities, consider the questions posed in figure 2-1. These questions will help you distinguish strategic capabilities from those processes simply necessary to function in your business. The first question must be answered yes for any process to be considered strategic. The capability has to be an important source, maybe the *most important* source, of your value proposition for customers. But, as we've already mentioned, being valuable is not the same as being strategic.

FIGURE 2-1

Diagnosing a strategic capability

When you are considering whether or not an organizational capability is strategically important, ask the following questions:

	Yes	No
1. Is the capability an important source of the value proposition you offer to customers?	☐	☐
2. Is this capability relatively unique among your firm's close competitors?	☐	☐
3. If your close competitors all rely on a similar capability, is your firm "head and shoulders" above the competition in the execution of that capability?	☐	☐
4. If your close competitors all rely on a similar capability, does your firm execute on par with industry standards (or well enough to remain profitable)?	☐	☐

Questions 2, 3, and 4 help you distinguish which among these valuable processes has more (or less) strategic value. You are looking not only for your most valuable capability, but also for the capability in which the value *difference* between you and your competitors is (or can be) the greatest and is sustainable over time. If you answer yes to question 2, the capability has the most strategic value. You are doing something different from your competitors that both increases the value delivered to your customers but also makes it more difficult for your competitors to copy your strategy. In some cases, as in service industries, the *differential* execution of the capability translates directly into the greater value experienced by the customer. It is the differential execution of the capability that gives it its unique and valuable quality. So being different is more than just executing better.

For example, in big-box retailing, logistics and distribution are an essential and valuable business process. But big-box retailer Wal-Mart has been able turn that common business process into a strategic capability through differential execution. Similarly, the regional bank, BankCo, we mentioned earlier competes in an industry in which every bank sees relationship management as a key business process. At BankCo, however, relationship management is a strategic capability because the bank can deliver innovative solutions from a portfolio of undifferentiated products in a way that translates directly into the customer value proposition.

If you cannot answer yes to question 2, but to question 3, then the strategic value is more limited. In effect, you are competing in the same way as your competitors, but you are better at the basic "blocking and tackling" when it comes to executing that capability. The differences between questions 2 and 3 can be subtle. What's important is that you focus on how you compete differently from your competitors, and where the competitive advantage is located. At one extreme (a resounding yes to question 2), you are a regional bank and all your competitors compete for commercial loans by attempting to provide innovative and unique product offerings. Your bank's products are up to date, but they would be considered relatively standard fare in the industry. In contrast to the competition, you rely on your relationship managers to craft innovative customer solutions based on those standard offerings. The strategic value is located in the relationship management capability rather than innovative R&D. Your strategic capability is different from your competitor's.

A more subtle difference is when you and your competitors all point to the *same* business process as a strategic capability, but your approach to that capability is completely different from your competitors. Again, take the example of BankCo. Let's assume all BankCo's competitors say they compete for business in commercial credit based on relationship management. BankCo might emphasize the role of the relationship manager in delivering its value proposition to the customer, while competitors might focus more on quality and accessibility of product information that supports the role. In reality, as the differences in the capabilities begin to resemble this example, your company is probably somewhere between categories 2 and 3.

While there can be gradations, if you answer yes to question 3, your organization would fall squarely into that category if your strategic capability was the same as your competitors, was structured in the same way, but your execution was simply head and shoulders above your competitors. In the example of BankCo, it would be as if BankCo and all its competitors competed for commercial credit business based on innovative productive offerings. But BankCo had a competitive advantage because it was routinely the first to offer more innovative offerings to its customers. The competitive advantage of this capability was limited, however, as BankCo's competitors could simply copy its offerings once they proved successful.

The last category is capabilities that can only be described as mimicking the competition (yes to question 4). They are a valuable part of your value proposition, but the same is true for the competition, and nothing your company is doing in this capability is differentiating it from the rest of the market. You are delivering the same value proposition, in the same way, as your competitors. This "me too" strategy keeps you in the game but isn't a basis for long-term, above-average performance.

Articulating the Strategic Impact of Talent

As we have noted, identifying your organization's strategic capabilities is probably much easier in practice than in the abstract. While terms like strategic capability might not be common parlance in some organizations, most senior managers find it fairly easy to determine their strategic capabilities when prompted with the kinds of questions posed in figure 2-1. But it's a big leap from putting a label on a strategic capability to creating a differentiated workforce strategy. What's missing is a clear articulation of how talent contributes to the success of a strategic capability.

Clarifying the strategic role that talent plays in your organization and therefore the potential value of a differentiated workforce strategy is a two-stage process. The first stage is to more clearly articulate how the strategic capability contributes to your organization's strategic goals and what organization drivers contribute to the effectiveness of that capability. What has to happen for that capability to create the intended customer value proposition? What are the strategic consequences of success? While your strategic capability is a basis of strategic differentiation, more important for our purposes, it also provides the basis for workforce differentiation. *Your strategic capability gives the workforce strategy its strategic focus.* The second stage, therefore, is to clearly articulate where and how talent drives your strategic capabilities.

The questions in figure 2-1 serve as a litmus test for the capabilities you might consider as the focus for your workforce strategy. Developing the right workforce strategy requires you to have a clear picture of how the workforce creates strategic value in your organization. In practice, that means understanding what part of the workforce is most responsible for driving a strategic capability and what kind of strategic performance is required of those positions. Defining very clearly what that strategic workforce performance looks like—what we have called *workforce success*—requires an equally clear description of the strategy drivers that execute your strategy. The strategy map process developed by Robert Kaplan and David Norton is the best way to identify those strategy drivers.[4]

Going through the mapping process forces you to think about two dimensions of strategy particularly relevant to your workforce strategy. First, developing a map will encourage you to think not only about the financial dimension of strategy, but also about the role of nonfinancial intangibles (e.g., customer buying experience, employee strategic focus, brands). Second, mapping your strategy highlights the temporal sequence of the value creation. The source of important outcomes and strategic results will be much clearer. Kaplan and Norton refer to this distinction as leading and lagging indicators, which is particularly useful for unraveling the strategic role of talent that typically is a leading indicator of strategic success. The map will make the relationship between talent and strategic success much clearer and more transparent.

To map your strategy, begin with the ultimate measures of strategic success and work back through the drivers of that success. For companies in the private sector, strategic success is almost universally measured in terms of financial performance. Most of these organizations have no shortage of financial metrics; the challenge is to winnow them down. Typically, the financials are divided into broad categories of profitability and efficiency, with profitability including a growth component. For nonprofits, strategic success might be measured in terms of service goals. In either case, it's the bottom line for the organization.

The next step is to identify the immediate drivers of that bottom-line success. Specifically think about your customers and the market success required to deliver the financial results identified in the first step. What kind of market success is required? For example, is growth based on increasing market share by adding new customers in existing markets, increasing wallet share of existing customers, or adding new customers in new markets? Likewise, what elements of the customer value proposition do you have to deliver in order to achieve that market success?

To this point, you have defined bottom-line strategic success, identified the type of market result required to achieve that success, and clearly specified the dimensions of the customer value proposition that produces that market result. The last step is to focus on the internal operations required to deliver the customer and market segment outcomes described. Attributes that might commonly be emphasized at this stage involve reliability, quality, delivery speed, efficiency, and so on. But those generic examples should be uniquely aligned to the specifics of your organization's value proposition.

As we have summarized, strategy maps describe the causal logic from internal organizational processes to customer value proposition to financial success. While we have used the more familiar term, "strategy map," our approach generates what is more accurately called a "talent map." It may not be as comprehensive as a true strategy map because the goal is not to provide a comprehensive template to manage the entire strategy. We are trying only to articulate the talent dimension of that strategy—what we call the workforce strategy. The links are intended to reveal the business case for talent's strategic impact. As in the case at BankCo, a company may develop separate talent maps for each of its most important business units.

Since the purpose of the mapping process is to reveal how talent drives strategic success, the way the talent impact is articulated in the map is a bit different from a traditional strategy map. Normally talent or people issues are in the fourth part of the map. Broad people-related issues like "strategic mind-set" might be included here as core considerations for the workforce strategy and HR function. Our approach, however, treats talent as a more systemic and focused (or differentiated) strategy driver. Therefore, in our approach, the influence of talent can appear not only in the fourth stage, but also as drivers in operations and at the customer level. Again, this reflects our primary interest in the mapping process—to clarify as much as possible the nature and locus of talent's impact on strategy execution. Without this clarity, there is no basis for a more differentiated emphasis in the workforce strategy.

When done correctly, developing a strategy map will involve various points (and organizational levels) in the strategy execution process and build consensus so that all the key players understand what achieving strategic success requires. Once you have agreement on what is strategically important, it is much easier to align and focus the workforce strategy and, as a result, you have a much clearer understanding of when and how the workforce makes a strategic impact. That this development process includes both line managers and HR professionals at every stage is essential.

A Multidivisional Business

The decision on where to focus a strategy map partly depends on the nature of your business. In this example, we return to the AA Systems case described in the previous chapter. The multidivision parts supplier manages strategy at the enterprise level. The strategy map focuses on capabilities that cut across the various business units. Figure 2-2 shows a strategy map for AA Systems. We have intentionally kept the map simple, while still illustrating its value for developing a workforce strategy.

Revenue growth is AA Systems' primary strategic concern. Since AA Systems' customers include the world's leading auto and aerospace companies, growing revenue means increasing sales to existing customers, rather than increasing its customer base. AA Systems considered the value proposition required by these customers. Not surprisingly, it determined that its customers valued high-quality, reliable products that were delivered on-time with shorter lead times for new products, all at lower cost. AA Systems realized that the key to delivering this value proposition was its product innovation process—a strategic capability that had to be executed flawlessly. The core of this process was a simultaneous engineering system that integrated both a systems focus and a customer focus in design and manufacturing. Several cross-functional product teams with representatives from each of the five

FIGURE 2-2

Mapping AA Systems' product development capability

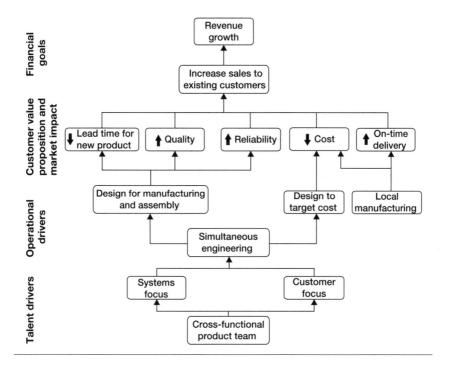

business units as well as marketing and finance managed the systems and customer focus.

This abbreviated analysis begins with bottom-line financial goals, identifies what has to be delivered to customers to achieve those goals, describes the internal processes that will deliver that value, and concludes by zeroing in on the part of the workforce that has the greatest impact on the overall process. The mapping process and the conversations in this process give two important results. First, the process begins to reveal the scope and structure of a strategic capability, in this case, the product innovation process. Once you begin asking questions about the critical strategy drivers in this causal logic, the truly strategic business processes—your company's strategic capabilities—are revealed. As important, the nonstrategic role of other processes and functions also becomes clearer. Second, by concluding this analysis with a discussion of jobs and roles that are most critical to executing this capability, you have begun to reveal how a workforce strategy contributes to overall strategic success.

AA Systems identified two positions as strategic jobs or what we call "A" jobs. These are positions where significant variation in job performance is possible *and* where that variation in job performance has a dramatic effect on the execution of the strategic capability. Identifying "A" jobs is the key to the stage 4 workforce differentiation described in chapter 1. (The process for identifying "A" jobs is discussed in much more detail in chapter 3.) For purposes of this example, AA Systems has identified two strategic jobs in the production innovation process: product introduction project managers and senior engineering managers.

Recall that the last strategic driver in figure 2-2 was the product introduction team, a cross-functional team led by a product introduction manager. When AA Systems looked at this process, it realized that there was considerable variation in performance across these teams and that this variation was due largely to the talent in the product introduction manager role. This was a classic strategic job. AA Systems also realized that among the more than seven hundred engineers in the company, the twenty or so engineering managers were critical to successfully executing the product introduction process. These roles were located in the operations level of the strategy map.

Figure 2-2 can make the process look more daunting than it really is. What are important are the discussions among line managers and HR professionals that lead to this diagram. Those discussions build a common understanding of what is strategic and how the workforce strategy can drive strategy. The strategy map itself is simply a device to articulate the results of those discussions. Yet it provides some important answers to questions that you should consider when developing your workforce strategy. These include:

- *What should be the focus of the workforce strategy?* At AA, it is delivering outstanding performance in two "A" jobs: product introduction manager and senior engineering manager.

- *Why are these jobs so valuable?* The talent in these jobs has the most significant impact on our strategic capability—the product innovation process.

- *Why is product innovation so important?* It is the key to delivering the customer value proposition to AA Systems' customers and the source of competitive advantage.

- *What does this mean for other jobs at AA Systems?* It doesn't mean that you ignore other jobs, but it does mean that they do not receive the same disproportionate investment as the "A" jobs. Investments in talent in the finance unit are scaled back.

A Business Unit

Sometimes it is easier to think about strategies at the level of the business unit. Products and services differ considerably across business units, so it doesn't make sense to focus on a corporatewide strategic capability. AA Systems ultimately came to think of itself as an engineering company, so a corporatewide focus on an engineering capability made sense. In the case of a regional bank like BankCo, that might not be the case. Capabilities are located within the business units, so those business units could be the focus of the mapping analysis. It also is sometimes easier to introduce a strategy map process to an organization unfamiliar with the concept, and HR is taking the lead in this process.

The experience of the regional bank, BankCo, is a good example. The bank's senior HR executives were interested in a more strategic approach for the function, but needed an approach that was as compelling to senior line officers as it was to HR professionals. The idea of a differentiated workforce strategy made sense in theory, but they wanted to see how it would work in practice. They decided on a demonstration project in one business unit, the commercial lending unit. The first step was the strategy map in figure 2-3.

Developing the strategy map was relatively straightforward and confirmed what senior line executives would likely have concluded with a more informal process. When HR met with the senior management team in this unit, they easily identified the financial targets. While there was interest in the general categories of revenue growth, profitability, and cost management, the executives' real interest was in revenue growth. How was the bank going to grow? Moving to the customer level, they acknowledged that acquisitions would continue to

FIGURE 2-3

Partial strategy map for BankCo's commercial lending unit

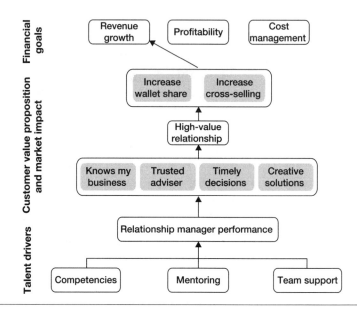

be targets of opportunity, but the most promising opportunity lay in expanding sales to existing customers. This meant greater wallet share from existing lending products, but also cross-selling other bank products to the bank's own customers.

BankCo had several choices for providing that value proposition to its customers. It could focus on developing innovative new products, but knew that wasn't really its competitive advantage. Instead it chose to emphasize creating *high-value relationships* with customers. BankCo then identified the key drivers of that value proposition. Customers were looking for a bank that understood their business, could be a trusted adviser, provided decisions and advice in a timely manner, and perhaps, most important, offered creative solutions to their business problems. This analysis made clear that while the commercial lending customers had a formal relationship with BankCo, the value in this relationship was created by the relationship manager position. This was one obvious strategic job for BankCo. The talent map for BankCo doesn't include the traditional operations dimension of a strategy map.

This omission highlights the direct, comprehensive effect of relationship management on the customer value proposition. In this case, the strategy impact of talent occurs right at the point at which the organization intersects with the customer.

Differentiating Your Workforce Strategy

So far, we have argued that you must begin with a clear articulation of your company's strategic capabilities, and we have described that process. We conclude this chapter with a brief description of *how* a differentiated workforce strategy follows from this capability analysis. While we discuss the particulars in more detail later, we briefly highlight some key features of a differentiated workforce strategy, using a strategic capability described in this chapter.

The Strategic Focus

The first design element in differentiating your workforce strategy is the *focus*. Getting the focus right means identifying the right capability and the right jobs. Making the workforce strategy concrete and operational isn't about managing talent in the abstract. It means managing the translation of that talent into strategic success and managing the performance of actual people in actual jobs. Many organizations have thousands of jobs and tens of thousands of employees. The first step is to narrow the strategic focus to those jobs that make a strategic difference. We do that by first getting the capability right, then getting the jobs right. In the case of BankCo's commercial credit unit, identifying relationship management as a strategic capability and articulating that capability (as described in figure 2-3), means disproportionately focusing the workforce strategy on the job of relationship manager (RM).

The Workforce Management System

Aligning the execution of the workforce strategy with the strategic focus is the next phase of differentiation. But align what? First, it means *systems alignment.* The various dimensions of the HR and workforce systems that influence strategic job performance must work together to maximize that performance. Creating value with these systems is like building an interlocking chain. How does the current compensation system motivate performance in strategic jobs and retain high performers? Are development opportunities broadly designed to service "high potentials," or are there specific programs focused on developing talent for strategic jobs? How are sourcing practices focused on the specific requirements of delivering performance in strategic jobs? Remember, in this system, one broken link can undermine the value of the rest of the system.

Once BankCo understood its strategic capability and the role of the RM position, it was clear that several aspects of its work system were not strategically aligned. For example, the RM position was located within a larger compensation and career structure, much as you might find at any other bank. While this system seemed to work well for the bank as a whole, it really didn't optimize the RM's strategic performance. BankCo was losing too many experienced RMs, generally the most valuable employees in the position. Why? They were moving into management positions where the rewards and career opportunities were more appealing. The bank's career structure was working at cross-purposes with its strategy.

Strategic Roles

Differentiation requires better alignment between managerial roles and strategic jobs. Line managers must be held accountable for the development and performance of strategic talent in the organization. Managerial compensation and performance reviews have to reflect their talent management role.

After mapping the relationship management capability at BankCo, it became clear that the leadership cadre in the RM units played a crucial role in unit performance. Much of the RM talent was developed through experience, rather than by formal programs. The mentoring and coaching by unit leaders was the foundation of that informal development process. But team leaders weren't held accountable or rewarded for that part of their job. Team leaders obviously regretted when an experienced RM left the unit, but they didn't consider it their responsibility to minimize the talent loss. Their response was simply to call HR and ask for replacements, sooner rather than later. The unintended consequences of this approach were quite costly.

The HR Function

A differentiated workforce strategy requires a differentiated HR function. Usually, a misaligned HR system is the natural result of an HR function organized by traditional functional silos. When HR professionals and line managers think HR's first responsibility is to deliver functional (i.e., compensation, development, employee relations) expertise, rather than strategic performance, there is a problem.

A functional structure guides the rationale and focus of an HR initiative. Major workforce investments in all likelihood do not have the clear focus on strategic performance we described earlier. Are you thinking of a new development program or whether one is required? The first question should be, how it will drive performance in your strategic jobs? A clear strategic rationale makes clear how to evaluate the success of these initiatives. You might track numbers trained or cost per trainee relative to some industry standard, but those are not strategic performance measures. If you are BankCo and develop a training program for RMs, the only real performance measure for that program is how it affects RM job performance.

The Measures

The last element of differentiated workforce strategy is getting the performance measures right. An interest in strategic performance measurement is often the motivation for thinking about the larger issue of workforce strategy. If the other elements of your strategy are appropriately differentiated, getting the measures right will be easy. Think back through the logic behind the strategic focus, the workforce system, and the strategic roles for HR and line managers we've described. The value of measuring strategic job performance rather than cost per hire should be apparent. Measures are answers to questions. Getting the focus and alignment right increases the chances that you are asking the right questions. Once you get the question right, you won't find yourself going through piles of employee survey results trying to figure out what they mean.

Conclusion

Differentiation involves making choices that have strategic consequences. By now, it should be clear why a differentiated workforce strategy is not only essential to the successful execution of your larger organizational strategy, but also the most effective way to increase the strategic contribution of both the workforce and the HR function. Beginning with the strategic logic, you choose which capabilities should be the focus of your workforce strategy. Next, the execution of workforce strategy is aligned with that focus. Those choices mean more differentiation. Finally, the workforce strategy is managed and evaluated with the appropriate measures. This is the big picture. In the next chapters, we continue to elaborate on these ideas and focus more specifically on workforce strategy implementation.

CHAPTER 3

Identify Strategic Positions

CLARIFYING YOUR firm's strategy and the strategic capabilities needed to execute it is a crucial first step in the process of developing a differentiated workforce. The next step in the process is to identify the strategic positions essential for delivering the firm's strategic capabilities, as well as the specific employee competencies and behaviors needed in these roles. These are the topics to which we turn in this chapter.

The process of identifying "A" positions begins with the development of a clear statement of the firm's strategic choice (how will we compete?) as well as the firm's strategic capabilities (what must we do exceptionally well to win?). Once you clarify these two factors, you can identify "A" positions. Then, the process of improving the performance of employees in the firm's most critical roles can begin. We outline the key elements of this process in figure 3-1.

Strategic positions have a significant impact on one or more of the firm's strategic capabilities. And, perhaps surprisingly for many managers, they might exist at almost any level in the organization. At Big Pharma, the strategic positions include R&D scientists focused on new product development. At Nordstrom, they are the personal shoppers. At Wal-Mart, they are the distribution and logistics specialists that make the firm's vaunted processes work so effectively.

In addition to their direct impact on the firm's strategic capabilities, strategic positions are characterized by a significant amount of variability

FIGURE 3-1

Creating a differentiated workforce

Determine strategic choice	Identify strategic capabilities	Identify strategic positions	Assess players in positions	Plan actions for all players in strategic positions
• Operational excellence • Product leadership • Customer intimacy	• List possible strategic capabilities • Review strategic capability criteria • Assess each for present and future wealth-creation impact • Determine 3–5 strategic capabilities	• List positions within each strategic capability • Assess each position on present and future wealth-creation potential • Identify strategic positions' performance variability • Finalize strategic positions • Review other positions (not in strategic capability for wealth-creation potential)	• Develop "A," "B," "C" criteria • Apply "A," "B," "C" criteria to all positions • List all positions by "A," "B," "C" designation • Assess all employees in positions • Determine percentage of "A," "B," and "C" players in all positions	• Remove "C" positions • Remove "C" players from "A" positions • Put "A" players in "A" positions • Develop "B" players in "A" positions into "As"
Exec team ✓	✓	✓		
Line managers		✓	✓	✓
HR function		✓	✓	✓

in the performance of the employees holding those jobs. Performance variability means that the difference between high and low levels of performance in a given job is substantial. For example, many managers are familiar with the wide variations in the performance of salespeople; a top salesperson might easily sell ten or twenty times more products than an average salesperson might. But such variations in performance can appear almost anywhere in an organization, and when they do, they have the potential to be an important driver of strategic success.

Strategic or "A" jobs provide the *context* for significant performance improvement, while variability in the incumbents' performance gives the specific *opportunity* for improvements in business performance. If everyone in a job were performing at a very high level, there would be little chance for significant performance gains. But in our experience, this situation is the exception and not the rule, especially in strategic positions.

In a single-product firm or division with few products, identifying strategic positions is usually straightforward. The few strategic jobs are usually apparent to managers (once they begin to look!). When a job (strategic or otherwise) affects multiple capabilities, matters get more complicated.

We recommend that managers spend time thoroughly understanding the strategic capabilities and the jobs most critical to ensure their firm's strategic success. They might be pressured to jump ahead in the process and anoint a certain group of jobs as key or strategic because they are obvious. But in the long run, this approach is shortsighted, as managers often misdiagnose the truly strategic positions. Managers might place too much emphasis on senior positions and not enough on the entry-level, customer-facing positions. We suggest that managers follow our process to ensure that they identify the truly strategic roles in their businesses, not just obvious ones.

Once you have identified the critical jobs, the next step is to specify, in clear behavioral terms, the employee actions and deliverables that constitute "A" performance in these positions. Performance differentials between "A" and "C" players in "A" positions can be on the order of twenty to one or more. So focusing intervention and improvement efforts first and foremost on the "A" positions is important, because it is where both the need and the payoffs are greatest.

Our approach to identifying strategic jobs and the staffing and development processes for ensuring that "A" players are placed in "A" positions is quite different from the processes most organizations use. In the next section we contrast the traditional process with our approach.

Traditional Approaches Are Not the Answer

Conventional approaches to job design use attributes of employees and the environment within which they work (in contrast to the strategy that must be executed) as the primary criteria to determine job structure. Historically, most large firms have used complex job-evaluation systems to allocate points to jobs, rank them, and then locate these jobs in the firm's pay system on the basis of these points. For example, the Hay System for job evaluation prices jobs based on the relative value of skill, effort, responsibility, and working conditions of a particular job. The typical job-evaluation process allocates points to benchmark jobs; then the remaining jobs are placed in the hierarchy. This process drives a number of organizational decisions, most notably, compensation.

But recently, job responsibilities have broadened considerably, and the pace at which jobs change has also increased dramatically. So, much like conventional accounting systems that are primarily focused on tangible instead of intangible assets, conventional job-evaluation systems are now much less useful than they used to be. The conventional approach looks both internally and to history for its definition of value; what we need is an approach based on future value creation and strategic job worth. More specifically, while the conventional approach might be effective in a world of stable companies, jobs, and (local) labor markets, *stable* doesn't describe the current competitive environment. A new and much more strategic approach to the design of work and the valuation of jobs is needed.

In our experience working with executives, many leading firms have come to this same conclusion and are substantially changing in the design and management of work and the workforce. In companies as diverse as American Century Investments, the American Heart Association, Biogen-Idec, Cisco, Colgate-Palmolive, Diageo, General Electric, GlaxoSmithKline, Haier, Honeywell, IBM, MetLife, Roche Pharmaceuticals, Telecom Italia, and Wyeth, managers are reconsidering how they invest in the workforce, and are increasingly recognizing that jobs differ in their contribution to strategic success, and they must be managed accordingly. Consider what some senior HR executives have to say about the importance of identifying strategic positions in the box, "Differentiating Strategic Positions."

The quotes in the box point to the potential problems associated with conventional approaches to job valuation, which we believe to be too slow, inflexible, and primarily focused on internal equity at the expense of strategic capabilities, value creation, and market competitiveness. Because the impact of history and inertia on job composition is substantial—job responsibilities, once set, are notoriously intractable

Differentiating Strategic Positions

"We must evolve new guidelines about how to manage our workforce to assure our future competitiveness, both within the U.S. and Europe."—Dan Phelan, senior HR vice president, GlaxoSmithKline

"In Telecom Italia Group, we are focused on ensuring that a good proportion of 'A' people fill the positions, particularly the 'A' positions. Our 'Management Review' process is designed to do that."—Carlo Bertelegni, vice president of HR, Telecom Italia Group

"Merely identifying strategic positions is not enough. You must assure a disproportionate representation of top talent in these strategic positions through recruitment, selection, development and rewards, as well as let them know how much we value them so we can retain them."—Ray Carson, senior HR vice president, Wyeth Healthcare

Source: All quotations are based on personal conversations with the authors.

---

in many organizations—it is important to reexamine periodically how jobs and work are designed. But most firms don't do this. The problem is exacerbated when strategy and the external environment are changing much more quickly than companies are adapting on the inside. Most need to be more adaptive in how they design and structure work. The question is how?

Effective talent management strategies resemble a world-class supply chain or logistics operation. In a supply chain, a firm focuses most of its efforts on acquiring and distributing its most profitable products and services. It doesn't use a "one size fits all" approach but puts considerable emphasis on understanding the profit and value chains and devising an acquisition, distribution, and logistics strategy uniquely tailored to its best customers.

Compare that approach to the talent-management supply chain in most organizations. Many staffing strategies resemble a first in, first out approach. For example, we've seen many strategic roles go unfilled while other, less strategic, roles were filled first. What if firms managed their supply chain processes for hot new products (e.g., the Nintendo

Wii or Apple MacBook Air) in a similar way? Investments in the work-force must be based on strategic capabilities or, more specifically, strategic positions.

How Our Approach Is Different

Firms should move from conventional approaches toward a model in which job value is determined by the specific strategic capabilities needed to execute strategy. Then they need to invest disproportionately in the most strategic positions, ensuring that "A" players are in "A" positions for "A" customers. They must also manage "B" and "C" positions effectively, acting quickly to remove "C" players from "A" positions (replacing them with "A" players) and ensuring that "B" players in "A" positions improve their performance. Similarly, "A" players in "B" positions might move into roles ("A" positions) that capitalize on their unique skills and abilities.

The workforce is the most expensive yet poorly managed asset in most organizations. In an era of global competition, both for talent and share of customer wealth, companies need a new way to manage talent. We believe that an inevitable trend toward increasing levels of differentiation in organizations is growing, and we are observing a movement from equality norms to equity norms.

Over time, organizations lose their focus on the importance of a job or position, and bureaucracy takes over. Over time, they tend to standardize and routinize HR processes and systems and iron variance out of the system. Firms focus on process improvement at the expense of strategic value. Six sigma processes contribute to this trend. The consequences are that workforce strategy becomes more homogenous and disconnected from business strategy.

How can we interrupt this process? As can be seen in the table 3-1, firms that are successful in workforce differentiation have a clear, widely shared view of the importance of identifying "A" positions and an action plan. In the remainder of this chapter, we demonstrate how to accomplish these tasks, beginning with a description of the key characteristics of "A," "B," and "C" positions.

TABLE 3-1

Successful workforce differentiation management

Firm	View of "A" positions	Firm's action	Comment
American Century Investments	• Explicit workforce and position differentiation	• Strategic position identification • Rigorous performance evaluation of strategic talent • Action plans to resolve gaps	Rigorous performance and rewards systems concentrate on investment positions and assuring "top talent" in these positions.
Biogen-Idec	• Not every position contributes to strategic capabilities	• Succession planning emphasized for strategic positions • Development and succession of those with potential in strategic positions are emphasized and carefully tracked	Differential investment and rewards are related to position value.
Cisco	• Historically reviewed "C" players and removed them • Focus of evaluation of managers and executives in customer success/wealth-creating positions	• Focus leadership on strategic customer-facing positions and redesigned incentive system to elicit wealth-creating customer behaviors	*"All executives must meet customer goals or incentives will not be paid."*—CEO John Chambers. Explicit recognition in a "techie" industry that customer solutions, not technical solutions, are the real wealth-creating positions.
Colgate	• Clear identification of strategic capabilities and strategic positions	• Explicit career development models for strategic positions within strategic capabilities • Rigorous assessment of career progress • Line managers know strategic positions	Investment in career development models appears to have a significant payoff in assuring strategic talent in strategic positions (e.g., consumer insight).
Diageo	• Explicit focus on strategic positions	• Refocused role of HR generalists to focus primarily on strategic positions	Strategic positions, largely in marketing, consumer insight, and supply chain, have been identified. LOB HR managers are responsible for delivering disproportionate capability in these positions and are evaluated on how well they deliver strategic talent in these positions.
General Electric	• Originator of "A," "B," "C" players concept ("organizational vitality") • Begin to focus on strategic positions	• Use explicit "A," "B," "C" player evaluation • Corporate owns strategic positions (e.g., leadership, M&A, etc.)	*"We can't afford 'A' players in all positions."* Therefore GE is moving, in one of five groups, to focus on "A" positions and realigning workforce strategy around these positions.

TABLE 3-1 (CONTINUED)

Firm	Issue	Firm's Action	Comment
Glaxo Smith Kline	• Workforce philosophy makes strategic positions explicit	• Have identified - Corporate strategic positions - LOB strategic positions • Line managers have explicit workforce accountabilities	To determine and leverage workforce investments in talent, a sequential assessment of strategic capabilities, strategic positions, and strategic players is used.
Haier	• Removing non-value-added positions	• Rigorous assessment of performance in wealth-creating work	Non-value-added work and "C" players are not tolerated. Thus both types of wealth creation (revenue enhancement and cost reduction) are maximized. The focus on value-added work is intense.
Honeywell	• Brought the GE model to Honeywell	• Rigorous assessment of "A" positions with GE criteria resulted in retention of "A" players—not the "new broom sweeps clean"	*"Differentiation is the mother's milk of a high performance culture."*—CEO Larry Bossidy. Assessing the value of the position as well as the player are critical but independent decisions.
IBM	• Strategic talent flexibility well beyond "lifetime employment"	• Explicit recognition of change in strategic talent requirements • Recognition that strategic talent is available externally	Building workforce agility around strategic and support positions, IBM clearly acknowledges that the nature of strategic work changes over time and workforce flexibility is essential to have the strategic talent instantly and continuously available without building expensive, embedded workforce platforms.
Roche	• Moved from competency model to strategic position model	• Removing non-value-added work • Making HR investment in strategic work	In a difficult European environment, they first attacked non-value-added work (i.e., surplus positions) and then the "C" players. More remains to be done, but they have now moved to identify and differentiate strategic talent through improved workforce management systems.
Wyeth	• Strategic positions require HR differentiation	• Clear recognition of strategic wealth-creating positions • Clear differentiation of HR focus on investing in strategic talent	Executive team has openly recognized wealth-creation positions and differentially invested in those positions using very nontraditional/differential investment workforce management systems.

Characteristics of "A", "B," and "C" Positions

To execute strategy with a differentiated workforce, organizations must clearly understand which positions are strategic and which are not. Understanding each position's level of impact on business success is the first step. While a number of factors contribute to a position's relative strategic impact, the most important are its *strategic impact* and level of *performance variability* (see table 3-2).

Primary Characteristics of Strategic ("A") Positions

Two elements are critical to the identification of a strategic or "A" position. First, the work must have strategic impact and directly affect one of the firm's primary strategic capabilities. Second, there must be a high level of performance variability among incumbents in those positions.

Strategic Impact. Jobs are strategic when they have a disproportionate impact on a firm's ability to execute business strategy through its strategic capabilities. For example, in a pharmaceutical firm focused on new products, a strategic capability at the firm level is likely to be R&D acumen, and the associated key jobs are likely to be research scientists. However, not all R&D scientists are likely to hold "A" jobs, just those associated with new product development in a particular domain (e.g., heart disease). Similarly, in a software firm, programmers associated with the development of the firm's core products are likely to have a greater impact on the firm's strategic capabilities than will programmers elsewhere in the firm (i.e., the firm's own internal IT operations).

As we mentioned in the first chapter, all a firm's jobs are important, but not all jobs are strategic; this distinction is critical for the design and implementation of effective workforce management systems. Strategic jobs are the very few (typically less than 15 percent) that directly enhance a firm's strategic capabilities. Strategic positions can appear at any level throughout the organization and affect one or more strategic capabilities. Jobs that affect more than one capability are

TABLE 3-2

Which jobs make the most difference?

An "A" position is defined primarily by its impact on strategy and by the range in the performance level of the people in the position. From these two characteristics flow a number of other attributes that distinguish "A" positions from "B" and "C" jobs.

Defining characteristics	"A" position Strategic	"B" position Support	"C" position Surplus
Scope of authority	Has direct strategic impact and exhibits high-performance variability among those in the position, representing upside potential. Autonomous decision making.	Has an indirect strategic impact by supporting strategic positions and mini-mizes downside risk by providing a foundation for strate-gic efforts, or has a potential strategic impact, but exhibits little performance variability among those in the position. Specific processes or procedures typically must be followed.	May be required for the firm to function but has little strategic impact. Little discretion in work
Primary determinant of compensation	Performance	Job level	Market price
Effect on value creation	Creates value by substantially enhancing revenue or reducing costs.	Supports value-creating positions.	Has positive economic impact.
Consequences of mistakes	May be very costly, but missed revenue opportunities are a greater loss to the firm.	May be very costly and can destroy value.	Not necessarily costly.
Consequences of hiring wrong person	Significant expense in terms of lost training investment and rev-enue opportunities.	Fairly easily remedied through hiring of replacement.	Easily remedied through hiring of replacement.

Source: Adapted from Mark A. Huselid, Brian E. Becker, and Richard W. Beatty, "'A Players' or 'A Positions'? The Strategic Logic of Workforce Management," *Harvard Business Review,* December 2005.

especially important, as they have the potential to have a leveraged or synergistic impact on the firm's performance.

Performance Variability. The second key driver of position impor-tance is *performance variability*, which means that the gap between low and high performers in this role is substantial. While strategic impact provides the context, performance variability provides the opportunity for improvement. If all employees perform at a very high level within a given role, then there is little opportunity for real strategic impact through more effective workforce strategy and management. But if a job has a direct impact on strategic capabilities *and* there are dramatic differences in the performance of job holders, managers can have a significant impact on firm performance through more effective workforce management. As Nathan Myhrvold, former chief scientist at Microsoft, commented, "The top software developers are more productive than average software developers not by a factor of 10X or 100X, or even 1,000X, but 10,000X."[1]

Few jobs exhibit the enormous variation on performance cited by Myhrvold. But differences in performance of twenty to fifty to one are common, especially in knowledge intensive roles, or in jobs with a substantial span of control or sphere of influence (i.e., where an employee's performance affects the performance of either subordinates or peers elsewhere in the value chain). Capturing the potential gains associated with this level of variation means that first we need to identify the key positions and then manage them differentially. But differentiation based on what? We focus on employee performance because there are often large differences from the lowest to the highest employee in any given role, and there are often large differences from the average to the top employees.

The impact of variability in workforce performance on firm-level outcomes is not just limited to highly complex jobs such as computer programmers or R&D scientists. Figure 3-2 gives an example from *Gallup* that describes the importance of developing a clear understanding of the processes through which variance in workforce performance creates value.

An important conclusion from the data is that firms would be better off paying the bottom 10 percent of the workforce to stay home! At an estimated $35,000 per employee per year in total compensation, the bottom 10 percent of the workforce (458 employees) generates cost to the business of over $16 million per year. Better yet, as the study's author noted, they destroy so much value, you should consider paying them to go to work for your competitors![2]

FIGURE 3-2

Performance variability is critical for a position to be strategic

Impact on customer attitude scores
This company, highly regarded for its customer service, surveyed about 45,000 customers to gauge the impact of its 4,583 service reps. It discovered that the top 10% had a positive effect on customer attitudes with 71% of the customers they talked to; the top seven reps created a positive effect with every customer. In sharp contrast, the bottom 10% had a net negative impact of 14% on customer attitude scores, while the bottom three employees alienated every customer they spoke with.

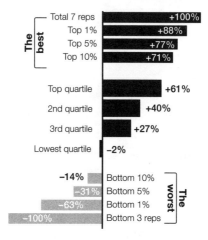

Source: Glen Phelps, "The Fundamentals of Performance Management," *Gallup Management Journal,* February 10, 2005:1–4.

Based on our experience with thousands of practicing managers and a careful reading of the academic literature, we believe that there is more variability in employee performance than many managers realize. Moreover, given the significant role of talent in the strategic success of most firms, we believe this gap is destined to increase. Just as the impact of the workforce on the firm's strategic success is increasing, so too is the variability in employee performance. As employee discretionary effort and knowledge continue to play a larger part in the creation of wealth within firms, the importance of managing these assets strategically increases as well. This means that managers will increasingly need to focus on managing the variability in employee performance.

To further complicate matters, not only are the average levels of variability increasing and the amount of variability differing substantially across roles, but the impact of workforce performance variability on firm performance can in many cases be asymmetrical; that is, the impact of an increase in workforce performance on firm performance can be either much larger or much smaller than the impact of a decrease in workforce performance. So, as the relative value of the workforce has increased, so too has the relative importance of high and low levels of employee performance. The very best employees (especially in strategic roles) are much more valuable, while the worst employees are more costly than ever in terms of lost profits.

Secondary Characteristics of Strategic ("A") Positions

Strategic or wealth-creating positions meet the criteria that we have outlined—they impact one or more of the firm's strategic capabilities, and the employees in those roles exhibit wide swings in performance. The strategic position identification process is partly empirical and partly clinical. Some key points to remember about strategic positions include:

- Strategic positions are those in which top talent significantly enhances the probability of achieving the business strategy.

- Employees are hard to get; top talent is difficult to attract and retain.

- Positions create wealth (by substantially enhancing revenue or reducing costs).

- Mistakes may be very costly, but missed revenue opportunities are a greater potential loss to the firm.

- Selection of the wrong person is expensive in terms of lost training investment and especially lost revenue opportunities.

- Poor performance is immediately detected.

- Strategic positions have major revenue-enhancing or cost-reducing impact on the firm.

- Strategic positions have strategic impact on the firm's customers.

- Substantial performance variability is possible, depending on the incumbent.

- These positions usually comprise less than 15 percent of the firm's positions.

- Strategic positions are not determined by placement in the firm's hierarchy.

Primary Characteristics of Support ("B") Positions

In contrast to high-impact strategic roles, "B" positions generally support or enable performance in "A" or strategic roles. World-class performance in these roles has only a neutral or modestly positive effect on firm performance. In addition, some positions are defined not so much by the wealth that they create but by the wealth that they can destroy. Said differently, although you can't win with "B" positions, you can certainly lose with them.

For example, imagine the case of a quality inspector in a pharmaceutical manufacturing plant. This is certainly an important role; an impurity or other manufacturing defect in a medicine that causes a product recall could cost the firm billions of dollars. Assuming that the job is structured correctly, however, an increase in the performance of quality inspectors, say from the seventieth to the ninety-fifth percentile, is unlikely to have much effect on the likelihood of a product recall (because the base rate is already so low). However, allowing job performance to fall below proficiency could be extremely costly.

Secondary Characteristics of Support ("B") Positions

In addition to the primary characteristics noted earlier, "B" positions can exhibit a number of secondary characteristics. No position is likely to have all these attributes, but the pattern of results is consistent with the following elements.

- "B" positions support wealth-creating positions.

- Mistakes may be very costly in that they can destroy wealth.

- Selection of wrong person is fairly easily remedied.

- Poor performance may be detected.

- Specific processes or procedures must be followed.

- Job level is the best predictor of compensation.

- Performance beyond a point has little potential for wealth creation or even diminishing returns to the firm.

- Performance variability may be substantial, but performance beyond "standard" has little strategic value.

- Usually most of the firm's positions are "B."

Primary Characteristics of Surplus ("C") Positions

Organizational success depends on *both* strategic success and operational excellence. Many "C" jobs, while having a small influence on strategic success, can be critical to operational excellence. A company might not even want to label them as "C" jobs or they may divide them into two categories: the jobs that contribute to strategic success and the jobs that primarily influence operational excellence. In any case, "C" jobs have the following characteristics:

- The work may be required in order for the firm to function, but it has little strategic impact.

- There is low performance variability in these positions.

Secondary Characteristics of Surplus ("C") Positions

"C" or surplus positions exhibit the following secondary characteristics:

- "C" positions have little economic impact.

- Employee mistakes and errors are not costly.

- Selection of the wrong person is easily remedied.

- Poor performance is often tolerated.

- There is little discretion in work, and procedures may be dictated by regulation.

- Market price is the best predictor of compensation.

Strategic Positions at Costco and Nordstrom

If we compare Nordstrom and Costco, we find a useful integration of the strategic capability and strategic position concepts. Both of these well-known retailers have been highly successful in the marketplace, and each is known for satisfying its customers. And while there is little overlap in the actual products that they sell, there is a significant degree of overlap in their customer bases (at least for the authors, who have often shopped at both stores, sometimes on the same day). But this is where the similarities end: despite a similar focus on retail sales and customer satisfaction, the processes though which they execute these strategies are quite different.

Nordstrom's customer intimacy strategy means that it needs to provide the latest, highest-quality, fashionable merchandise, professional expertise, and personalized service (via the personalized shoppers who have made the store famous). Delivering on these promises means that the firm must have world-class strategic capabilities in customer-facing sales, purchasing, supply chain, and marketing. Thus, a few strategic positions are key to its success: personal shoppers, fashion buyers, systems designers (in the supply chain), and customer-insight specialists (in marketing).

In contrast, for Costco, delivering on its operational excellence strategy means that customers must perceive it as providing the best value, product variety, convenience, and speed of transaction. The strategic capabilities that matter most at Costco involve real estate sourcing, purchasing, logistics, merchandising, and membership management (customers who consistently pay the $50 annual membership fee are a significant source of revenue for the retailer). As a consequence, the strategic positions at Costco are likely to be site-location analysts and specialists in category purchasing, logistics, layout, and membership management.

FIGURE 3-3

Wealth-creating workforces

Nordstrom		Strategic choice: Customer intimacy				
Customer perception of firm attributes	Strategic capabilities	1. Consumer-facing sales	2. Buying	3. Supply chain	4. Marketing	5. Leadership
• Best solution	Strategic positions	1.A. Sales counselors	2.A. Fashion buyers	3.A. Systems designers	4.A. VP-marketing	5.A. CEO
• Fashion forward	• Wealth impact	1.B. Category supervisors	2.B. Purchasing contractors	3.B. Logistics engineers	4.B. Consumer insight specialists	5.B. Store managers
• Professional expertise	• Performance variability				4.C. Brand managers	
• Personalized service						

Costco		Strategic choice: Operational excellence				
Customer perception of firm attributes	Strategic capabilities	1. Real estate	2. Purchasing	3. Logistics, distribution and information systems	4. Merchandising	5. Membership maintenance
• Best value						
• Convenient	Strategic positions	1.A. Site-locating analysts	2.A. Category purchasing specialists	3.A. Logistics analysts	4.A. Layout specialists	5.A. Membership marketing specialists
• Variety	• Wealth impact			3.B. Distribution contract negotiators	4.B. Store managers	5.B. Membership systems manager
• Speed	• Performance variability				4.C. Promotions specialists	

Personalized service and advice are key at Nordstrom, while product availability and low prices are key at Costco. As a result, the key jobs differ as well. Figure 3-3 describes the significant differences in workforce philosophy, mind-set, culture, and workforce management systems at Costco and Nordstrom.

Impact of Performance Variability on Wealth Creation

We've argued that strategic impact provides the *context* and performance variability provides the *opportunity* for creating shareholder wealth. The quickest route to increasing shareholder wealth is to increase employee performance in strategic positions, which is done by simultaneously increasing average employee performance and reducing the associated variance in these roles. Surprisingly, while the goal is to increase the average performance, you want to focus on the two ends of the performance distribution, which is why understanding variability is so important. Jobs characterized by high performance variability yield substantial increases in *average* performance from significant improvements at *either* end of the performance distribution. High performers make disproportionately higher contributions, and low performers are a disproportionate drag on strategic success.

As a consequence, managers need to pay much more attention to performance variability and the potential for *asymmetry* in outcomes. There are some jobs where significantly improved performance won't help you much, but where lower performance can have disastrous effects. And, there are some jobs where very high *or* very low performance won't make much difference. Our work shows that there are at least three broad categories of jobs: those that create wealth, jobs that are wealth-neutral, and jobs that have the potential to destroy wealth, depending on the level of employee performance, as we describe in figure 3-4.

Wealth-creating jobs. An "A" position is one in which improved employee performance leads to enhanced strategic capabilities, which leads to improved strategy execution, and ultimately, to increased revenue, cash flow, and shareholder wealth. So it is with wealth-creating jobs. In the airline industry, an example is the fuel hedge fund manager. In big-box discounters, it is the distribution or supply chain manager. In pharmaceuticals, it is the vice president of discovery (R&D). In the fashion apparel industry, it is a designer or buyer. Not only is each role an "A" job in its respective industry, as improved job performance will lead to enhanced shareholder value, but "the sky is the limit" for increased performance. That is, there is no inherent limit on the wealth-creating opportunity in these roles, and managers should be encouraged to continually upgrade the performance of employees who hold them.

Wealth-neutral jobs. In contrast to wealth-creating jobs, some roles have little opportunity to improve shareholder wealth. These jobs are important, but they aren't strategic; for example, cabin cleaners in the airline industry, cashiers in big-box discounters, field sales

FIGURE 3-4

How the impact of performance level varies by position

	Airline industry	"Big-box" discounter	Pharmaceuticals	Fashion apparel
Impact if job performance: Is significantly above standard	**Creates wealth**	**Creates wealth**	**Creates wealth**	**Creates wealth**
	• VP consumer insight	• Distribution/supply chain manager	• VP discovery	• Designer
	• Brand manager	• Purchasing manager	• VP marketing	• Buyer
	• Fuel hedge fund manager	• Promotions manager	• Field sales manager	• Supply chain manager
	• Events planner/ broker	• Merchandising manager	• Field sales	• Floor sales
		• VP real estate		
Meets standard	**Wealth neutral**	**Wealth neutral**	**Wealth neutral**	**Wealth neutral**
	• Cabin cleaners	• Cashier	• Field sales trainer	• Floor sales
	• Ground crew	• Department manager	• VP marketing	
	• VP consumer insight			
Is below standard	**Destroys wealth**	**Destroys wealth**	**Destroys wealth**	**Destroys wealth**
	• Airline pilot	• Store manager	• Field sales	• Buyer
	• Ground crew	• VP real estate	• VP discovery	• Designer
	• Fuel hedge fund manager		• VP marketing	• Supply chain manager
			• Quality control engineer	

trainers in pharmaceuticals, and floor salespeople in fashion apparel. These are all important and necessary roles, but not worthy of the same level of investment as strategic positions.

In wealth-neutral jobs, significantly increased employee performance isn't likely to create much wealth, and lower performance is likely to have extremely damaging long-term consequences. We want to ensure that employees in these roles meet the standard, but because of the job's structure and its place in the value-creation process, significant efforts to improve employee performance is unlikely to make much difference.

Wealth-destroying jobs. The third category has the potential to destroy significant shareholder wealth, for example, pilots in airlines, store managers in big-box discounters, quality control engineers in pharmaceuticals, and buyers or designers in fashion apparel.

Even if the average level of performance among pilots or hedge fund managers is very high, one or two lower performers can have disastrous effects on shareholder wealth. In the airline industry, for example, the level of investment in pilot training is substantial, even though most pilots join an airline after training and certification by the military. So the level of current investment in pilots is very high, and their error rate is very low. As a result, doubling the investment in development for pilots is unlikely to create much wealth for shareholders. Conversely, the opposite is not true: a reduction in safety and skills training for pilots could conceivably lead to increased errors and potential accidents, with catastrophic effects for all.

The amount of performance variability in a given role and where the variability is placed in the distribution is a variable of choice for firms (whether or not they have made a conscious explicit decision). By "choice," we mean that the level of variance is a direct result of how managers manage. But unfortunately, managers tend to focus on managing average levels of performance, not the variance. Just as with quality, managers need to think not only about average levels of employee performance, but also about the range or variability in employee performance. So managers need to choose how much variance they want in employee performance, as well as where they want it to be in the distribution. For example, for hedge fund managers, you want high performance and low variance. You'll probably have to pay high salaries and invest substantially in developmental efforts to attract, select, and retain only the best. You can't tolerate low performance, and the strategic impact of the hedge fund roles suggests that the investment will be worth it.

Identifying "A," "B," and "C" Positions

Building a differentiated workforce requires that you first clearly understand the role of each job in executing your firm's strategy and how employees need to perform within that role. The process is to identify the strategic impact of jobs as part clinical and part empirical, and you need to pay careful attention to both elements. Identifying the first few positions is relatively simple; after that, the process becomes much more challenging.

The next phase is to assess the positions based on the key elements that we have described: *strategic impact*, *performance variability*, *top-talent impact*, and *top-talent scarcity*. But for many firms, even the relatively simple question, how many jobs do we have?, can be surprisingly difficult to answer. Sometimes the same title can mean different things in different locations, due to history, mergers and acquisitions, transferred employees who retain their titles, and so on. At other times, the same job has different titles across locations, for many of the same reasons. So, a first step in the due diligence process is to determine which clusters or families of jobs have similar work across locations. The next step is to evaluate each position on its level of strategic impact and performance variable, along with a number of secondary characteristics that we outline later.

The most effective approach for doing this combines survey data with clinical judgments. Starting with a clear definition of the firm's strategic capabilities and a list of potential strategic positions, key subject-matter experts evaluate each job (or cluster of jobs) based on certain criteria. Then the jobs that they rate at approximately the seventieth percentile or higher on these dimensions are further evaluated by a committee of five to ten experts, who identify the top jobs and document the rationale. Finally, the list of jobs is returned to the initial subject-matter experts for their comments and feedback. These are the specific questions we use to begin this process.

- *Strategic impact.* Once you have developed an understanding of your strategic capabilities following the process outlined in chapter 2, you should be able to answer the following questions:

  - Does this capability enable us to capture a disproportionate share of the wealth created in our current markets?

  - Will this capability enable us to capture a disproportionate share of wealth created in future markets?

- Does this capability positively influence our firm's brand image?

- Does this capability add significant intangible value to our firm's market capitalization?

- Does this capability significantly influence our firm's wealth creation by enhancing revenue?

- Does this capability significantly impact our firm's wealth creation by reducing costs?

- Does this capability primarily reside in a unique wealth-creating process within our firm that is not easy to replicate?

- Does this capability primarily reside in positions that have a significant impact on our firm's ability to create wealth?

- *Performance variability.*

  - To what extent is there a significant performance gap from the highest to lowest in this role? In the example of BankCo, there were 250 individuals in the relationship manager job. When BankCo sorted them by the annual revenue they produced, it found that the average revenue produced by the top 25 percent was ten times that produced by the average of both the third and fourth quartile.

  - To what extent is poor performance in this role immediately detected? For example, how difficult is it to identify poor performance? While we can all think of jobs where it might be difficult to assess individual performance, when it comes to the truly strategic jobs, poor performance is fairly obvious. What's important is that strategic performance be evaluated, rather than the often unrelated metrics found in many performance evaluation systems.

- *Top-talent impact.*

  - To what extent would improved employee performance in this role significantly improve firm performance? This is the combined product of both the strategic impact of the job and the potential variation in job performance. The ability to identify the strategic contribution of the job is traditionally what is missing in this assessment. However, it should now be clear what high performance means and, more important, what it's worth. A simple analysis should indicate the value of increasing the average performance in the third and fourth quartile up to the current average of the first and second quartile. Alternatively, you could simulate what would happen if you replaced the performance in the fourth quartile with the performance in the first quartile, either through development or replacement.

- *Top-talent scarcity*.

  - Is top talent in this role difficult to attract and retain? (See figure 3-5 for a summary of this process.)

- *Summary points*. In addition to the criteria that we have outlined, the following points are important:

  - Strategic positions feature a high degree of variability in performance, even if there is only one incumbent in the role.

  - Strategic positions often require a high level of expertise.

  - Strategic positions aren't determined by hierarchy.

  - Strategic positions aren't defined by how hard they are to fill; workforce scarcity doesn't equate workforce value.

  - Not all positions in a job category have to be considered strategic for some of the positions in a job category to be considered strategic.

  - Strategic positions typically represent less than 15 percent of the workforce.

Are All Leadership Positions Strategic?

We have argued that whether a position is "A" or strategic does not necessarily depend on its level in the organization. In fact, we have

FIGURE 3-5

"A" position assessment

Strategic impact

Capability:

VALUE:

1. Does this position directly affect one or more of our strategic capabilities?

Not at all
1   2   3   4   5   To a great extent

2. Does this position directly affect the creation of new wealth?

Not at all
1   2   3   4   5   To a great extent

3. Does this position directly affect the creation of significant cost savings?

Not at all
1   2   3   4   5   To a great extent

4. Are mistakes by incumbents in this role very costly?

Not at all
1   2   3   4   5   To a great extent

5. Is the potential to generate new wealth via this role virtually unlimited?

Not at all
1   2   3   4   5   To a great extent

6. To what extent is the selection of the wrong person in this role costly in terms of lost revenues?

Not at all
1   2   3   4   5   To a great extent

Performance variability

7. To what extent is there a significant performance gap from the highest to lowest in this role?

Very little
1   2   3   4   5   Some-To a great what   extent

8. To what extent is poor performance in this role immediately detected?

Very little
1   2   3   4   5   Some-To a great what   extent

Top talent impact

9. To what extent would improved employee performance in this role significantly improve firm performance?

Very little
1   2   3   4   5   Some-To a great what   extent

Top talent scarcity?

10. Is top talent in this role difficult to attract and retain?

Very little
1   2   3   4   5   Some-To a great what   extent

Strategic position?

Yes ☐

No ☐

worked with a number of firms that have started the process by arguing that all executive or leadership positions are strategic. This is rarely the case (see table 3-3). We believe that many, but not all, leadership positions are truly strategic.

The key point is that the strategic importance of a job is not just defined by its level in the hierarchy: strategic impact and performance variability are the important factors. Strategic positions can appear at any level throughout the organization, and they will differ significantly across industries and even across firms within the same industry.

Identifying and Managing "A" Positions at IBM

IBM is a firm that has carefully identified their "A" positions and now manages them differentially based on their contribution to IBM's strategic success. IBM has recently completed strategic workforce planning initiatives to drive disproportionate investments in people, pay, and positions, with outstanding results.

Managing "A" Positions in IBM Central and Eastern Europe, Middle East and Africa

In 2005 many of IBM's Central and Eastern Europe, Middle East and Africa (CEMA) operations were experiencing substantial and rapidly expanding growth. At IBM, growth is expected, and in growth markets specific focus on building and managing disciplined growth is core. Upon their arrival in Europe in 2005, Garrett Walker, director of HR for IBM CEMA, and Brendon Riley, general manager of CEMA, evaluated the situation carefully and came to the conclusion that, to build and sustain growth in their territory, significant changes would be needed in IBM's people and business management systems. Within a month of assuming their new roles, Walker and Riley established a country GM board to focus on strategic workforce issues and scalable solutions to use throughout the region.

As of February 2008, IBM made the decision to group growth markets together on a global basis under the direction of a single global

TABLE 3-3

Wealth-creating leadership positions

Industry	Wealth-creating leadership roles			Non-wealth-creating leadership roles		
Pharmaceutical	Lead scientist, discovery process	Vice president, product development	Vice president, product marketing	Chief dietician	Director, building maintenance	Chief legal counsel
Automotive	President, North American operations	Director of brand management	Vehicle lead engineer	Director, security services	Manager, customer survey unit	Director, medical services
Financial services	Chief investment officer	Head, broker dealer management	Partner-in-charge, mergers and acquisitions	Manager, teller services	Technology lead employee transaction services	Director, employee publications
Lockheed Martin	Chief propulsion engineer	Chief lobbyist, government relations	Chief of contract negotiations	Manager, chauffeur services	Corporate treasurer	Head groundskeeper
Manufacturing	Chief, product engineering	Director, brand management	Chief procurement officer	Director, plant security	Director, workforce diversity	Manager, payroll
Hospitals	Manager, guest relations	Head, oncology	Chief medical officer	Chief, security services	Manager, gurney services	Manager, soiled linen services
Technology	Director, new product development	Lead software engineer	Chief, product design	Director, employee assistance program	Director of benefits services	Manager, accounts payable
Fashion design	Head fashion designer	Lead, brand management	Manager, New York showroom	Director, maintenance	Chief tax accountant	Manager, employee credit union
Airlines	Manager, airline fuel hedge fund	Manager, convention events	Director, special promotions	Airline captain	Manager, luggage services	Chief, airplane cleanliness

leader. This change facilitated IBM's desire to invest disproportionately in growth markets—and to focus on refining the supply chain and developing "ecosystems" of talent.

However, high-growth markets posed a number of significant talent-development challenges for IBM; and more so because of IBM's strong preference for sustainable and managed growth. Walker and Riley found that they had a leadership and management team with varying levels of experience and expertise throughout the forty-one countries that make up CEMA. The rapid growth in these markets was accelerating so quickly it would soon be—and was already in some cases past—the level of local leadership talent expected by IBM. Walker describes managing and leading in this environment as akin to "catching fast-balls every day," a skill set in short supply in IBM's high-growth markets. As a result, ensuring that they had the right people in the right roles to manage and sustain growth was a top priority for Riley and Walker.

The first step in addressing these issues was to recognize that growth market leadership, development requirements, and skills and capabilities differed substantially from major markets, and as a consequence, the strategic capabilities needed for success in Eastern Europe, Russia, and the Middle East differed as well. Indeed, IBM Asia Pacific and Latin America had made similar discoveries. Because the strategic capabilities were different in these high-growth markets, the jobs and roles that created wealth differed as well. As a result, both jobs and employees in IBM's growth markets would need to be managed in quite another way than in its major markets. This conclusion represented a significant philosophical shift for IBM, whose HR function now targeted growth regions for talent-development investments.

Riley makes the point that "you can fall into a trap if you try to apply a mind-set from a developed economy in a developing economy. For example, management systems designed to generate incremental change are not likely to be successful in a high-growth market. Incremental thinking is just not enough; [say] if our expectation is that the business will triple in the next five years, you need to be thinking about how you will develop the talent that you need *right now*." In addition, and more broadly throughout IBM, it has become important for executives to gain experience managing in high-growth markets such as Latin America, Asia Pacific, and Eastern Europe. Riley believes that becoming "more scientific in how we develop talent is one of the most important things we can do as leaders."

Riley and Walker evaluated their growth regions very specifically, sub-categorizing them into *growth, high-growth, conditional growth, developing,* and *emerging.* Each country or region had unique characteristics in terms of the market, culture, talent levels, and availability. In contrast to the major markets (e.g., North America), the challenges and opportunities in each of these growth markets differs substantially. Specialized recruiting and hiring, management development, compensation, rewards, and recognition, would need to be carefully tailored to each stage in the growth process in each market, as described in figure 3-6.

In addition to differentiating management systems for each stage of the growth cycle, IBM managers also concluded that they would also need to differentiate investments in the workforce based on their roles within each market. The jobs that create the most wealth in a high-growth environment differ substantially from the wealth-creating roles in a major market—and in fact might not even exist in the fully developed major market organizations.

In the process of identifying "A" positions, for example, Walker found that many of the wealth-creating positions in Eastern Europe and Russia were relatively junior in status. As a result, these positions were off the radar to many high-potential IBM managers, and the firm had a difficult time attracting internal candidates into these positions. Left unaddressed, this problem could have a negative impact on business growth. Growth markets require the infusion of highly experienced technical, sales, and leadership talent, since the business growth often outpaces the existing local talent. To directly address this challenge, Walker and Riley developed targeted plans and processes to ensure that the opportunities within their growth region had the necessary "visibility" to attract highly skilled candidates for these roles. Currently, IBM runs a highly sophisticated Global Opportunity Marketplace, which ensures all IBMers around the world can access online every open job anywhere in the world, and through an automated process matches qualified candidates, regardless of location, to open roles.

FIGURE 3-6

IBM's market categories

Structural options/changes—human resources

	Major markets	Growing markets	High-growth markets	Conditional-growth markets	Developing markets	Emerging markets
				Growth Markets		
Recruitment and hiring	Maintain and leverage	■ Integrated recruitment/university relations process to improve IBM employment brand, campus visibility, influence curriculum, access to top talent, internships, research				
Management development		■ Sustained overinvestment and customized development programs accelerate the growth of key roles/leadership positions beyond the traditional organization structure				
Compensation/ reward/recognition		■ Differentiated and more flexible programs for compensation across local employees to maintain competitiveness and special focus on simplified sales plan				

For example, detailed assessments of the key roles within each country were conducted, and incumbents and top talent were assessed for both existing performance and ultimate potential. They then placed highest-rated managers (potential executives destined for key roles) in unique development programs, significantly enhanced on-the-job training opportunities, mentoring relationships, and short-term assignments in other parts of the country or the world for the experiential learning that they believed these people would need to manage growth and create wealth in their emerging markets.

They also built a Growth Market General Manager Academy specifically designed for critical roles in IBM. The GMGM Academy was designed to take young local high-potential managers and to help them get ready for their new roles as IBM leaders in the growth markets. This process exposed those who might be considered "lower-level" managers elsewhere in IBM and gave them extensive mentoring and senior executive development designed specifically for the challenges unique to management roles in high-growth markets. Former IBM Chairman and CEO Lou Gerstner and current Chairman and CEO Sam Palmisano came and spoke with these young future leaders, which helped to reinforce both the expectation and the support that the entire company had for their performance, growth, and development. These programs were very highly rated, and were subsequently replicated in Asia and South America.

Managing "A" Positions in IBM Russia

Kirill Korniliev, country GM for IBM Russia, has also successfully adopted a workforce differentiation strategy. IBM Russia has grown sixfold in recent years, in large part, they believe, through transforming the role of the line leader in talent development. As a result of this growth, IBM Russia has become much more complex, with managers responsible for a much greater span of control. Indeed, IBM Russia now has as many managers as it had employees six years ago. This unit found the market for technical talent and managers to be very "hot," and was very difficult to hire "ready now" management talent. This meant that IBM Russia needed to increase the pace with which they developed both newly acquired and existing talent—and to leverage talent from elsewhere in IBM. Fundamentally, the key challenge was that IBM Russia's talent needs were growing faster than its ability to acquire and/or develop critical skills and people.

Recognizing the workforce challenges facing IBM Russia, Korniliev and Walker put in place a plan to address the tactical recruitment, hiring, and retention issues facing them, as well as a strategy and plan to rapidly build the skills and capabilities needed now and three years out.

According to Walker it has generally taken two to three years to recruit and prepare a competent employee to lead in IBM's complex environment. "In a major market this development process works well and is highly defined, [but in a growth market] time is the enemy," states Walker. IBM Russia has also found that four out of five new managers will fail in the environment if they are not provided with significant development resources and efforts; the unit has also found that investments in workforce development yield lower turnover and significantly higher productivity. However, it is important for these developmental efforts to be strategically focused and not generic.

At IBM, there is no escaping the idea that managers are accountable for the talent which reports to them, and they communicate this expectation in a wide variety of ways. Weekly meetings among executives help to air issues. Regular teleconferences focus on talent and culture. Developing soft skills will likely be the most significant challenge for IBM Russia in the coming years.

To facilitate the development of these leaders, IBM Russia's HR leader, Sonia Budjacova, leveraged the investments IBM HR is making in growth markets, and in partnership with the Worldwide IBM Learning organization developed a customized solution for Russia's requirements. HR constructed a profile of leadership skills, developed a series of structured interviews used to identify those skills, and subsequently implemented a series of individual leadership development plans to quickly develop the needed skills, which included the use of a leadership development center, and a three-day assessment workshop. Subject matter experts (SMEs) were brought in to help consult on the design and delivery of this program. As of late 2008 the top one hundred leaders (e.g., the leadership team) have been exposed to this process. After completion of this program, most managers are promoted and moved into a higher-level managerial position. In the near future, this process will be modified for use with lower-level managers.

Similarly, in IBM Slovakia, country GM Roman Brestovansky and HR leader Tatiana Kotrusova have made a number of important changes in their segment of the business. They have identified key jobs and created a strategic talent inventory within IBM Slovakia. They have also restricted the organizational chart and grouped jobs by strategic capabilities. In addition, they have:

- Clearly communicated their strategic priorities to the workforce: to be number one in the marketplace within the next three years.

- Carefully analyzed revenue and profitability by product line.

- Conducted a personnel audit to identify talent inventories by position.

- Made the needed personnel changes.

- Set priorities and executed on them.

The leadership team at IBM Slovakia doesn't believe that they have done anything extraordinary, but that they have focused significant attention on executing the "basics" brilliantly. The results from these changes, however, have been almost immediate: business productivity has improved dramatically, employee morale has measurably improved, and the focus on performance differentiation within the management team is "maniacal."

Managing "A" Positions in IBM Middle East and North Africa

Takreem El-Tohamy, the GM for IBM's Middle East and North Africa (MENA) regions, also came to similar conclusions about the strategic importance of the workforce. In his highly competitive marketplace, GDP has been growing at 6 to 7 percent per year, while IT spending has been growing at roughly 10 to 11 percent per year. There is virtually zero percent unemployment for the desired technical and sales talent within the markets in which he operates, creating an extreme war for talent, and a critical need to be able to acquire and retain top talent.

In the MENA region, El-Tohamy has identified *relationship managers* and *global business services managers* as strategic positions. Historically, the relationship manager role had not attracted much attention from the executive team: now it is seen as one of the key "chairs" that one must sit in to be successful in the organization. Similarly, the global business services manager role was historically filled by an expat; now IBM MENA has clearly defined an internal job ladder for the role and has staffed it with a local person. These were significant advances for the MENA team, in part because these roles didn't even exist in the major markets, and relatedly, because few managers were interested in taking these roles before they were identified as strategic positions.

As a result of this process, IBM MENA's culture gained a greater emphasis on high performance among employees. In addition, the unit adopted a model of increased accountability among line managers of workforce success: at IBM, even if you "meet your numbers" but don't develop people adequately, you won't be able to stay in the business. The company just can't afford to lose good people or not develop them quickly enough as a result of poor workforce management. Now, candidates for key roles are highlighted in the talent development process, and much more emphasis is placed on ensuring that they are ready to be promoted. As a consequence, low-potential employees tend not to even apply for jobs within the organization. El-Tohamy's only regret was that he didn't move more quickly to make these changes. Indeed, while he initially expected that there might be resistance from the workforce to these concepts, he actually got very little pushback once the key concepts were clearly communicated and understood by the workforce.

Managing "A" Positions in IBM's IT Delivery Business

After IBM's successful experience with workforce differentiation in Europe and in MENA, the team replicated this approach in the IT Delivery business, when Garrett Walker returned to the United States in his new role as vice president of HR for IBM IT Delivery. As in CEMA, IBM focused on identifying "A" positions that had a significant impact on the creation of new wealth at IBM (via increased revenue or reduced costs), and pinpointing where significant variability in current employee performance exists (i.e., where the consequences of poor performance in this role was significant and could destroy value, and where the economic significance of increased employee performance in this role was substantial). IBM's goal was to place its very best employees in these roles or in feeder positions for employees preparing to take them, and also to develop an action plan to ensure that these roles would be visible to employees or, as Walker noted, "making them the roles that everyone wants to compete for."

The team discovered that some of the most important jobs in the IT Delivery business are no longer in corporate headquarters, but are in the field and in growth markets. To build and sustain the expected business performance meant that IT Delivery would have to provide employees in these roles with substantially enhanced managerial attention and development.

IBM also discovered that an important part of the implementation process was to ensure that these jobs would be attractive to high-potential candidates. The solution was to develop a model of "sustained overinvestment" in key leaders, which was intended not only to build management skills but also to ensure that the IBM values and leadership DNA were instilled in these high-potential managers. IBM also developed a systematic "career road map" to help high-potential employees gain a better understanding of the pathways to success in the "A" positions it had identified. It then provided significant training opportunities, as well as substantial "face time" with IBM's leadership.

Walker describes this process as delivering "sportscar leaders for a track that hasn't yet been developed." More broadly, IBM managers describe the outcomes associated with their new focus on "A" positions as "hugely successful."

Managing "A" Positions in IBM's Software Group Sales Business

Garrett Walker, now vice president of HR Software Group Sales, is leading the work to establish IBM focus on identifying "A" positions that have a significant impact on the creation of new wealth at IBM (via increased revenue or reduced costs), and where significant variability in current employee performance exists, that is, where the consequences of poor performance in this role were significant and could destroy value.

Central to the success of IBM's Software Group Sales organization are the investments made to develop, deploy, and motivate the best sales leaders in the business. The "A" positions within SWG Sales are clearly defined in organizational models for growth and major markets; the roles and the individuals who fill those roles are carefully managed by the very senior line executives within SWG Sales.

For example, SWG Sales disproportionately invests in the pipeline for future sales leaders. The Delta program consists of the fifty highest-potential sales leaders worldwide. Members of Delta are nominated annually by their regional GMs, and then must pass through a rigorous review by senior sales leaders to be selected. Each year the Delta class starts at zero members. Specialized sales and leadership training are provided, and each Delta is assigned a senior executive coach and mentor. The goal of this program is to identify the best of the best of SWG sellers and then to make them even better. Garrett Walker describes the program as an "elite sales leadership program. [B]eing a Delta is about developing elite sales leadership skills, potential is interesting but performance is everything in this program." Success in the Delta program is being promoted into an "A" SWG Sales leadership role somewhere in the world.

"A" position career paths. SWG Sales has defined a dual career path for sales professionals, one that provides for career paths for individual sellers to traditional sales management and one that leads to executive sales roles considered to be "A" in terms of the value they create for clients for the IBM business. These roles are known as the *rainmakers*, and world-class industry expertise coupled with exceptional consultative sales skills are the fundamentals required to be considered for promotion to these elite positions. Within SWG Sales, these positions sit at the very top of what are known as *tiger teams*. These "tigers" have a unique compensation scheme, specialized development, and ongoing training and mentoring, and serve as role models for the career aspirations of sales professionals within SWG Sales.

Summary

Establish Leadership Accountability for Workforce Success

The Line Manager's HR Role

HOW DO WE ensure that firms clearly understand the unique strategic capabilities required to execute their business strategies and develop a differentiated workforce strategy?

The first step is to recognize that the workforce is not just HR's problem, and that line managers and HR leaders have joint responsibility for developing talent throughout the organization. However, while the workforce is the single biggest expenditure for most firms (averaging almost 70 percent of all spending), it is also the last "unaccounted for" resource in most businesses. Thus, companies must devote substantial effort to understanding managers' workforce management responsibilities and how they must differentiate workforce investments and outcomes to create greater economic and customer value.

Management must ensure that top talent is allocated to the strategic roles that create the most value—those that drive the firm's strategic capabilities and create customer and investor wealth. In this chapter, we turn our attention to the leadership role and how real leaders create a differentiated workforce to execute the strategy of their work units. We make five key points:

1. Line managers and leaders influence the mind-set of the workforce and its capabilities more than HR function leaders and managers do.

2. But both line managers *and* HR should be held accountable for the development of a successful workforce.

3. Workforce accountability begins by creating performance expectations for both line managers and HR.

4. Accountability requires inspection to determine if the workforce is meeting those expectations.

5. Workforce accountability becomes a reality when there are consequences for meeting, exceeding, or failing to meet expectations, for both line managers and HR.

Thus, this chapter is about talent and leadership's role with respect to *effective* strategic talent management.

The Role of Leaders in Workforce Strategy Execution

The classic definition of management is "getting things done through others." Most introductory texts on management describe the distinction between managerial and nonmanagerial jobs as the accountability for people (i.e., the workforce). Yet most organizations do not see this accountability as important as the accountability for other resources (e.g., financial, material, information, time, and so on). For most organizational resources, there are systems for allocation, management, and measurement, with consequences for effective or ineffective utilization. But on balance, the workforce lacks these systems and accountabilities, and is frequently not well managed. As a result, strategy execution suffers.

There is a substantial opportunity to have an impact on a firm's strategic success by managing its least well-managed resource, its workforce. We view this as a way that firms with the foresight, willingness, and courage can implement workforce accountability systems for line managers. This is not rocket science; it is simple. It requires creating expectations, inspecting against those expectations, and, most important, holding managers accountable for their workforce just as they are held accountable for other resources. There must be consequences for effective or ineffective workforce management. An investment in time and resources is required to build an accountability system of workforce measurements and commensurate consequences for managers who successfully (or unsuccessfully) manage talent.

Effective strategy execution begins with the right leadership team—leaders who fully understand the strategic pursuit of the firm and the work that adds customer and economic value to deliver that strategy. Leaders must ask if their workforce understands the strategy and whether the business has the right talent in the right roles. These major challenges require leaders with the courage to communicate the strategy, expect the workforce to clearly understand and accept the strategy, and achieve that strategy. Leaders need the courage to make necessary changes in order to constantly enhance the value created for customers and investors. Such changes demand that leaders differentiate every resource that they manage, including the workforce.

Effective leaders create the kind of mind-set that fosters a strategic understanding of each role and customers' and investors' expectations. That mind-set pervades the entire organization—to the lowest levels. For example, at Zingerman's restaurants, even the dishwashers know the firm's operating profit and how they can improve it. It takes effort for a firm to be filled with "missionaries" who can proudly and spontaneously explain to its stakeholders what the firm does, why it does it, and why the company is good to do business with. Managers must constantly communicate the firm's strategy and its strategic issues.

In addition to creating a mind-set, leaders have a significant role in developing a workforce. The workforce should be disproportionately populated with top talent in the roles that enable the firm to realize strategic capabilities at the level necessary to create its intended value. In addition, the organization should be overpopulated with emerging talent (i.e., "B" talent with "A" potential) in strategic roles. Talent should be a primary concern of managers (and the HR function), especially the strategic talent that delivers the firm's value proposition. These strategic roles have a far more profound impact on customers and

A- Versus B-Level Leaders

A-Level Leaders

A-level leaders continually focus on leveraging the firm's competitive advantage by increasing value to customers and creating wealth for investors. Employees, especially those in strategic roles, are clearly aware of the firm's strategy for winning in the marketplace. Work is constantly revised to find ways to add more strategic value to customers and to eliminate work (and bureaucracy) that no longer adds value. A-level leaders identify roles that add strategic value and demand they be filled by the best talent available in the labor market and will not settle for less than the best. Performance expectations are clear and consistently raised; employee performance is continually inspected against these expectations, and specific feedback is provided. Rewards are disproportionate, reflecting the strategic contribution/performance of the employee. Considerable time is devoted to developing the strategic workforce through coaching, rotations, and external training programs. Leaders are evaluated on their leadership capability based on a 90-degree instrument (i.e., from director reports) that assesses how strategically they manage their workforce.

investors than other roles. The care, feeding, growth, and retention of strategic, wealth-creating talent are essential and require a strategic workforce accountability metric for line managers.

The box, "A- Versus B-Level Leaders," describes two types of leaders—one who focuses on the current situation and one who is constantly changing, upgrading, and differentiating. Leaders separate, break away, and change things; they don't just manage. Leaders lead, distance themselves, and break from the past. Leaders at the top have the responsibility for creating unique strategies. Firms win by becoming different, but becoming different requires leaders' courage. Leaders below top management must understand how they can make strategy a reality. Maintaining the status quo is not the job of a leader but the job of a manager. In some

B-Level Leaders

B-level leaders maintain the status quo rather than create change. They focus the workforce internally, primarily on today's work. Work is based on job descriptions (how it was done in the past), rather than future value added to customers. Once created, few positions and little work are eliminated. The objective of selecting employees is to fill the position, often based on political considerations, not rigorously seeking the best candidate (either inside or outside the firm). Performance expectations are often unclear (or based on job descriptions), and little feedback is provided during the performance period. There is little variance in performance ratings, and many employees are highly rated. Rewards are about the same for everyone, irrespective of actual performance. Most "merit" variance can be explained by the employee's base pay, rather than performance. Development is driven more by convenience, rather than by design, with many high-potential candidates identified, regardless of their strategic role in the firm. Managers' competencies are assessed, in part, using a 360-degree instrument (often purchased from a consulting firm), where the manager often selects who provides the data. The 360-degree instruments are developmental-only tools, with the results provided only to the manager profiled.

organizations, there are pillar roles that are always done the same way to provide stability. But seldom do those roles create customer and economic value.

In order for work to change, leaders must lead the change of work. This differentiates A-level from B-level leaders. We may want some "B" leaders who may be moved from one position to another. But if an organization has only "B" leaders, it will be made obsolete by a competitor strongly populated with "A" leaders in strategic roles.

In the box, "Leadership's Role in Workforce Accountability: Talent Management," we itemize the fundamental expectations for talent development. The eight steps are leaders' specific workforce activities to help them determine the positions that drive strategic success, evaluate

Leadership's Role in Workforce Accountability: Talent Management

1. Determine which positions drive strategic success.

2. Assess the talent in these positions: performance/benchmark/ future.

3. Assess whether the talent we have will enable us to achieve our success expectations.

4. Develop action plans for each strategic position.

5. Develop action plans for each employee in a strategic position.

6. Work with HR to assure enough "top talent" in strategic positions.

7. Review strategic talent often.

8. Submit strategic talent updates to HR frequently.

the talent in those positions, and assess whether the talent available will enable the company to achieve its strategy.

In this chapter, we significantly expand on the remaining steps where there is significant work for line managers. Each line manager needs to develop a strategic human capital plan and action plans for each strategic position and for incumbents in those strategic positions, and work with HR to ensure sufficient top talent in those positions. Each line manager should constantly review and assess strategic talent to determine what needs to be done and share updates with HR on the essential level of talent.

HR Practices to Deliver Business Results

Effective workforce strategy execution requires managers to focus on five broad workforce practice areas. These include selection of employees, their development, assessment and reward of performance, design of work, and a process that we developed called *strategic human capital planning*. We detail each practice area and managers' accountability for them later. The process culminates with some questions to use in surveying line managers to determine how effective leadership is in all five practices.

Leaders, by definition, have followers, and how those followers are managed determines a firm's success. Leaders are expected to separate, to differentiate, to take higher ground, and to change the organization. The best source of leader behavior data is from those individuals who report to a manager. Thus, instead of using the traditional 360-degree tool, we propose a top-down or 90-degree instrument as more appropriate. Direct reports provide data about their leaders, about how well they lead, communicate, design work to provide strategic value, articulate competencies required of the workforce to deliver value-added work, develop emerging talent into top talent, articulate and monitor performance expectations, and reward employees for their value-added contributions.

These are similar to the expectations of the HR function, which is to ensure that an organization leverages its workforce to deliver a level of proficiency that makes a strategic difference. HR cannot do this alone; leaders have much more effect on the workforce than does HR. Thus, creating expectations of leaders and judging how well they discharge their workforce management responsibilities is essential. How effective leaders discharge workforce practices is a major component of their accountability to the business.

Leaders can be held accountable for top talent, the extent to which strategic positions are occupied by top talent, and the efforts to close perceived strategic capability gaps attributable to talent. The FridgeCo example later in the chapter describes what is necessary to build a significant accountability metric for the quality of a leader's strategic talent.

Line Managers' Expectations of Their Workforce

Line managers should first expect their workforce to understand the current status of the organization, where the organization is going, and their role in that journey. Such understanding is not commonly held. Many individuals, if given a quiz, have little idea of the firm's customer constituency, its success in serving its investors, or its goals. Employees need to know the frame within which they work. Knowing and understanding

TABLE 4-1

Assessing your workforce mind-set: Where are you? Where do you want to be?

| | My unit's strategic understanding | | | | |
	Not at all	Somewhat	Mostly	To a large extent	Full
External environment – The workforce for which I am responsible understands:					
1. our firm's strategy	1	2	3	4	5
2. our firm's financial targets	1	2	3	4	5
3. that our firm must serve both its customers and its consumers	1	2	3	4	5
4. that we must enhance our firm's image in all interactions with external constituents	1	2	3	4	5
Internal environment – The workforce for which I am responsible understands:					
1. who are the customers we must serve	1	2	3	4	5
2. how well we must serve them	1	2	3	4	5
3. the strategic focus/culture that we desire	1	2	3	4	5
4. the capabilities we need to achieve our financial and customer targets	1	2	3	4	5
Workforce management – The workforce for which I am responsible understands:					
1. that identifying strategic positions that impact our firm's competitive advantage is critical to our firm's strategic success	1	2	3	4	5
2. the strategic talent needed to achieve our financial and customer targets	1	2	3	4	5
3. that line managers must be accountable for their workforces	1	2	3	4	5
4. that line managers must hold their workforces accountable for creating wealth for our firm	1	2	3	4	5

TABLE 4-1

HR capability – The HR workforce for which I am responsible understands:

1. that we are to deliver a work-force that can execute our firm's business strategy	1	2	3	4	5
2. the skills required to develop a workforce that can execute our firm's business strategy	1	2	3	4	5

Deliverables – The workforce for which I am responsible understands:

1. that we must leverage our firm's competitive advantage through our LOB's workforce	1	2	3	4	5
2. that it must enrich our firm's wealth creation over last year's	1	2	3	4	5
3. what HR skills are needed to manage culture/change of our firm's workforce	1	2	3	4	5
4. that HR must have the ability to create cultural change within our firm's workforce	1	2	3	4	5

that frame is a tool for helping employees decide what work is worth delivering and which work should not be done. It's critical that the workforce understand what is expected and to develop a workforce mind-set (see table 4-1).

Line Managers' Role in Selection

Once a line manager has determined what an employee's job is, the next step is to figure out *who* should do it. Figure 4-1 presents a simple model depicting how we believe the workforce should be managed. It assumes that once an individual understands the strategy of the firm, expectations about performance can be created. Essentially, *performance management* is a system of creating expectations and inspecting against those expectations. Once expectations are clear, however, managers must answer the question of who will do the work. Every selection decision is a prediction of who is going to best perform the work. We

FIGURE 4-1

Basic workforce management

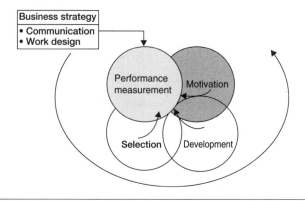

think line managers should be intimately involved in the selection decision. Line managers should own the work and know the work, its value, and its impact on the firm's strategic capabilities and ultimately performance. How well does it need to be done? How good must the talent be to do it? For a strategic position, obviously we want *great* talent. For a "B" or support position, we want good talent. For a "C" position, a lower level of talent is appropriate.

Line Managers' Role in Workforce Development

Next we address the line manager's role in developing a workforce. Development means different things to different people. In the near term, it can mean enabling people to get up to speed to perform a particular job or task within a job. It can also mean enabling experienced employees to improve so they can meet changing performance standards. In terms of career development, it can mean enhancing people's competencies for higher strategic positions in the long term. Thus when we refer to development, we include all three, but especially the growth and retention of strategic talent to move up in the organization.

Line managers need to be intimately involved in the various ways to do this. It is outside the normal performance management process, so it takes significant time, independent of that process. Especially for strategic talent, development is absolutely critical. Young, talented people often ask two things of an employer: "pay me and keep me marketable." The pay is obvious; "keep me marketable" has to do with growth of individual competencies. What we know about competency growth is that most (approximately 70 percent) takes place through assignments. Assignments may include jobs, projects, tasks—work experiences throughout an employee's work life. Second, coaching and mentoring explains about 20 percent of an individual's professional competency portfolio, and formal training programs, only about 10 percent.

What is the role of line managers in development? They can provide experiences and continue to challenge and stretch people, especially talented people who want to grow their careers. They can give a part of their own job away, such as a project or specific deliverable, or ensure that they move to other positions to not only grow but also retain them. But development is a long-term proposition and if a firm is faced with severe talent challenges, selection may be the best option. However, if firms are going to invest in people, doing so in strategic roles and working assiduously to retain developed talent may be the prudent course.

Line Managers' Role in Assessment and Rewards

Line managers play a significant role in the reward and recognition of the workforce. How talented people are treated from a reward and recognition perspective is essential for their retention and motivation. As we said earlier, talented people are most interested in pay and career development. The pay issue is critical, because we know that everyone can go online to Vault.com to check the profiles of other firms and Salary.com to compare the salaries for their position. The availability of such information has a profound influence on how people perceive their current circumstances. Thus we see much mobility of strategic talent not only in North America but across the globe. In many areas such as in Shanghai or Mumbai, the movement of individuals for the best opportunities and compensation is increasing, so much so that it severely challenges organizations and their HR functions to retain staff, especially in strategic roles.

Line Managers' Role in Work Design

Design of work, another critical practice in the line managers' role, has an impact on what work is done, how well, and to what extent employees are growing their professional portfolio of skills. Work design can be profoundly affected by constantly questioning what work is worth keeping, what work should be abandoned, and how to leverage the appropriate identification of work to the advantage of customers and investors. Some firms are moving to customer-based job designs, creating work from the customer back and avoiding (or eliminating) the traditional job descriptions where employees explain what they did in the past as a prologue of the work's current and future requirements. The perception of a leader who focuses his or her workforce on constantly expanding value-added work and including or eliminating all other work is also included in a 90-degree survey of direct reports.

Line Managers' Role in Strategic Human Capital Planning

The final (and most important) workforce management practice is a process we developed called *strategic human capital planning*. This process involves determining and evaluating your firm's unique strategic capabilities and then identifying the strategic or "A" positions required to execute your strategy. You then develop a talent inventory for each position, which helps you generate an action plan capable of delivering the needed talents. Finally, you determine specific managerial workforce accountabilities, which are then captured in each manager's performance appraisal.

An example of the strategic human capital planning process can be seen at FridgeCo (real name disguised). FridgeCo, a large appliance division of a major corporation, is located in the Midwest. It produces retail appliances primarily for big-box vendors such as Best Buy and Circuit City. FridgeCo is under severe competitive pressure, not only domestically but from global high-end and low-end competitors (especially from Haier, the Chinese multinational). Haier is a fierce competitor that is manufacturing and marketing in at least sixteen nations.

FridgeCo recently experienced serious problems in customer satisfaction, revenues, and profitability, all significant indications that the value it needs to create and the value it is creating are not aligned. Its current workforce of six thousand has been reduced substantially over the past several years. The company has a new CEO and a new senior vice president of human resources. Both are very focused on talent and believe that many of the current employees (especially executives) are not a team that will enable the organization to succeed.

FridgeCo's strategy is one of operational excellence in a highly price-sensitive market. Using the process we described in chapter 2, it identified four strategic capabilities: executive leadership, manufacturing excellence, sales and marketing, and R&D and new product development (see table 4-2). FridgeCo also assessed the gaps between where it is and where it needs to be in each capability.

FridgeCo subsequently identified twelve strategic positions with a total of 111 incumbents. Using the talent designation criteria shown in table 4-3, it assessed these individuals, categorizing them into top, emerging, and career-level talent. It used these criteria to determine talent and preliminary action plans for the near term. It determined where it intends each position to be within eighteen months. FridgeCo knows if it is not aggressive, it may not survive.

FridgeCo concluded that it cannot continue to operate as it is now. It has two or three years until it could be sold or closed. The new CEO and the new vice president for HR are determined to keep the plant open and save many of the jobs, as well as continue the contributions that the firm makes to the local community.

It is easy to recognize from the data in table 4-2 that although the firm wishes to be world class in manufacturing, forty of its sixty-four strategic incumbents are identified as career level, with an additional seven labeled as "moves"—that is, it plans to move them out of strategic positions. These forty-seven incumbents are a serious problem for FridgeCo. Moving to world-class levels is not a linear but an exponential target. Only a few organizations are defined as world class. The question FridgeCo needs to ask is: Do we have the talent to enable us to achieve that level within eighteen months? The answer is no. Thus FridgeCo leaders must decide on its message and how to redesign the jobs of plant

TABLE 4-2

FridgeCo strategic human capital plan

Business leader recap
Line of business: Retail appliance division

Strategic talent HCP
Position scorecard

Strategic capabilities:

- Executive leadership
- Manufacturing excellence
- Sales/marketing
- R&D/new product development

			Status		
	Abysmal (1)	Less competitive (2)	Competitive (3)	Very competitive (4)	World class (5)
Executive leadership			3 →→→→→→→		↑
Manufacturing excellence				4 ↑	
Sales/marketing				4 ↑	
R&D/new product development		2 →→→→→→			

Strategic positions:	Number	Top talent	Emerging talent	Career level	Move	Action plans
• Executive leadership						
– VP marketing	1		1			Develop more talent from sales and marketing.
– VP manufacturing	1			2		Consider early replacement of VP manufacturing.
– CFO	1	1				
• Manufacturing						
– Plant managers	16	4	2	7	2	Exit moves and "careerists." Hire developing talent. Hire and
– Area supervisors	48	7	3	33	5	move "top talent" into the 38 career level/move positions.
• Sales/marketing						
– Marketing directors	6	2	1	1	2	Exit moves and initiate campus recruiting and career devel-
– Brand managers	5	1	1	3	0	opment plans to strengthen marketing talent at all levels.
– Consumer insight specialists	7	2	4	0	1	
– Merchandising managers	6	1	0	5	0	
• R&D/new product development						
– Design engineers	11	3	0	8	0	Initiate external hiring program for "top talent" at all levels. Begin to exit careerists – we have 14 of 20 in this category.
– Cooling specialists	4	1	1	2	0	
– Laundry specialists	5	1	0	4	0	
	111	Σ = 37		64		
		Mentors needed				

TABLE 4-3

Determining "player" status at FridgeCo: Criteria considerations

"Player" status/criteria	Top talent	Emerging talent	Career level	Exit
External benchmark	Among the top 10% available for this position in the external labor market; often sought by best competitors for strategic roles	Highly sought after in the labor market; may be a promotion and substantial increase in pay	Unlikely to be recruited by a major competitor in this or higher role in this function, with major pay increase	No better than midpoint of talent available in the labor market; substantially below average talent in the labor market
Current performance	Excellent performance/ outstanding by most any standard	Very good performer and continues to improve; seeks and succeeds in developmental challenges	Could be an outstanding performer, but often solid performer meets most expectations; exceeds some, fails some	Below expectations at present and well below expectations for the more competitive environment we face
Internal bench strength	Clearly a succession candidate for a vertical move in a strategic role, in this strategic function or another	Clearly in the succession pool for advancement in this strategic function	Not in succession pool for advancement in a strategic role in this function or another, may be moved to a nonstrategic support role	Certainly not in succession pools or slates for strategic positions and not seen as a fit for our future strategy
Developmental action	Certainly in succession pool for several openings in strategic/developmental roles or slates and will be selected; a critical part of our future strategy	Performance warrants developmental move in a strategic role within this function; clearly must in a substantial developmental move in a strategic role to retain this person and build our bench strength	Potential does not warrant promotion in a strategic position; may be a developmental candidate in a nonstrategic role	Find a better fit or remove from the organization

managers and area supervisors. They must articulate necessary performance expectations. Leaders must also determine the appropriate rewards and incentives for plant managers and area supervisors. Finally, the leaders must decide which developmental efforts are necessary, especially for emerging talent, to enable them to quickly make extraordinary contributions and deliver the business results to keep the plant operating. Finally, they need to ask, What is our selection strategy? How do we recruit? Who do we recruit? Where do we recruit? And how are we able to track the level of talent that is absolutely necessary?

As with most organizations, the managers got FridgeCo into this dilemma. Can they get FridgeCo out of it? The executive vice president of manufacturing is a career-level individual. Perhaps new leadership is required at the very top of manufacturing.

The situation is much the same in sales and marketing, although they believe they are very competitive and need to remain so. Although there are twenty-four incumbents in strategic positions within sales and marketing (marketing directors, brand managers, consumer insight specialists, and merchandising managers), there are nine at career level and three who the firm has already targeted as "moves." Thus, 50 percent of the existing marketing organization is not considered top talent. The question now is, how critical is this talent gap and what does FridgeCo need to do? Further, FridgeCo recognized that its sales function was less critical than the marketing function. It needs real marketers, people who can help FridgeCo pull product through the big-box retailers. It needs people who can promote, market, and ensure that new demand is created for its products, even in a price-sensitive market.

So how can FridgeCo create more demand for its products, beyond price? The difficult question is, does FridgeCo have the sales and marketing workforce that can do this? In fact, we recognized that selling to big-box retailers was not the challenge. The real challenge was marketing to the consumers who buy appliances from the big-box retailers.

The same analysis was necessary for R&D and new product development. Ideally, FridgeCo needs some new products or innovations that would differentiate it from competitors despite price competition. Looking at the R&D talent data, there are twenty incumbents in strategic positions, and fourteen at career level. Thus 70 percent of this workforce is at the top of their careers and highly unlikely to significantly improve their talent levels. The question is, can these individuals create and have the market impact FridgeCo needs, through innovative offerings in the very near term? Some may be able to achieve what we expect; others may not. In this instance, the reality was that FridgeCo needed new R&D and some way to differentiate its products through product development. Thus the firm decided to remove the current staff and recruit new talent.

Fortunately, FridgeCo found several young engineers who were thrilled to join the organization. FridgeCo decided to expand its hiring beyond people who would require time to bond and be able to create the product innovations and hired a team of five skilled individuals (all from the same firm), who knew each other and brought excitement about designing, engineering, and marketing appliances. Hiring this team was fortuitous, but it taught FridgeCo a lesson. At times, it may be best to recruit not for an individual but for a team. In addition, because new product development can create real customer value and subsequent economic value, the organization decided to hire a human resources vice president for product development, who reports to the CEO. In the past, all R&D people reported to the senior vice president of manufacturing.

Table 4-4 outlines the early actions taken to hit the relatively stringent targets at FridgeCo. These are the beginning steps, as FridgeCo needed to significantly upgrade its talent to remain in business. The organization decided that it was going to rigorously analyze its organization by identifying the appropriate workforce actions necessary for "A," "B," and "C" positions. The table shows the severe differentiation in the deployment of HR practices in selection, development, performance management, rewards, communication, and work design.

FridgeCo has had the second largest market appreciation on the New York Exchange in this decade. It has been extremely successful in acquiring properties and rigorously managing talented people to its best advantage. This example shows only one of several major steps FridgeCo took to deploy strategic talent for strategic positions, creating significant customer and economic value. If FridgeCo had done this earlier, the threat to the company and the workforce might have been averted.

TABLE 4-4

Aligning HR practices to deliver strategic talent at FridgeCo

	"A" positions	"B" positions	"C" positions
	Target: Attracting, growing, and retaining candidates/employees from the top 10% of the available labor market for strategic positions.	Target: Attracting and growing candidates/employees from the middle of the labor market for positions that support the success of the strategic workforce.	Target: Attracting candidates from below the midpoint of the labor market for necessary positions that are neither strategic nor support strategic positions.
Selection	• Talent is constantly top-graded. • Never wait for a vacancy to recruit. • Constantly in the market for top candidates. • Seek referrals from very top performers. • Assiduously screen all referrals using specific, high-expectation criteria.	• A vacancy must occur before recruiting begins. • Use an agency for recruiting. • Allow screening to be conducted by recruiter. • Permit only referrals from recruiters who are below the market midpoint in compensation. • Positions eliminated if not contributing to the strategic success of the firm.	• Each vacancy scrutinized for its necessity. • Recruit with newspaper ads. • Use an agency screen and hire from applications. • Positions eliminated if adding little or no value.
Performance management	• Set performance expectations at very high levels; among the highest in the Industry or establish world-class standards using both outcome and behavioral standards. • Performance is continuously monitored and employees given frequent feedback on the status of their contributions. • Immediately separate employees in strategic positions who are not performing at very high levels.	• "Success" is defined as meeting a market standard for performance. • Outstanding performance is slightly above what is considered the market standard. • Occasional feedback provided for standard and above-standard employees. • Employees performing very poorly are removed.	• Standard performance is at or below market midpoint. • Feedback is given only if employees fall significantly below standard performance. • If employees in this position continue to come to work and meet minimum standards, they are retained.

Rewards	• Base compensations is well above the third quintile in the market; may even have internal midpoint as high as the ninetieth percentile. • Significant "at risk" variable pay is used as an incentive with top-performing employees, often doubling or tripling their base compensation (or even higher in many instances). • Incentive pay does not become a part of base pay.	• Base compensation is about the midpoint of the market. • Incentive pay is provided based on the range of market movement for the position (e.g., 3%–4%) with top performers getting twice the maximum increase if they are below market. • Gain sharing/goal sharing is encouraged. • Low performers receive no increase in pay.	• Base compensation is set with the midpoint at the lowest quartile or the market for the positions. • Increases are based on market movement for the positions. • Productivity incentives (and technology) that reduce cost of this work are encouraged.
Development	• Significant developmental resources are set aside for investing in individuals in these positions. • Each employee in these positions has a mentor (or external coach); is considered for rotational assignments and provided internal and external training opportunities. • Best practices are encouraged and efforts devoted to the development, identification, and sharing of best-practice examples. • Funds are readily available for attending professional conferences and best-practice audits. • Attendance at a special orientation designed for strategic positions is mandatory.	• Employees are encouraged to attend programs designed to enhance their skills in their specific area of expertise. • Leaders/managers in these roles are encouraged to attend the leadership development offerings provided by the firm. • Attendance at organizationwide orientation is mandatory.	• Employees are expected to attend training efforts designed to enable them to meet the minimum performance standards. • Managers/supervisors can attend companywide developmental programs when space is available. • Attendance at organizationwide orientation is optional.
Communication	• Messages acknowledge employees' value to the firm and that their roles make the firm's business strategy become a reality.	• Incumbents are informed that their role is to support the strategy of the business by enabling strategic roles to deliver more value to customers and leverage the firm's margins in doing so.	• Messages are designed to indicate that these roles are designed to provide a stable, safe, and secure work environment for the organization.

TABLE 4-4 (CONTINUED)

	"A" positions	"B" positions	"C" positions
	• They are often in contact with "stretch" customers to learn new ways of enhancing the value of their efforts in meeting customer requirements. • Messages from top management make them intimately familiar with the firm's business strategy. • Supervisors consistently assure top performers in these positions of their value to the firm now and in the future.	• They are to understand that their value is focusing on work that makes strategic roles successful. • They are admonished that creativity and innovation in providing support to strategic roles is encouraged and recognized.	• Unacceptable performance will not be tolerated. • Exceptional performance may not be recognized.
Work design	• New and improved ways of adding strategic value are demanded and revered. • Efforts are designed to remove all bureaucratic non-value-added work from these positions. • All work is constantly assessed for its strategic value. Work once considered highly valuable but devalued in competitive markets will be eliminated regardless of who designed the work or work processes. • Special "best practices" training sessions are developed to train the strategic workforce in new, improved ways of creating customer and economic value for the firm. • No work is sacred. If it does not leverage the firm's competitive advantage in these positions, it is eliminated.	• Improving work processes that reduce costs and/or deliver enhanced levels of strategic support to the firm's business strategy are highly encouraged. • Monitoring internal and external best practices is encouraged and suggestions to audit best practices taken seriously and implemented. All non-value-added strategic work is to be eliminated. • Offshoring/outsourcing may be implemented when it provides sufficient value to the firm's strategy.	• New ways to eliminate work are encouraged and acted on immediately. • All unnecessary work is to be eliminated. • Outsourcing and offshoring are constantly considered for these positions.

Assessment of Line Managers' Success

Organizations measure many things, but the measurement of the workforce and holding line managers accountable for this expensive resource is not well practiced. We need to develop far more effective tools to hold line managers accountable. In designing such tools, we consider three components: (1) assessment of line managers on the workforce's mind-set, (2) management of strategic talent, and (3) the line manager's behavior in exercising workforce responsibilities. The line manager can be held accountable for each of these elements (see table 4-5). The questions in the table relate to the message the firm wants to communicate to its entire workforce, such as how to grow, what are the obstacles to growth, what the firm is doing about marketplace growth, how it can accelerate change, how well it is doing on the metrics that indicate strategic success, and the workforce's understanding about their role in the firm's success.

This relatively simple and straightforward tool assesses the extent to which leaders are perceived as delivering on expectations, provided by the best source of that information—their direct reports. Direct reports have a unique perspective, especially for performance measurement, rewards, and development. They also have an opportunity to assess selection, especially the external candidates brought into the organization, how new hires compare with internal candidates (who were aspirants for the position), and their impact on wealth creation. In the areas of work design and communication, employees are a critical source of data input, because they know what has been communicated and their level of strategic understanding of where the firm is going, its obstacles, and work allocation is crucial. They often have better ideas for what work needs to be done and by whom than the leader does. This tool can be used to assess leaders as they attempt to deliver their workforce responsibilities.

TABLE 4-5

The line manager's HR responsibilities

	Manager's rating				
	Not at all	Somewhat	Well	Very well	Extremely well
Communications: How well does this manager...					
1. provide strategic direction for our group?	1	2	3	4	5
2. continually remind us how we must grow (improve our group's contributions)?	1	2	3	4	5
3. remind us of our obstacles and what we need to do to remove them?	1	2	3	4	5
4. admonish us of the metrics indicative of our success and where we stand?	1	2	3	4	5
Work design/redesign: How well does this manager...					
1. continually redesign work to add greater strategic value?	1	2	3	4	5
2. eliminate work which no longer adds value?	1	2	3	4	5
Performance management: How well does my manager...					
1. detail what is expected of me in my job?	1	2	3	4	5
2. detail how well I am performing?	1	2	3	4	5
3. provide feedback on how well I am performing throughout the year?	1	2	3	4	5
4. conduct year-end reviews with no surprises?	1	2	3	4	5
Selection/staffing: How well does this manager...					
1. detail performance and competency expectations in preparing to make staffing/selection decisions?	1	2	3	4	5
2. interview candidates and provide detailed feedback to HR?	1	2	3	4	5
3. ask HR for a list of internal candidates?	1	2	3	4	5
4. review internal candidates and provide feedback on each?	1	2	3	4	5

Development: How well does this manager...

	1	2	3	4	5
1. demonstrate interest in my professional development and provide me with stretch experiences?	1	2	3	4	5
2. hold individual one-on-one development sessions separate from performance appraisals?	1	2	3	4	5
3. discuss career opportunities and offer developmental assignments to enhance eligibility?	1	2	3	4	5
4. contact their manager to aid in employees' career growth?	1	2	3	4	5
5. provide candid feedback about reality of career advancement?	1	2	3	4	5

Rewards and recognition: How well does this manager...

	1	2	3	4	5
1. provide me recognition throughout the performance period?	1	2	3	4	5
2. inform me of what more I need to do to get more rewards?	1	2	3	4	5
3. make recognition of outstanding performance in public?	1	2	3	4	5
4. communicate the value of our team incentive and why we receive it?	1	2	3	4	5
5. provide equitable rewards and recognition based on my performance?	1	2	3	4	5

Strategic HR planning: How well does my manager...

	1	2	3	4	5
1. identify strategic wealth-creating positions?	1	2	3	4	5
2. identify strategic positions which have a significant impact on customers?	1	2	3	4	5
3. assure that we have "top talent" in these strategic positions?	1	2	3	4	5
4. remove "C" and "B" players from these strategic roles?	1	2	3	4	5
5. identify emerging strategic talent and enable their rapid growth into "top talent"?	1	2	3	4	5
6. assure that "career level" talent in strategic positions are outstanding performers?	1	2	3	4	5

Summary

In this chapter, we have focused on the role of leadership in effective strategy execution. Our approach begins with the definition of clear expectations by the leadership team, which are then implemented by specific actions taken by leadership to differentiate the workforce through selection, development, assessment and rewards, work design, and strategic human capital planning. The last of these elements is crucial, as it is through the process of talent inventories and action plans that leaders can help to ensure that they place "A" players in "A" positions for "A" customers.

In the next chapter, we describe how to build an HR architecture to support a differentiated workforce. We discuss the importance of developing a culture of accountability and a workforce philosophy to drive successful strategy execution through the workforce. We show how to design an integrated system of HR management policies and practices to help execute strategy. We conclude with a discussion of the HR practices that must be specifically differentiated by strategic capability, versus those which need to be the same for everyone.

CHAPTER 5

Design an HR Architecture for the Differentiated Workforce

W E HAVE EMPHASIZED the importance of ensuring that a firm's workforce strategy—and its workforce—is as differentiated as its business strategy. Developing a differentiated workforce requires that the HR management policies and practices a firm adopts be differentiated as well, not just by business strategy but, more important, by *strategic capability*—the bundle of information, technology, and people needed to execute your strategy.

Making meaningful and lasting changes in your workforce management systems requires a clear understanding of *why* change is necessary, *how* to change, and an *action plan* to ensure that it happens. It is important to create a system not only where the parts and pieces fit together in a way that makes sense to the workforce, but also where they are specifically designed to execute strategy.

After identifying strategic capabilities and strategic positions, many managers feel the pressure to jump right in and make changes, but a poorly planned execution strategy can often backfire. The HR policies and practices in most firms have developed and evolved slowly over a long time, and can be very resistant to change. Thus, the change-management intervention process should be carefully designed and appropriately resourced.

We start this chapter with a discussion of the importance of developing a culture of accountability and a workforce philosophy to help drive successful strategy execution. We then show how to design an integrated system of HR management policies and practices to help execute strategy, focusing on the distinction between HR practices that must be specifically differentiated by strategic position and those that need to be the same for all jobs. Finally, we describe the key roles, accountabilities, and infrastructure needed in the HR function to support this process of strategic transformation.

From Strategic Intent to Corporate Culture

All firms have cultures. Sometimes firms actively choose and manage their culture; at other times, it seems as though the culture chooses the firm and the workforce is just along for the ride. Managers need to ensure that they develop a corporate culture by design, not by accident. Managers need to ask tough questions about their firm's culture: What do we want our culture to look like? How do we embed values and assumptions throughout the organization? What needs to happen for us to develop the culture we need? Who will be accountable for making this happen? Where do we start? While thousands of books and articles have focused on the topic of organizational culture, the literature on developing a culture of accountability in support of strategy execution and the workforce is surprisingly sparse.

In a culture of accountability, everyone in the firm focuses on executing the strategy, helping each other improve, and holding each other accountable for the outcomes. This is much easier said than done. In the global business environment, successful strategy execution requires consistently higher levels of performance—and much higher levels of internal and external differentiation. A clearly articulated culture of accountability helps to enable successful strategy execution. But few firms are able to create such a culture, instead settling for "feel good" cultures that make everyone comfortable but do little to ensure success.

Consider the two scenarios in the box, "What Mind-set and Culture Do We Want?," based on our work with a wide variety of companies. The

What Mind-set and Culture Do We Want?

Firm X—Employer of Choice

We are an *employer of choice*, and we work hard to hire the best employees for all positions in our business. Once we hire them, we try to make sure that they are committed to our firm and never want to leave. We provide them great salaries and benefits. We also make certain they have the tools to do their jobs and recognize their good work. Our supervisors care deeply about our employees and encourage each employee's career growth. Our employees also know the values of our firm and that caring about them is an important part of our firm's mission. Our firm also believes it is important to have friends at work. Most important, we are committed to do the very best work we can in all our jobs. Few people ever leave our firm voluntarily.

Firm Y—Employee of Choice

We hire the *very* best employees (from the very top of the labor market) for strategic positions that create wealth for the firm. We will do whatever is necessary to attract, grow, and develop employees in these roles. Our leaders create stretch expectations for these employees and inspect their performance rigorously, extremely candidly, honestly, and accurately. We have career growth models to stretch these employees and expect extraordinary contributions and growth from them. We believe in removing all bureaucratic obstacles (including employees and leaders) that get in the way of positions with wealth-creating impact and affect our ability to attract or retain this talent. We are an employee-equity firm and proud of it.

"feel good" culture of firm X is much more common and significantly less effective than that of firm Y. Y-type firms are more likely to consistently and effectively execute their strategies, in large part because they have open and honest conversations with the workforce about what the firm needs to do to be successful and how the workforce can contribute.

From Corporate Culture to Workforce Philosophy

A comparison of firms X and Y highlights the importance of workforce mind-set and culture in strategy execution and firm success. Developing a mind-set and culture of accountability involves two steps. The first is to develop a workforce philosophy that outlines the firm's expectations and accountabilities for the workforce. An effective workforce philosophy—a concept that we introduced in our previous book *The Workforce Scorecard*—is an important teaching tool to help managers communicate strategic intent and also to clarify accountabilities for line and HR managers. The second is to develop a unique and differentiated system of HR management policies and practices to translate the workforce philosophy into strategy execution.

An effective workforce philosophy has several dimensions that explain the roles and responsibilities of managers and employees. It describes the nature of the work relationship between employees and the firm in clear behavioral terms. In addition, it outlines the roles and responsibilities of each primary functional area and describes where the firm will and will not invest in the workforce. This type of document is also an important recruiting tool for high-potential talent, as it demonstrates to employees that the firm has thought carefully about their development and will invest in them.

The process of developing a workforce philosophy is partly empirical and partly clinical. In *The Workforce Scorecard* we presented the fifty-item scale shown in figure 5-1. This tool is very helpful in working with management teams to raise points of agreement and disagreement and measure progress toward consensus on the firm's workforce philosophy.

This tool is also useful in uncovering a firm's current and desired workforce philosophy, especially when data is collected from high-potential employees at various organizational levels.[1] We typically feed the data back to the executives, showing them (1) highest-rated items, (2) lowest-rated items, (3) items with the highest level of agreement, (4) items with the highest level of disagreement, and (5) items with the highest discrepancy between the "have now" and "will need in the future" categories.

Collecting such data is an important step in the process of developing a workforce philosophy. The workforce philosophy should be a joint

FIGURE 5-1

What is your workforce philosophy? Which choices must your firm make to deliver its competitive advantage?

Workforce strategy: Developing a strategically successful workforce
Listed below are examples of principles that could be the basis of your firm's workforce philosophy. They are intended to stimulate your thinking as you consider how to design and build the best workforce to deliver your firm's strategy. Please check those that represent your firm now and those you believe are necessary to deliver your firm's strategy and to build the most successful workforce in your industry. These are but a sample of workforce philosophy statements taken from various firms. You may wish to add others.

Now Future

☐ ☐ 1. All employees deserve "lifetime job security."
☐ ☐ 2. All employees are entitled to an annual increase.
☐ ☐ 3. Equality is more important than equity.
☐ ☐ 4. Leadership competencies for top positions should be based on our leaders today.
☐ ☐ 5. Replacement planning for all top positions is critical.
☐ ☐ 6. Employee advocacy by the HR function is critical.
☐ ☐ 7. Staffing strategic capabilities is an imperative.
☐ ☐ 8. Each employee's performance must improve annually.
☐ ☐ 9. Every employee must contribute more value to the firm than they receive from it.
☐ ☐ 10. Successful staffing of "A" positions is critical.
☐ ☐ 11. Having effective leaders at all levels is critical to strategic success.
☐ ☐ 12. Corporate "owns" and manages the careers of most "A" positions.
☐ ☐ 13. Developmental investment should be made in "A" players in "A" positions.
☐ ☐ 14. Developmental investment in "B" players with "A" potential is critical.
☐ ☐ 15. Performance management is a tool to execute strategy.
☐ ☐ 16. "C" players must be developed or exited.
☐ ☐ 17. All employees must contribute to customer/consumer success.
☐ ☐ 18. No employee "owns" a position.
☐ ☐ 19. Line managers have workforce responsibilities: mind-set, competency growth, and employee behavior.
☐ ☐ 20. Line management is to execute workforce strategy.
☐ ☐ 21. We must topgrade in all "A" positions.

Now Future

☐ ☐ 22. "A" players must be in "A" positions.
☐ ☐ 23. Competency growth is required in all positions.
☐ ☐ 24. All employees are strategic resources, operational resources, or surplus.
☐ ☐ 25. Generating ideas and high levels of performance are the criteria for employee advancement.
☐ ☐ 26. Differential investment in employees is necessary.
☐ ☐ 27. "B" players are expected in "B" positions.
☐ ☐ 28. "C" positions (and "C" work) must be eliminated.
☐ ☐ 29. Managers must be accountable for their workforces.
☐ ☐ 30. Knowledge sharing is indispensable to strategic success.
☐ ☐ 31. Retention of "A" players in "A" positions is vital.
☐ ☐ 32. Our workforce is HR's major deliverable.
☐ ☐ 33. Management of the workforce should represent at least 25% of a line manager or executive's performance evaluation.
☐ ☐ 34. Active learners in all "A" positions are needed.
☐ ☐ 35. "A" positions are not hierarchical, but based on strategic value to the firm.
☐ ☐ 36. All employees must be given timely, candid feedback on their performance.
☐ ☐ 37. Managers should be the advocate of their employees based on their performance.
☐ ☐ 38. Employees should be their own advocates.
☐ ☐ 39. Replacement planning for all strategic positions is critical.
☐ ☐ 40. Building a deep, broad succession pool is critical.

FIGURE 5-1 (CONTINUED)

☐ ☐ 41. "A" positions should have a midpoint at the 75th percentile, "B" positions at the 50th, and "C" positions (if we must have a few) no higher than the 25th percentile.

☐ ☐ 42. Outsourcing is a tool we must use to provide us focus and reduce our costs.

☐ ☐ 43. Offshoring is a competitive tool we must use to strengthen our competitive advantage.

☐ ☐ 44. The primary focus/customer of HR's work is line management.

☐ ☐ 45. The focus/customer of HR's work is the firm's external customers.

☐ ☐ 46. HR and the CHRO must serve as the firm's corporate conscience.

☐ ☐ 47. Accountability must become a capability within our firm.

☐ ☐ 48. The CHRO must become responsible for corporate governance standards.

☐ ☐ 49. All leaders are expected to communicate the firm (or business unit's) strategy to the workforce.

☐ ☐ 50. All leaders will be assessed in part on how well their workforce understands the firm's strategy and its status.

Source: Mark A. Huselid, Brian E. Becker, and Richard W. Beatty, *The Workforce Scorecard: Managing Human Capital to Execute Strategy* (Boston, MA: Harvard Business School Press, 2005), 4.

product of both line and HR managers to both improve its overall quality and generate buy-in and acceptance of the final outcome. For example, a team of line and HR managers at Lockheed Martin, a military contractor, worked on developing a workforce philosophy (see the box, "Lockheed Martin's Workforce Philosophy"). Lockheed Martin's business has changed dramatically in recent years, based on its customers' needs. Going forward, Lockheed Martin needs a more integrated, team-based approach to effectively execute its strategy. It reorganized the business, but lacked a mechanism to communicate the needed changes throughout the workforce. By developing the philosophy and communicating it to the workforce, Lockheed Martin's managers came to a consensus about which elements of the workforce were crucial to successful strategy execution and, as a management team, became committed to the process as they spread the ideas throughout the organization. Specifically, Lockheed Martin concluded that it needed to ensure that the workforce clearly understood the challenging environment the firm faced, the importance of strategic focus, the criticality of delivering customer success, the need for workforce differentiation and diversity, the importance of leadership accountability, and the role of the HR function and its managers in ensuring strategic success.

We can't overstate the importance of developing a shared understanding of the workforce philosophy. When senior executives devote attention to this topic, they often find that they have very different

Lockheed Martin's Workforce Philosophy

1. **Challenging Environment.** The United States competes with other nations for military and nonmilitary technological superiority and is faced with new entrants in a variety of emerging markets. Lockheed Martin's goal is to be *the* solution provider of choice. This requires talent superiority, despite critical skill shortages in the available labor market, and extraordinary teaming with internal and external partners in providing customer-focused solutions.

2. **Strategic Focus.** We must establish strategies that address the changing global environment and diversified customer needs in current, adjacent, and emerging markets. This requires superior technical capabilities that deliver innovative solutions and provide the best value to our customers and end-users. Thus our workforce must embrace growth and readiness capability to precisely meet business and customer expectations. Business decisions must balance short-term results with long-term gains, which requires the workforce to have the skills and agility to meet current and future customer needs.

3. **Delivering Customer Success.** We must view all business activities from the customer's perspective, ensuring our customers' success. In order to achieve this, we must cultivate enduring, strategic customer relationships and help them shape the future. We must understand the environment that customers and end-users face and provide solutions that combine innovation with operational excellence, provide *one* face to the customer, and deliver exceptional value.

4. **Workforce Differentiation and Diversity.** An inclusive workplace values diversity of thought to provide unique customer-focused solutions. It is essential that we have key talent in strategic positions and that these careers will be managed and deployed across the enterprise. Lockheed Martin must differentiate investment in the development, recognition, and compensation of key talent. Employees must understand that those who collaboratively share

ideas, knowledge, and solutions, and align their performance in order to deliver business results will be disproportionately rewarded. Our future success will require workforce agility as never before; thus cross-organizational development and assignments will be necessary to ensure our competitiveness.

5. **Leadership Accountability.** Full Spectrum Leaders are accountable for their workforce. This requires communicating business strategy, creating a high-performance culture, clarifying performance expectations, and assessing each employee's performance, relative to these expectations. Each leader is to be accountable for his or her behavior and the behavior of the workforce. This will require honest, accurate assessments of every employee and rewards commensurate with strategic contributions to business success. In doing so, leaders will make our Workforce Philosophy a reality.

6. **The Role of HR.** We must recognize that our business success is increasingly more dependent upon strategic talent to provide the solutions necessary to meet customer expectations in an ever-changing environment. HR's primary responsibility is to partner with leadership in the advocacy and delivery of strategic talent for our customers. The workforce is the deliverable of HR.

values and beliefs. As a result, this process is vital for raising divergent views and achieving consensus.

From Workforce Philosophy to Workforce Management Systems

The development of a clear workforce philosophy is also a crucial step toward building an HR architecture to execute strategy. An explicit workforce philosophy helps both line and HR managers carry on the process of creating a differentiated workforce. Once the philosophy is developed, the next step is to understand how the firm's HR management processes and systems drive this outcome.

HR practices affect firm performance indirectly by altering the knowledge, skills, abilities, and motivation of the workforce, which in turn produces some type of goods or service, which is purchased by customers (or not), which in turn generates revenue and profits. None of this is guaranteed, and the increasingly competitive markets and long lead times between workforce investments and the profits generated make this task daunting. Recognition that firm performance is the outcome of a long string of actions is an important component of the design and implementation of an effective workforce management system.

Being very clear about what you want the workforce to understand and be able to do, and what, very specifically, you need employees to *deliver* to the business is important. Think of the information employees need in terms of *business strategy*, *strategic focus*, *performance focus*, *performance management*, *performance consequences*, and *employee outcomes*, as we outline in table 5-1.

> *Business strategy.* Employees must have a clear understanding of the firm's competitive strategy, being able to answer questions such as: How will we grow our business? How will we win a disproportionate share of customers in the markets where we compete? What is our competitive advantage? What strategic capabilities enable our competitive advantage to become a reality? What strategic capabilities will be necessary to win our future?

> *Strategic focus.* Employees need to clearly understand the strategic capabilities essential for delivering the strategy. What customer and wealth-creating capabilities are essential? What are the obstacles to our growth and what should we do about them? How do we accelerate our growth? What metrics indicate our growth or strategic success?

> *Performance management.* Employees need to see how their job fits with the other jobs and roles in the organization. Who has an

TABLE 5-1

What do you *really* want your workforce to understand?

Business stategy	Strategic focus	Performance focus	Performance management	Performance consequences	Employee outcomes
• How will we grow our business?	• What customer and wealth-creating capabilities are essential?	• What is expected of me?	• Who has an impact on my work?	• What happens to me if I do a great job?	Employees:
• How will we win a disproportionate share of customers in the markets where we compete?	• What are the obstacles to our growth and what should we do about them?	• How well am I to perform?	• How well am I doing?	• What will happen if I do not perform at the expected level?	• Understand strategy
		• Do I have the competencies I need?	• How do I get specific, timely feedback on my work?		• Are able to deliver strategy
• What is our competitive advantage?	• How do we accelerate our growth?	• Do I need new/different competencies?	• Who do I go to to remove obstacles to my efforts that impact our competitive advantage and create wealth for the firm?	• Is extraordinary performance expected / highly rewarded in roles that impact our competitive advantage and/or create wealth for the firm?	• Engage in strategic behavior
• What strategic capabilities enable our competitive advantage to become a reality?	• What are the metrics indicative of our growth/ strategic success?	• What work impacts our success with customers?			• Create wealth
		• What work impacts our ability to change our desired price?			
• What strategic capabilities will be necessary to win our future?		• What work reduces production costs?			
		• What do I do that creates wealth for the firm?			
		• What are my work priorities?			
		• What should I spend very little time doing?			
		• What should I stop doing?			

impact on my work? How well am I doing? How do I get specific, timely feedback? Who can help me remove obstacles to my efforts that affect our competitive advantage and create wealth?

Performance focus. On a personal level, employees must understand the implications of the business strategy and strategic capabilities for their own jobs, performance, and careers. What is expected of me? How well am I to perform? Do I have the right competencies or do I need new or different ones? What work affects our success with customers? What work affects our ability to change our desired price? What work reduces production costs? What do I do that creates wealth for the firm? What are my work priorities? What should I spend little time doing? What should I stop doing?

Performance consequences. The workforce must understand the consequences of high and low performance. What happens to me if I do a great job? What will happen if I do not perform at the expected level? Is extraordinary performance highly rewarded in roles that affect our competitive advantage and/or create wealth?

Employee outcomes. Everyone must know what the end game is— what is likely to happen to us if we are able to effectively execute our strategy? What will success look like in our organization from our key stakeholders' perspectives?

Attributes of a Differentiated Workforce

Developing a differentiated workforce is much easier if the firm has a clear workforce philosophy and a change management program. For many firms, this represents a new way of thinking about talent and the role of the workforce in the firm's strategic success. Managers, who only recently grew comfortable with differentiating based on employee performance, are now asked to differentiate by position as well. And many HR leaders have spent their careers ensuring that all employees are treated *equally* instead of *equitably*. As a result, much resistance may come from HR leaders themselves.

There are four key domains that distinguish a differentiated approach from a more conventional (undifferentiated) approach to workforce management: a focus on *equity instead of equality*; a focus on *engaging the right employees*, not necessarily all employees; an emphasis on *hiring choice employees*, not becoming the employer of choice; and finally, a focus on *earned increases, not entitlement*. (See tables 5-2 and 5-3.)

TABLE 5-2

Attributes of an *undifferentiated* workforce

Philosophy/ assumptions	Examples of common workforce practices	Workforce outcomes	Firm outcomes
Equality	Practices are designed to be "fair" and treat everyone the same; compensation for all jobs is at the market midpoint.	Few top performers in strategic roles; "high potentials" identified across the organization in all roles.	
Engagement	Employees are aware the firm has a mission and values; are informed that they are all valued and asked for their loyalty.	Employees are "loyal" and do not seek alternative employment; employees often cannot describe the firm's strategy, objectives, and success metrics.	Underperforming vs. best competitors
Employer of choice	Company promotes itself as a great place to work and encourages all candidates to become employees.	Employees and the marketplace learn that it is a great place to work; all job hunters apply.	
Entitlement	Employees feel secure in their jobs and are not looking for employment alternatives; expect annual compensation increases and incentive pay regardless of their performance.	High-performing employees are "underpaid" and eventually leave for more attractive opportunities; low-performing employees are overpaid and have very long tenure and low turnover.	

TABLE 5-3

Attributes of a *differentiated* workforce

Major themes	Workforce practices	Workforce outcomes	Firm outcomes
Equity	Differentiation in selection, rewards, etc., to assure the very best talent is in positions that leverage the firm's competitive advantage; outstanding performers are highly motivated to remain with the firm.	Strategic talent becomes a competitive advantage.	
Employee focus	Employees, especially strategic talent, understand the firm's strategy and how to win customers; these employees are engaged in delivering customer success and know the metrics of their success and how the firm creates wealth.	All strategic (and support) talent can easily answer how the firm intends to win its customers and how well it is doing in the pursuit of customers and what needs to be done to accelerate firm performance.	Outperforms *best* competitors
Employee of choice	The firm makes certain it focuses all recruitment efforts on strategic talent (the talent that leverages its competitive advantage) and discourages lesser talent and outstanding individuals seeking nonstrategic roles from applying.	Number of candidates who apply is reduced; a much more focused and qualified workforce is attracted; best employees remain and enable the firm to attract outstanding strategic talent.	
Earned increases	Employees do not expect increases/incentives unless they have added significant customer or economic value to the firm.	Best performers are highly rewarded and remain; poor/mediocre performers are not rewarded and asked to vacate their strategic roles.	

Equity, Not Equality

Conventional HR management practices are often designed to be fair and treat everyone the same way. For example, in many firms, compensation is set at the market midpoint for all jobs, and the degree of differentiation between low and high levels of performance is limited. As a result, few top performers appear in strategic roles, and high-potential employees quite often become dissatisfied with their pay and leave. As a corollary, a much higher percentage of low performers are retained. In contrast, firms seeking to develop a differentiated workforce focus on distinctions in selection and rewards as well. The goal is to ensure that the very best talent is in positions that leverage the firm's competitive advantage, and that outstanding performers have the incentive to remain with the firm.

Engaging the Right Employees

In undifferentiated firms, employees are aware that the firm has a mission and values, are informed that they are all valued, and are asked for their loyalty. Employees are loyal and do not seek alternative employment, although in many cases employees cannot describe the firm's strategy, objectives, and success metrics.

In differentiated firms, all employees, especially those in strategic positions, understand the firm's strategy and how to win customers. These employees are engaged in delivering customer success and know the metrics of their success and how the firm creates wealth. As a consequence, all employees can easily answer how the firm intends to win its customers and how well it is doing in the pursuit of customers, as well as what needs to be done to accelerate firm performance.

Hiring Choice Employees, Not Becoming the Employer of Choice

A company with an undifferentiated workforce promotes itself as a great place to work and encourages all candidates to apply for employment. As a result, employees and the marketplace learn that it is a comfortable place to work. All job hunters apply, and the firm is overwhelmed with applicants, many of whom, however, are ill suited for the firm.

In differentiated firms, managers focus most of their recruitment efforts on strategic talent (the talent that leverages its competitive advantage) and discourage low-performing individuals from applying for employment. As a result, the numbers of candidates who apply are reduced, but the proportion of qualified applicants is greatly enhanced. The company attracts and selects a much more focused and qualified workforce, with employees who are more likely to remain.

Earned Increases, Not Entitlement

In undifferentiated firms, employees feel secure in their jobs and are not looking for employment alternatives. They expect (and receive) annual compensation increases and incentive pay regardless of their performance. The result is that high-performing employees are underpaid and eventually leave for more attractive opportunities; low-performing employees are overpaid and have no incentive to leave.

In differentiated firms, employees do not expect increases or incentives unless they have added significant customer or economic value. As a result, the best performers are highly rewarded and stay; poor or mediocre performers are not rewarded and are asked to leave their strategic roles.

Work System Organizing Principles

Firms have almost complete discretion (subject to applicable legal requirements) in how they manage people, one of the few truly strategic levers under their direct control. Firms can't change the rate of competitors' new product introductions or oil prices or geopolitics, but they can act quickly and decisively to improve how they manage their workforce. So HR management systems are important because they create significant shareholder wealth, and they are a feature of the business that managers can directly control.

We call this system of HR management policies and practices an *HR architecture*. As we've described, designing and implementing an effective HR architecture begins with the development of a culture and workforce philosophy. All firms have an HR architecture, that is, they have designed jobs and recruited and selected employees, they have compensation systems in place, and so on. They use these systems to make decisions about employees—who will be hired, fired, promoted— every day. The portfolio of talent currently in any firm is a direct result of the HR management policies that have been in place for the past ten to twenty years. Moreover, given that HR management systems are slow to change, the leadership team currently in your business may have been recruited, selected, brought on board, trained, and promoted with HR management practices designed and implemented in the 1970s or 1980s! So, the choice isn't whether to have an HR architecture or not—you already have one. The question is whether you have the *right* HR architecture, and whether it will build talent in your strategic positions and lead to your ultimate success.

Our colleague Randall Schuler has described the five key elements of an HR architecture: *philosophies, policies, programs, practices,* and *processes.*[2] An HR philosophy is a high-level statement, much like a mission or vision. HR policies describe the general framework for people-related programs and practices. HR programs are the specific, coordinated efforts to solve a business problem, for example, a performance management system. HR practices are the specific activities that constitute the program, for example, a 360-degree performance appraisal is one element of the overall performance management system. Finally, HR processes are the specific elements, activities, and transactions that make up the constituent parts of the HR practices.

Schuler's "5-P" model makes clear that two firms might have the same philosophy about performance management, but could have adopted very different practices to support this philosophy. Social scientists often describe this concept as *equifinality*—there may be two roads to the same destination. This explains how two otherwise successful firms can have very different HR architectures; they may either have different strategic capabilities or have found distinct ways to achieve the same goal. For example, many firms want to develop a performance-oriented and high-accountability culture, so they will often use performance management and incentive plans. But while one firm might use a 360-degree approach, another might use the more conventional top-down approach of providing feedback. Each may well be effective, but the important issue is not which performance appraisal practice the firm has adopted. It is that the firm has made the philosophical commitment to developing a culture of accountability.

Within the context of HR philosophies, policies, programs, practices, and processes, Schuler also showed that there is a myriad of choices for planning, staffing, appraising, compensating, and training employees that firms have at their disposal (see figure 5-2).[3] Managers need to recognize that this menu represents a substantial opportunity to structure an HR architecture for competitive advantage. The key challenge is to think carefully through all the potential design options.

In designing an HR management system, the challenge is to figure out the core elements of the workforce philosophy and the resulting HR management systems that need to be the same for everyone and the elements that must be differentiated by strategic capability and strategic position. This is an important distinction. There are some things that companies want everyone to know and understand such as: How do we compete? Who are our key competitors? Which jobs are key or strategic? And as a consequence, there are some things that we do the same for all employees. For example, communication systems are likely to be undifferentiated. But at times, companies should differentiate on how they manage the workforce; not all jobs are managed in a similar manner.

As shown in figure 5-3, firms generally attempt to create the same mind-set for all employees, at least within strategic capability. Managers need to ask what kind of understanding they want everyone to have and how to hold all accountable for the appropriate level of understanding. And within the HR function, many of the HR transactions will be identical for strategic and nonstrategic positions. But beyond that, the specific HR management policies and practices needed for strategic success will differ markedly for strategic and nonstrategic roles.

As we showed in figure 5-2, there are multiple levels of analysis to consider when developing an HR architecture, and within each level, there is a menu of different choices and opportunities to consider. We stress the importance of beginning with clearly defined objectives for

FIGURE 5-2

Human resource management practice menus

Planning choices

Informal	....	Formal
Loose	....	Tight
Short term	....	Long term
Explicit analysis	....	Implicit analysis
Narrow jobs	....	Broad jobs
Segmental design	....	Integrative design
Low employee involvement	....	High employee involvement

Staffing choices

Internal sources	....	External sources
Narrow paths	....	Broad paths
Single criteria	....	Multiple criteria
Limited socialization	....	Extensive socialization
Closed procedures	....	Open procedures

Appraising choices

Loose, incomplete integration	....	Tight, complete integration
Behavioral criteria	....	Results criteria
Purposes: developmental, remedial, maintenance		
Low employee participation	....	High employee participation
Short-term criteria	....	Long-term criteria
Individual criteria	....	Group criteria

Compensating choices

Low base salaries	....	High base salaries
Internal equity	....	External equity
Few perks	....	Many perks
Standard, fixed package	....	Flexible package
Low participation	....	High participation
No incentives	....	Many incentives
Short-term incentives	....	Long-term incentives
No employment security	....	High employment security
Hierarchical	....	Egalitarian

Training and development

Short term	....	Long term
Narrow application	....	Broad application
Spontaneous, unplanned	....	Planned, systematic
Individual orientation	....	Group orientation
Low participation	....	High participation
Extensive organizational structure	....	Minimal organizational structure

Source: Adapted from R. S. Schuler, "Human Resource Management Choices and Organizational Strategy," *Readings in Personnel and Human Resource Management*, 3rd ed., ed. R. S. Schuler, S. A. Youngblood, and V. Huber (St. Paul, MN: West Publishing, 1987). Used with permission.

FIGURE 5-3

Common and unique elements of the HR architecture

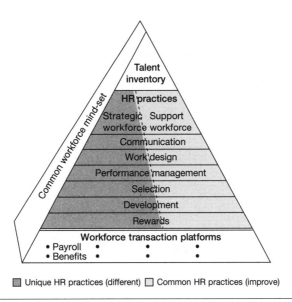

Talent inventory

HR practices

Strategic workforce   Support workforce

Communication

Work design

Performance management

Selection

Development

Rewards

Workforce transaction platforms
- Payroll
- Benefits

Common workforce mind-set

▨ Unique HR practices (different)   ☐ Common HR practices (improve)

the workforce, so you can then design a system to specifically deliver on those objectives.

An important threshold issue is to develop a clear sense of the HR management practices (selection, development, performance management, and so on) that you wish to *improve* versus those you would like to *do differently*. Generally speaking, investments in strategic positions need to be at the seventy-fifth percentile or greater (i.e., much higher than the overall average investment in the workforce), while investments in support positions, considerable less so. The former typically correspond to support positions, while the latter, strategic positions, as shown in figure 5-4.

Designing an HR Architecture

HR as a science was built on the concept of differentiation, on making distinctions between employees (or potential employees) on a wide variety of attributes, such as personality characteristics, academic achievement, and

FIGURE 5-4

The new HR: Workforce deliverables

Workforce	HR practices	Practice strategy	Target workforce
Strategic	Selection Development Performance management Rewards Work design Communication	Different	Quartile 3 and above
Support	Selection Development Performance management Rewards Work design Communication	Improve	Quartile 2 and below

Workforce mind-set

Workforce success → Strategic success

☐ Common practices   ☐ Differentiated practices

job performance. Selection, training, a focus on measuring individual differences, and so on, all form the basics of HR as a science, beginning with the publication of the first text on human resource management (personnel) in the early 1900s. Along the way, the HR function became the "equality police," advocating *equal* treatment of all employees at the expense of *equitable* employee treatment. Instead of facilitating good decision making about the workforce, many firms opted for homogeneity and avoiding difficult but often necessary decisions about the workforce.

An undifferentiated approach to workforce management can make a lot of sense in certain situations. For example, when jobs are simplified and standardized, when the workforce adds little to the production process, and when unions are strong, standardization and simplification of workforce management systems work well. However, none of these attributes characterize the current economic environment.

Our research and practical experience has shown that firms must differentiate their HR management practices and systems to effectively execute their strategies. There is a causal order or time lag that occurs in the design, implementation, and impact of HR management practices.

For example, before we can hire employees, we need to structure work into jobs. Before we make selection decisions, we need to recruit a pool of candidates. Before we can develop and train employees, they have to be brought on board and socialized. Before we can pay any types of incentives, we need to conduct performance appraisals. Before we can project the need for the number of promotion or exit decisions, we need to have developed workforce planning models.

In addition, not all HR practices have an equal impact on firm performance. So, in designing an HR architecture, it is important to consider not only the timing or causal order of the expected impact of any changes, but also the relative magnitude of the expected impact of each category of practice on firm performance.

For example, as we show in figure 5-5, selection systems are likely to have the greatest impact on the ability to execute strategy because they have the greatest opportunity to reduce variance in employee behavior. If we have an effective selection system to help us determine which five candidates out of one hundred applicants to hire, we remove a substantial

FIGURE 5-5

Relative impact of different HR practices

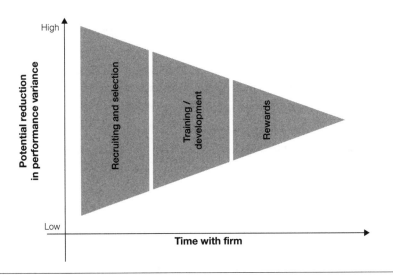

amount of negative variance from the workforce. This is also true for pro-motion decisions, although the selection ratio (proportion of hires to applicants) is less favorable for proportions than is typical for external hires. This effect is mitigated by the fact that most promotions occur at a higher job level.

After selection, the HR practices with the next largest opportunity to reduce variance and increase performance include training and develop-ment efforts. Finally, there are performance management and incentive compensation systems, which have an economically and statistically significant impact on firm success.

Our point is not that organizations should invest all their efforts in the best and most valid selection system available (although the empir-ical evidence overwhelmingly suggests that such an investment pays off handsomely in most organizations). Our point is that if you select the wrong person, the subsequent investment needed to rectify the situa-tion is substantial and, in many cases, might not even be possible, because HR practices after selection have relatively less impact. Thus, managers must ensure that the HR management practices they adopt are internally consistent, and that the entire bundle of practices is based on the needs of the business and helps to execute strategy.

The workforce strategy team at Lockheed Martin provides an excel-lent example of this process in action. For each of the HR functional areas, Lockheed Martin carefully described both its current situation and where it needed to be in the future. The document became an important communication and teaching tool throughout the organiza-tion. (See figure 5-6.)

Next we highlight some key elements to remember when designing an HR management system for a differentiated workforce. This is not a comprehensive review of all possible elements of a work system, but focuses on those elements likely to differentiate strategic from non-strategic positions.[4]

Work Design

The goal of work design for the differentiated workforce is to ensure that strategic jobs are structured to maximize contribution of talent to

FIGURE 5-6

Workforce strategy: process flow for HR practices

Current state	HR practice changes	Strategic differentiation
• Same process for all positions • Recruit on demand • HR driven	**Staffing**	• Constant recruiting for key positions • Line ownership • Competency-based
• Once a year • Leaders not skilled with development planning and feedback • Reluctance to address issues	**Performance management**	• Ongoing/proactive for key positions • Leaders well trained and accountable • Performance issues managed
• Most development offered to all employees • Some differentiation for "key talent" • "Random" approach to career pathing	**Development**	• Greater differentiation of investment to build strategic capabilities • More career guidance for key areas/positions • Competency approach
• No assessment or process for key positions • Success factors not well-defined • "Tough" calls are sometimes avoided	**Talent management**	• Leadership development programs and assessments well-defined • Success factors well-defined for key positions • Process ensures that key talent occupies key positions
• Pay at market • Pay for performance • Universal retention strategy	**Compensation**	• Increase pay for key positions • Pay for performance, greater at-risk pay for key positions • Targeted retention plans
• Messaging for HR and leadership is unclear	**Communications**	• Processes are well-defined and communicated to HR and leadership

business success. For many firms, the outside world is changing more quickly than they are able to adapt on the inside. Jobs are notoriously intractable and tough to change. As a consequence, it is important to ensure that they are designed correctly at the outset. Jobs must be periodically evaluated to ensure that they contribute to strategic success. This is even more important for strategic positions, because their impact on the company's ability to execute strategy is so substantial.

But old models of job design, which focus on fairly reductionist approaches to maximizing efficiency, are not useful in the new, interconnected organization. We need approaches that maximize employee effectiveness and design jobs from the top down, not the bottom up, as is typical in most businesses. The key is to start with the strategy, not with the employee.

Recruitment and Selection

The primary goal of recruitment and selection policies and procedures is to maximize the probability that they place the right people in the right roles at the right time. While true for all jobs, it is especially important for strategic positions. For example, "A" players will be placed in key jobs, "B" players in less strategic roles. The timing of the process is important to monitor as well. A company simply doesn't have time to wait for an open position. It needs to be proactive in building bench strength, especially in the strategic roles.

As we've shown, selection (and promotions, which are also a selection decision) is likely to be the highest-impact HR management practice for "A" positions. For key roles, there are reliable and valid selection tools designed to maximize the probability that high-potential candidates are selected from the pool.

Development

Conventional approaches to workforce planning and development are too slow to be useful in the current economic environment. Talent takes time to build, so it is crucial to be proactive when developing a workforce capable of executing strategy. A key challenge for HR leaders is ensuring that they are able to aggressively develop the best and the brightest so they are prepared for cross-functional moves. Similarly, the challenge for line managers is to develop their subordinates to maximize their potential.

Performance Management and Rewards

The goal of performance management and reward systems is to execute strategy by aligning rewards and feedback with actual levels of employee performance. Managers need to ensure that key performers in important positions are highly compensated, good performers are moderately compensated, and poor performers are helped either to improve or to find employment elsewhere.

How should performance management and rewards differ for strategic positions? As we show in table 5-4, the assumptions, practices, and

TABLE 5-4

Conventional vs. strategic approaches to compensation

	Conventional	Strategic/differentiated workforce
Assumptions	Pay should be determined primarily by a set of factors that highly correlate with labor market prices for jobs. The factors are selected to represent how all firms value positions in the labor market.	Pay should be determined by the value of the job to the firm. Positions that have strategic value (i.e., influence customer value, price, or cost to produce) have greater value to the firm.
Practices	Firms (or consultants) allocate points to these factors to determine overall "job worth," then group jobs with similar value, select a "key" job, find a labor-market price for the key job, and price all jobs of similar value equally.	Firms find the market price of the job and price the job based on its strategic value to the firm (e.g., Q1, Q2, Q3, etc., or above the top price in the market, if it has that value to the firm).
Consequences	Jobs are priced based on the consultant's (or firm's) selected factors, and these factors determine the value of the job to the firm. All positions, especially those without market data, can be priced based on these factors.	Jobs are paid based on market value, but in terms of the strategic value to the firm, not a set of factors that correlate with the labor market.

consequences differ markedly for strategic and nonstrategic roles. For strategic roles, companies determine pay by the value of the job to the firm. Positions that have strategic value (i.e., influence customer value, price, or cost to produce) have greater value to the firm and should be compensated accordingly. The compensation practices for strategic positions seek to find the market price of *the* job and evaluate the job based on its strategic value to the firm (e.g., quartile 1, quartile 2, quartile 3, etc., or above the top price in the market, if it has that value to the firm). As a consequence, for strategic roles, jobs are paid based on market value, but in terms of their *strategic* value, not on a set of factors that correlate with the labor market.

How does our approach differ from conventional approaches to performance management, such as General Electric's Topgrading approach? A forced ranking system encourages managers to rate 20 percent of their employees as high performers, 70 percent as average, and 10 percent in the "needs significant improvement" category. This approach recognizes that there is almost always variability in employee performance and that many managers need help overcoming their natural resistance to differentiation. Thus, this approach rewards the highest-performing employees, develops those in the middle, and deals effectively and humanely with the lowest-performing employees. In many firms, managers are held accountable for the twenty-seventy-ten ranking system, based on the assumption that average performance will improve over time.

Mathematically, of course, this is true: if you consistently weed out the lowest-performing employees, average performance increases. But in our approach, we challenge the idea that a company can or should have a normal distribution of employee performance. We believe that having only 20 percent of world-class performers in strategic positions is not enough. Conversely, it might not be financially viable to place 20 percent of the best performers in "B" or "C" positions. Those resources might be better spent on the "A" roles. Firms should carefully consider the proportion of top talent that they need to have in each category (see table 5-5).

TABLE 5-5

Differentiating incentive compensation by performance and position

DIFFERENTIATION BY PERFORMANCE

	"A" POSITION	"B" POSITION	"C" POSITION
"A" player	20%	20%	20%
"B" player	70%	70%	70%
"C" player	10%	10%	10%

DIFFERENTIATION BY PERFORMANCE AND POSITION

	"A" POSITION	"B" POSITION	"C" POSITION
"A" player	60%	30%	10%
"B" player	30%	60%	70%
"C" player	10%	10%	20%

The Talent Responsibility Matrix at FridgeCo

The FridgeCo example, introduced earlier, shows that the identification of strategic capabilities and positions allowed the executive team to pinpoint critical talent gaps in the workforce. These talent gaps led FridgeCo to develop specific actions to ensure that the firm can place "A" players in "A" positions for the benefit of its "A" customers. FridgeCo was very systematic throughout this process, but just as important, line and HR managers jointly conducted the analyses. This created a direct line of sight from business strategy to strategic capabilities to strategic positions to the roles and responsibilities of line and HR managers to specific HR management practices designed to fill the gap between existing talent and needed talent.

For each strategic capability—*executive leadership, manufacturing excellence, sales and marketing,* and *R&D/new product development*—FridgeCo identified a specific set of initiatives that the senior executive team agreed to (see table 5-6).

TABLE 5-6

Strategic talent responsibility matrix at FridgeCo

Initiatives required	Line manager	HR function
Executive leadership		
We need to strengthen executive talent bench strength. We should review our "top talent" in sales and marketing and begin cross-functional rotations and external, university-based programs to broaden them through finance and manufacturing experience/education.	The president of this division must assume responsibility for the development of "top talent" for executive leadership positions. Tracking of the development of these individuals' progress through rotations, external programs, and mentoring is essential. Two "ready now" executive caliber leaders are expected within 18 months.	Corporate HR must be involved in developmental efforts and explore potential executive "top talent" available for this division. CHR must also assess and suggest external programs to develop the available talent. CHR must be involved in the hiring of at least one external "top talent" executive this year.
Manufacturing excellence		
We need to develop manufacturing talent faster and provide openings to acquire "top talent" manufacturing professionals. We must reduce the number of the CLs and moves (38 of 48) to provide space for hiring manufacturing talent. Of our 64 employees in strategic manufacturing positions, 47 are at career level or identified as "moves." This situation must be quickly corrected.	The president of this division and the vice president of manufacturing must devise a plan to significantly enhance manufacturing talent and track the results. At least a dozen "top talent" hires from the best schools or best-practice firms must be accomplished in the next year. The hires must be familiar with the latest manufacturing tools (e.g., six sigma, etc.). The president and vice president of manufacturing are responsible for significant progress in the next two years. At least one-half of the 47 must be addressed. This will be a significant part of their performance evaluation.	Corporate HR must begin both a college recruiting program (6 hires) for manufacturing positions and develop a manufacturing leadership program (MLP) for the new hires. They must also identify, recruit, and be involved in the selection of external manufacturing talent with cutting-edge skills. CHR must also develop a manufacturing skills training program to update all manufacturing supervisors. Significant overall competency enhancement is expected in manufacturing in the very near future, and HR must be up to this challenge!
Sales/Marketing		
We must get rid of our "move" individuals and significantly upgrade our brand management talent from our consumer insight talent. We should also develop better merchandising talent; 50% of these positions are staffed with CL or move incumbents.	Vice president of sales and marketing is to initiate the hiring of two marketing directors and provide developmental plans for brand management and consumer insight specialists targeted on marketing director positions. The leadership of sales and marketing is accountable for measurable progress in workforce development in the next two years.	CHR must develop career growth models for the brand manager and consumer insight series to accelerate the development of "top talent" in these positions. CHR, in conjunction with vice president of marketing, must acquire/develop at least one new brand manager and exit all "move" individuals.

TABLE 5-6

R&D/New product development

There are way too many career-level individuals in this group and not enough top talent. We need at least four new design engineers who can develop new products and improve old products, especially our "hardy perennial" in-service problems.	Vice president of marketing and vice president of manufacturing must be honest in the assessment of talent in this group and devise a plan to achieve "top talent" status to not only better market new products, but also to reduce the cost of production through design.	CHR must explore how they may be involved and help this group, even if it is merely referrals to external recruiting sources. Perhaps they might design new product idea business proposal process (for all employees) to "jump start" product innovation.

FridgeCo used these analyses to drive specific changes in how it managed the workforce. For example, for manufacturing excellence, FridgeCo managers concluded that it was vital to develop manufacturing talent faster and provide openings to acquire top-talent professionals. They also concluded that it was important to reduce the number of managers rated as career level and "move" (thirty-eight of forty-eight) to provide space for hiring manufacturing talent. Of the sixty-four employees in strategic manufacturing positions, forty-seven were at career level or identified as moves. Executives concluded that they had to correct this situation quickly.

In delivering these initiatives, both line managers and the HR leadership team played important but different roles. The president of the division and the vice president of manufacturing needed to devise a plan to significantly enhance manufacturing talent and track the results. They needed to hire at least a dozen top-talent hires from the best schools or best-practice firms in the next year. The hires had to be familiar with the latest manufacturing tools (e.g., six sigma, etc.). The president and vice president of manufacturing were responsible for significant progress in the next two years, by reducing at least one-half of the forty-seven career-level managers. Delivering on these objectives became a significant part of their annual performance evaluation.

Corporate HR's role included the development of both a college recruiting program (six hires) for manufacturing positions and a manufacturing leadership program for the new hires. HR also needed to identify, recruit, and be involved in the selection of external talent with cutting-edge skills. Corporate HR also developed a manufacturing skills training program to update all manufacturing supervisors. Significant overall competency enhancement was expected in manufacturing in the near future, and HR needed to help achieve this goal.

After determining the specific deliverables for the line and HR managers, the HR team developed a detailed strategic human capital plan for FridgeCo (see table 5-7).

Work design. The HR leadership team redesigned the area supervisor positions to assume more of the plant managers' roles early in their careers. The effort accelerated learning and helped build bench strength for these roles.

Selection. The HR team knew from the previous analyses that they needed to remove or relocate at least 25 percent of career-level staff. They moved more of the developing manufacturing talent into the thirty-seven career-level and "move" supervisor positions and hired twelve top-talent hires from the best schools or best-practice firms within twelve months. They replaced them with top-talent hires or individuals designated as emerging talent elsewhere in the firm. All these efforts drew on a college recruiting program for manufacturing talent, which they developed.

Development. Building bench strength in manufacturing required a manufacturing leadership program for all new manufacturing hires and new skills training program for manufacturing supervisors.

Performance management. Effective performance management in manufacturing mandated a new emphasis on competency acquisition as a significant component in the appraisal of manufacturing supervisors. The HR team also decided to evaluate all manufacturing staff in company-sponsored training programs on their progress, using a competency-development model the team developed.

Rewards. FridgeCo's HR team developed a pool of "spot awards" to reward extraordinary competency growth by manufacturing talent (especially for area supervisors). They also developed productivity incentives as plantwide awards for all employees.

TABLE 5-7

FridgeCo human capital plan

Strategic capability:
Manufacturing excellence

Strategic positions:
- Plant managers
- Area supervisors

HR leader strategic talent recap

Action plans:
- Exit moves and "careerists."
- Hire developing talent.
- Hire and move "top talent" into 38 career-level / move positions.

HR PRACTICE ACTIONS

Work design	Selection	Development	Performance management	Rewards	Communication
• Redesign area supervisor positions to assume more of the plant managers' roles earlier in their careers.	• Get rid of or move at least 25% of career-level (CL) staff. • Move more of the developing manufacturing talent into the 37 CL/"move" area supervisor positions. • Hire at least 12 top-talent hires from the best schools or best-practice firms within next 12 months. • Reassign and replace at least one-half of CLs and move manufacturing staff incumbents. • Replace with top-talent hires or individuals designated as emerging talent elsewhere in the firm. • Initiate a manufacturing college recruiting program.	• Develop a manufacturing leadership program for all new manufacturing hires. • Develop a manufacturing skill training program to update all manufacturing supervisors.	• Add competency acquisition as a significant appraisal of manufacturing supervisors. Weight as 25% of the evaluation of these individuals. • Evaluate all manufacturing staff in company-sponsored manufacturing training programs on their progress using a competency-development model developed by HR.	• Develop a pool of "spot awards" to reward extraordinary competency growth by manufacturing talent (especially for area supervisors). • Develop productivity incentives as plantwide awards for all employees.	• Communicate to all managers and supervisors in this area that they must significantly grow their manufacturing competencies annually.

Communication. Finally, FridgeCo's management team made clear to all managers and supervisors in this area that they had to significantly increase their manufacturing competencies annually.

Summary

In this chapter, we have shown that managers must specifically and intentionally design workforce management systems to execute strategy, and that the basis of this differentiation should be the strategic capabilities needed to execute the firm's business strategy. HR management practices are notoriously intractable and difficult to change. It is exactly this difficulty in replication and implementation that gives HR management systems a potential long-term source of competitive advantage.

In the 1970s, 1980s, and 1990s, managers, consultants, academics, and students looked at the success of Hewlett-Packard's vaunted management practices and asked, how do they do it? HP's approach to workforce management has been documented in countless books, articles, case studies, and videos. Someone once asked an HP executive why the company was willing to publicly detail the specifics of the HR management practices when it believed that they were a source of competitive advantage for the firm. If competitors knew exactly how they managed the workforce, wouldn't this pose a significant risk for the firm? The executive replied that there is a huge difference between knowing how another firm manages talent and being able to copy it in your own firm. Even if competitors had a detailed description of the process, they wouldn't be able to replicate the outcome, given the differences in culture and workforce philosophy. Even if competitors were able to duplicate HP's current approach, by the time they achieved it, HP would have continuously improved the process to a new level. The HP executive was exactly right.

Change—especially differentiation—is hard work, and managers avoid it if they can. They prefer to deal with resources that don't talk back. But they must overcome this inertia. The process must start with a clear statement of strategic goals, a clear understanding of the strategic capabilities that each firm must master, as well as the workforce and behavioral outcomes needed to make the strategy a reality.

In practical terms, certain elements of the firm's HR management system and strategy need to be absolutely consistent throughout the business, and other elements need to be highly unique and customized to the particular situation and job. Not only must we understand our business well to develop both the diagnosis and the treatment plan, but we must also communicate both our intent and the reality to the workforce. Differentiation can be challenging and hard work, but it is absolutely necessary for effectively executing strategy in the global environment.

Is this worth all the trouble? Yes. The workforce represents the greatest potential source of opportunity for value creation, but realizing this potential requires more than simply asserting that "people are our most important asset." Using HR management systems to improve the performance of employees in strategic positions is the best and most effective way. In the next chapter, we take this process to the next level and show how to develop measurement systems to track strategy execution progress.

CHAPTER 6

Develop Strategic Workforce Measures

W HEN THINKING strategically about the workforce, senior managers are almost always motivated by concerns about both employee performance and, ultimately, firm performance. Sometimes senior HR executives are asked to demonstrate HR's contribution to firm performance during a discussion of measures. Often, the available measures generate more questions than answers. For many organizations, the transition to a strategic focus on the workforce and the HR function begins (and sometimes ends) with a very frustrating experience with workforce measurement.

The only way to ensure that you know what your measures mean and that you have the right measures is *first* to have the right workforce strategy and *second* to develop your strategic workforce measures based on that strategy. Our previous two books, *The HR Scorecard* and *The Workforce Scorecard*, focused on the measurement challenge in depth. The purpose of this chapter is to highlight the key principles of strategic measurement described in those books and show how to apply them, building on the examples from earlier chapters.

By now, you might realize that questions about what measures mean and which are appropriate are in many respects the same. If you have the right measures, you know what they mean and why the results are important and useful. The problem for most organizations is that they have workforce measures, but they have the wrong ones. Our perspective on *strategic* workforce measures begins with a simple premise—measures are answers to questions. As a result, measures are important and useful when they answer important and useful questions. For our purposes, important means strategic and useful means they serve as guides for executing the firm's strategy.

Six Principles of Strategic Workforce Measures

Discussions of workforce measurement often turn quickly into recommendations of the best measures or the minutiae of measurement construction. The first encourages you to give up all responsibility for developing your own measures, while the latter tends to be of interest only to measurement specialists. This chapter is intended for senior line managers and HR professionals, so the goal is not to make you a measurement technician, but rather an informed consumer. You should understand what a good workforce measure looks like and recognize a bad one. For this purpose, we think in terms of measurement principles that you should keep in mind as you develop a workforce strategy. These can be conveniently divided into three do's and three don'ts. We begin with three mistakes to avoid.

Principle 1—Don't Start with the Measures

For many reasons, a manager might mistakenly start with the measures. HR professionals might be under pressure to justify and explain HR's contribution to the firm's performance. Maybe there is a vague goal to transform HR into a strategic role. Since we manage what we measure, if we have a new batch of measures, HR might manage more strategically. Line managers, used to having good measures for the rest of the business such as financial measures, just assume that similar measures ought to be available for the workforce.

Where do you find these measures? The most common question we hear is, "Do you have a list of measures I can use?" There is no useful list of best-practice measures. The best practice is the process itself, not the measures that result from that process. Just as the particulars of your workforce strategy should be unique to your company or at least your industry niche, the really meaningful measures of workforce performance are equally unique to your firm. In other words, a differentiated workforce strategy requires a set of differentiated measures to manage and evaluate performance.

So where do you begin? Strategic workforce measurement should reflect the workforce's contribution to the firm's strategy implementation process. In order to measure that contribution, an organization needs to begin with how its strategy will create value. Where are the strategy drivers that culminate in successful firm performance? Given the framework we described earlier, the answer is clear. You start at the top, with your strategy, and work backward to identify the appropriate workforce measures. One of the biggest challenges to managing the workforce strategically is the long line of sight between what HR professionals do and the ultimate strategic outcome. The logic of the strategy map serves to clarify those strategic decisions and is the basis for the workforce measures. But you can't develop the measures before you understand that strategic logic.

Principle 2—Don't Rely on Benchmarking

The tendency to "start with the measure" has a corollary. Starting with the measure probably indicates that your company hasn't focused on how the workforce uniquely contributes to strategic success in your company. When you have no strategically justified basis for determining what a measurement result means, looking to external benchmarks might seem to make sense. After all, if there is no obvious internal relationship between measures like cost per hire and firm performance, comparing your results to external benchmarks may be your only option. This is particularly true for the HR function, where the line of sight to the firm's bottom line has traditionally been difficult to unravel. But relying on benchmarking for your performance measures is more a symptom than a solution.

When the HR function is managed as an administrative cost center, efficiency metrics are probably an apt description of its performance. However, when HR professionals increasingly take responsibility for strategic workforce performance, these efficiency metrics are inadequate and misleading. Managing the workforce as a strategic asset implies measuring strategic workforce performance in terms of its impact on strategy implementation. Looking to external benchmarks for measures of strategic performance implies that every firm has the same strategy and the same implementation system. Relying on benchmarking is an undifferentiated workforce strategy, instead of a differentiated one. Effective strategy implementation is not a commodity, and workforce drivers of strategy should not be measured like commodities. External validation that is appropriate for efficiency-based measures is inappropriate for strategic workforce performance.

For example, at BankCo, HR professionals were held accountable for time-to-fill rates, the quicker the better. BankCo could easily use time-to-fill, a common HR metric, as one benchmark of HR's performance against other banks in the industry. But think of the strategic implications of so much attention on time-to-fill. Is this really a strategic performance measure? The relationship manager (RM) position was a strategic job at BankCo, and the overall strategic contribution of that position depended on the level of the RMs' performance at any time *and* the vacancy rate. In other words, BankCo's challenge was not only the level of performance of employees currently in the position, but also the fact that in several high-growth markets, it couldn't fill all the positions required to fully take advantage of the growth opportunity. Focusing on time-to-fill might have made sense if just about any level of performance in an otherwise vacant position is better than zero, but at best that is a short-term solution. Besides, our earlier analysis suggested that to deliver the kind of value proposition expected of its customers, the warm-body test just wasn't going to be enough.

So what kind of measures should BankCo use in this situation? Time-to-fill is fine to track, but ultimately, both line managers and HR should pay more attention to RM performance and the vacancy rate.

The vacancy rate, in turn, is affected not just by the pace of external sourcing, but by the turnover rate among current RMs. Turnover rates for high performers is especially important. And, of course, the line managers are at least as responsible for the turnover rates as HR. The point of this analysis is that strategic measures should guide strategic decision making. Focusing so heavily on time-to-fill sends the message that speed is the most important concern. This could, and has in some organizations we know, encourage HR to change recruiting channels, with the result that the new applicant pool is not of the same quality. In BankCo's case, this would have meant both lower RM performance in the future and possibly even higher vacancy rates. These unintended consequences would be fairly obvious to both line managers and HR professionals if they were to consider the selection of workforce measures within the context of a larger strategic analysis. It's not so obvious when the context is a benchmarking analysis.

Principle 3—Don't Expect Human Capital Alchemy

The third principle is a variant of the first, because it sometimes explains why managers want to begin with the measures. HR professionals, in particular, might believe that they have a strategic impact on the organization, but it is simply not reflected in the current measures. We call this human capital alchemy: the gold in the current strategy will be revealed, once the leaden efficiency measures are replaced by more strategically focused measures. Maybe all you are missing is the right measures to reveal the strategic impact of your workforce. Changing the measures might turn out to be useful, but only because the new measures reveal how little value is actually being created. The current workforce strategy is more likely not delivering the strategic impact you need, and no change of measures will transform this lead into gold.

BankCo's experience with workforce measures reflected this evolution. The senior leaders knew they wanted their HR professionals to be business partners with the line managers. A consulting report indicated that the HR professionals were good at the administrative role, but the line managers wanted them to think in terms of business solutions, not just HR solutions. (Many HR professionals will recognize their own companies in such an assessment.) BankCo's first step was to look for new measures to capture HR's strategic contribution. But once it considered the measures typically used in HR, it realized that the line managers would not see this as much progress. With this new perspective on measurement, it stepped back and went through the analyses we've described. The difference was remarkable. Now the bank has measures that reflect the real business problems facing line managers and HR's impact on those problems. The best evidence that it was on the right track was the comment of a line manager at a subsequent meeting, either in praise or in surprise, "You guys don't sound like you are from HR."

Beware of These Common Workforce Metrics

Before moving on to the good measures, we briefly highlight the problems with some common workforce metrics, based on the principles just discussed. We alluded to several of these in the examples of the three don'ts, but want to emphasize that those limitations apply more generally and are not limited to the specific situations we described.

Measures that we routinely find in use that should be avoided as *strategic* measures include:

- *Cost per hire and time-to-fill.* These commonly used efficiency measures should not be confused with indicators of strategic performance. The research literature actually shows a positive relationship between these measures and firm performance. Efforts to minimize these measures encourage recruiters to be less selective in the choice of both applicants and recruiting channels. A better alternative is some measure of subsequent performance for these hires and retention of "A" players in "A" positions.

- *HR expense factor.* More profitable firms spend more on HR administration than do low-profit firms. This may in part be due to the profitable firms having more resources. However, it is clear that with the right workforce strategy, a portion of HR's expenses should be considered investments. Simply relying on a summary expense measure for HR's strategic role is misleading.

- *Human capital ROI or human capital value added.* With a differentiated workforce strategy, think very carefully about what you mean by human capital ROI or value added. Any ROI measure of your strategic human capital is very specific to your own company. It depends on your strategic capabilities and the role of talent in driving those capabilities. An overall measure can be constructed by aggregating the contributions of this strategic talent, but it is a bottom-up process. Beware of summary ROI formulas that attempt to compare overall workforce expenses to financial outcomes and purportedly apply to all firms in all industries. You cannot simply reconfigure existing financial and workforce data and miraculously reveal the strategic impact of the workforce.

- *Training expense factor.* In the research literature, there is a modest, positive relationship between training expenses and firm performance. But these studies don't account for either quality or the strategic focus on these development programs. We don't recommend spending *less* on training, but neither do we believe that simply spending more is the best approach. What's important is how you spend those training dollars, not how many you spend. Those investments should be disproportionately focused on strategic talent.

- *Turnover rates.* There is a modest, negative relationship between overall turnover rates and firm performance. But these studies don't have the data on type and quality of turnover to usefully guide management decision making. The impact of turnover on firm performance depends on whether that turnover is occurring in "A" jobs and among "A" players. High turnover among "C" players could actually be a plus. Again, turnover rates can be useful, even strategic measures, but they need to be strategically focused rather than aggregated to large segments of the workforce.

- *Turnover costs and vacancy costs.* The problem with these measures is that they tend to focus on the wrong costs, the incremental recruiting, selection, and training costs associated with a new hire. Strategically, however, the much more important cost is the lost performance. The lost revenue associated with the departure of an upper-quartile relationship manager at BankCo is many multiples of the total replacement expense for that individual.

Principle 4—Focus on the Strategic Impact of the Workforce

Thinking of talent as an asset is familiar to most managers. The problem comes when they try to *measure* talent like an asset. Accounting systems make it difficult to capitalize investments in skills and other intangibles. So what is the best way to measure human capital? First, since measures are answers to questions, they are not ends in themselves. Determining the appropriate measure depends on the question you are trying to answer. If your organization wants to drive out costs and the HR function is being asked to justify its performance based on efficiency, you might focus on the cost of talent (i.e., annual expenditures on training or cost per hire). If you compare talent to another intangible—research and development—focusing on cost and efficiency would be equivalent to valuing the R&D function by the size of the annual R&D budget. Alternatively, if you are interested in how intangibles drive strategy so you can better manage firm performance, efficiency measures of this kind are a blunt instrument at best.

Another possible measure is the stock of talent, where the level of talent is compared against a desirable benchmark. This approach includes measures such as hours of training per year, leadership competency levels, or other methods that capture the level of talent in the firm. If there is a war for talent, presumably it's important to know how much talent you have. The R&D equivalent of focusing on stocks might be the number of new products developed per year or even the number, education, and experience level of the R&D staff. This is a common approach for many organizations where the emphasis is on counts and activities such as number of employees trained per year, number of courses offered, and so on. These measures capture a type of functional performance, but tell us nothing about the value of those outcomes. At best, they are the first step in a long value chain that culminates in improved firm performance. At worst, they turn out to be well-intentioned initiatives with no evidence of any influence on the firm's strategy drivers. Line managers see them as overhead to be controlled, while HR professionals are hard-pressed to demonstrate their contribution to strategic success.

By contrast, the real focus should be on the productive results of talent, what we call the strategic impact. Strategic impact, as seen earlier, is the impact of the workforce on strategy implementation. Therefore, the most important workforce measures focus on how the workforce influences the key strategy drivers. Returning to the R&D analogy, the equivalent focus on productive results is to value R&D performance by the annual change in revenue attributable to new product ideas.

What would these measures look like at BankCo? In order to fully capture how workforce strategy influences the bank's ultimate financial success, measures are required at all levels of the strategy map (see the map for BankCo in chapter 2). Let's think about the measures that would answer the question, what is the impact of the workforce on strategic success? The focus should be on the strategic job performance part of the map, namely, where workforce performance has the most significant impact on strategic success. That is the point at which strategic jobs link to the strategy map. At BankCo, it is the job of RMs.

Based on the strategy map, the bottom-line measures for the workforce strategy should be (1) customer satisfaction measures on the five dimensions of the relationship value proposition, and (2) the vacancy rate of the RM position. Why these two measures? One reflects the *actual* strategic impact of the workforce, and the other captures *potential* strategic impact. Both are important. The customer satisfaction measure, particularly if it can be linked to individual relationship managers, exactly captures what we mean by strategic performance in this job. But what if BankCo needs nine hundred trained RMs in place to fully realize the growth potential of all markets, and the average staffing level is eight hundred twenty for the year? BankCo is underperforming on the execution of its strategy.

While the focus is on the two underlying measures of customer satisfaction and vacancy rates, these measures should also be translated into their financial equivalents. In other words, it is not enough to logically understand the strategic importance of these two workforce measures, BankCo should estimate the financial impact of a 1 percent increase in the vacancy rate among "A" players in the RM job. Likewise it should understand the revenue impact of improved customer satisfaction and the consequent changes in market share or wallet share. This not only makes the workforce measures more salient to line managers, but also guides resource allocation decisions going forward.

Just as the strategy map reveals leading and lagging strategy drivers, there are corresponding measures for the drivers. For example, a company should analyze typical recruiting and sourcing measures that HR professionals might follow in terms of how likely they are to drive one or both of the bottom-line measures described earlier. Likewise it should evaluate the return on investments in development programs based on their impact on the bottom-line measures. Typical measures like numbers trained and cost per trainee might still be useful to reflect the administrative efficiency of the HR unit, but would have *strategic* value only to the extent they influence the bottom-line measures.

Let's look a little closer at turnover rate in the context of our strategic analysis. Now we can see exactly how turnover rates might be strategically significant. Turnover isn't a bottom-line workforce measure, but it probably affects both bottom-line measures directly. First, we aren't talking about turnover broadly, but the turnover rate of RMs specifically. The effect of turnover on overall RM performance depends on who is leaving. Turnover among inexperienced, low performers is much less costly than turnover among experienced "A" players. So when we say turnover is important, we really mean turnover rate among high-performing RMs. Second, as overall RM turnover increases, we expect the vacancy rate to increase as well. Here the measure might not be as narrow as turnover among "A" players, but would include turnover among all RMs with satisfactory performance. The difference is that even a "B" player in a strategic job is probably better than a vacancy.

Principle 5—Think in Terms of a Strategic Workforce Architecture

Managing and measuring strategic workforce success in an organization is challenging because of the confusion about what it is, who should have responsibility for managing it, and how it should be managed. Is it a characteristic of individual employees? Is it the responsibility of the HR function or line managers? How is it influenced by the HR system and other organizational policies? Line managers and HR professionals need a new perspective on workforce management that must include the central role of a strategic workforce architecture. It is important to think in terms of architecture, because the creation and management of human capital, as well as the measurement of strategic workforce performance, are by necessity interrelated processes. Firms need to manage the component parts with an eye toward these interrelationships or they can't expect to transform that architecture into a strategic asset.

Figure 6-1 shows all three dimensions of strategic measures that must be considered when managing your workforce strategy. The upper level—the primary focus of the balanced scorecard approach—reflects the impact of the workforce strategy. In the case of BankCo, the upper-level measures included customer satisfaction with the bank's relationship-based services in commercial credit, market penetration like wallet share and new customer growth, and a variety of financial measures. The next two levels describe the architecture of the workforce strategy. At the foundation is the HR function, and the appropriate strategic measure is the HR Scorecard. The key elements are the competencies of the HR professionals, the functional areas within HR, and the system of HR practices that drives workforce success. HR may have multiple roles, but its *strategic* responsibility is to deliver the workforce attributes in the second level, in particular, the workforce mind-set, competencies, and the performance required to execute the organization's strategy.

The HR function is the administrative home of the HR professionals who take the lead in managing talent. The HR system is the set of organizational policies and practices that acquire, develop, motivate,

FIGURE 6-1

Managing human capital to execute strategy

		Customer success	Financial success
	Workforce scorecard	What specific customer desires and expectations must be satisfied?	What specific financial commitments must be met?
	Leadership and workforce behavior Are the leadership team and workforce consistently behaving in a way that will lead to achieving our strategic objectives?	**Workforce success** Has the workforce accomplished the key strategic objectives for the business?	**Operational success** What specific internal operational processes must be optimized?
HR Scorecard **HR systems** • Align • Integrate • Differentiate	**Workforce mind-set and culture** Does the workforce understand our strategy, embrace it, and do we have the culture we need to support strategy execution?	**Workforce competencies** Does the workforce, especially in the key or "A" positions, have the skills it needs to execute our strategy?	
HR practices • Work design • Staffing • Development • Performance management • Rewards • Communication	**HR workforce competencies** • Strategic partner • Change agent • Employee advocate • Administrative expert		

Source: Mark A. Huselid, Brian E. Becker, and Richard W. Beatty, *The Workforce Scorecard: Managing Human Capital to Execute Strategy* (Boston, MA: Harvard Business School Press, 2005), 4.

and appraise the human capital in the organization. While HR professionals take the lead in developing the HR system, line managers share responsibility in managing that system. We mentioned that turnover rates among certain categories of RMs are probably an important measure for BankCo. Understanding that line managers have a shared responsibility for managing workforce success, which at BankCo means keeping the performance up and the vacancy rate low, also tells us something about the level at which these measures are tracked. BankCo should measure turnover rates among RM "A" players, for example, not only at the level of the bank, but at the level of the line manager. Again, understanding the overall strategic logic of the underlying workforce strategy makes it much easier to identify the right measures.

Thinking about the architecture of a workforce strategy means examining how the workforce policies and practices fit together to deliver the desired workforce success. The architecture should send a clear and consistent message about what is strategically important. The experience at BankCo reflects the norm rather than the exception. Career paths and both tangible and intangible rewards encourage bank professionals to move into certain management jobs, but relationship manager is not one of them. As a result, the bank has difficulty keeping some of the best RMs in that position, because the professional rewards and bank culture send a different signal. BankCo's career structure is no doubt very much in line with a best practice in the industry. But that's the problem. It needs to be differentiated to more effectively implement its current strategy.

BankCo also has a clear policy that limits promotion salary increases to no more than 10 percent. Expense management is a dominant strategic theme, and the across-the-board cap on promotion increases is consistent with that. However, there are no such limits on how much BankCo will increase the current salary for external hires. Both policies make sense on their own, but not when considered as part of a larger strategic system. Together they encourage BankCo employees to leave in hopes of getting a higher salary on their return. The 10 percent cap on promotion increases is not inherently a bad policy, but it has consequences that depend in part on the value of the employees leaving and the value of the employees who may or may not be returning. From the perspective of a differentiated workforce strategy, such a policy is likely to result in a disproportionate share of "A" players leaving, but a disproportionate share of "B" and "C" players returning.

The appropriate workforce measures should follow directly from your strategy map. However, the emphasis on architecture means that you should also track measures that reflect how the elements of the architecture fit together. This is a kind of measure in the workforce strategy that you won't find on any top-ten list of best measures. Given the consequences of an HR system out of alignment, however, it is vital not to ignore it. A measure of fit is more important as a management prompt than a performance measure. In that sense, any measure of fit that is routinely collected and discussed is better than no measure. What matters is the discussion of the measure and the continuing attention to the alignment of the workforce system.

Measures of fit can exist at several levels. For example, at the employee level, you can survey all employees in strategic jobs about how the elements of the HR system affect their performance and likelihood of leaving. This could include the performance reviews and cues, formal and informal, from different levels of the organization's leadership. Are you saying one thing, but being held accountable for something else? Are you rewarding A, developing for B, recruiting for C, and hoping for D?[1] HR professionals and line managers could quickly come up with a long list of practices that tend to work at cross-purposes; they just don't systematically track this problem as a strategic measure.

Another measure of fit focuses on HR professionals. The measure tracks how HR professionals in each functional area rated the fit of policies with the strategic workforce goals. For example, BankCo asked the compensation professionals to rate how the compensation and benefits policies fit with the strategic performance objectives for RMs. What's important is that the notion of strategic performance for the RMs had already been clearly articulated, and the HR professionals had a clear picture of what good fit meant. In particular, fit measured the alignment with performance and continued tenure of "A" players in these jobs. Measuring each functional area also provides a point of comparison to the employee survey on the same issues. Obviously, if employees don't see the same fit as the HR professionals, there's a problem.

Figure 6-1 suggests how more traditional HR functional measures might rise to the level of a strategic measure. Thinking in terms of the strategic architecture, activities at the HR functional level play a role when you can trace the line of sight to the upper-level outcomes. The clearer the line of sight, the more important the measure. For example, think of development programs at BankCo. One measure might track the percentage of development resources allocated to development of employees in "A" jobs. A similar measure might be used in each HR function.

Companies are interested in ROI measures for development programs or HR programs more generally. Without an appropriate perspective on workforce strategy, they are left with fairly clear indications of the costs, but struggle to measure the benefits. Even when HR comes up with a benefit measure, line managers typically don't find such measures as persuasive as more traditional financial measures. With a differentiated workforce strategy in place, however, ROI measures can actually capture strategic return. The benefits can be described in terms of the workforce success in "A" jobs. At BankCo, for example, the upper quartile of RMs produced *eight times* the revenue of the bottom half of RMs. These are clearly the "A" players in an "A" job. One simple development ROI measure at BankCo could focus on several variations of "revenue produced by RM graduates per development dollar invested." This can be tracked one year after the program and three years after. BankCo can also track the percentage of graduates that fall into the upper quartile, compared to a pretraining baseline for current RMs. In other words, is the development program increasing the number of "A" players in the RM job?

Principle 6—Measure Both Levels and Relationships

The sixth principle reminds us that talent has value when it drives business results. This doesn't mean that workforce performance always has a direct influence on bottom-line measures of financial performance. Workforce performance is a leading indicator of strategic success, as are most of the activities of HR professionals. The influence of workforce strategy on the financials is indirect via its influence on the strategy drivers. This indirect line of sight poses a challenge for measuring workforce performance. Organizations have to focus on more than the *levels* of strategic workforce measures. They also have to focus on the *relationship* between workforce measures and the drivers of firm financial performance.

Sears undertook perhaps what was the most systematic effort to quantify the relationships between human capital and firm performance. First it developed a clear, strategic logic linking human capital, customer service, and financial performance. What set the Sears approach apart, however, was that it was able to calculate the quantitative magnitude of those links in a way that allowed it to forecast future financial performance based on current human capital measures. For example, it found that "a 5 point improvement in employee attitudes will drive a 1.3 point improvement in customer satisfaction, which in turn will drive a .5% improvement in revenue growth."[2] In *The Workforce Scorecard*, we described how Allstate Insurance Company used a more sophisticated analysis of relationships to underscore the impact of its workforce strategy. HR professionals at Allstate believed in their leadership competency model, but there was no evidence of the business impact. However, they were subsequently able to establish a statistical relationship between managerial scores on the Leadership Index and business outcomes like claim satisfaction and policy renewals.[3]

At BankCo, there are several opportunities to measure relationships that provide direct evidence of how the workforce strategy drives strategic success. For example, HR professionals tend to think in terms of managing employee attributes like skills and motivation, while line managers worry about customers and market share. Using our perspective on workforce strategy, line managers and HR professionals should have a shared interest in both. They both should think about how much employee attributes, such as RM competencies, affect customers' perception of BankCo's value proposition and the implications for market and wallet share. That means thinking in terms of relationships, or thinking in terms of impact. What effect do RM competencies have on customer satisfaction? How do changes in customer satisfaction with the relationship management experience translate into revenue changes in market and wallet share? Similarly, RM competencies are typically a function of experience on the job, focused development programs, performance management, and initial selection decisions.

Focusing on relationships among measures rather than just their level is a natural result of thinking strategically about leading and lagging indicators. The strategy maps we've discussed describe relationships. So those same relationships should be reflected in the way an organization takes advantage of the measures available to it. At BankCo, customer satisfaction is measured on the five dimensions of the value relationship for each RM position. Competencies are also measured at the level of the RM. A simple statistical analysis calculates the change in customer satisfaction associated with a change in those competencies. More importantly, the bank can also estimate the relationship between customer satisfaction and customer revenue. These two analyses together allow BankCo to understand how a 10 percent change in RM competencies affects customer satisfaction and, in turn, how that change in customer satisfaction translates into additional revenue.

Moving further into the HR Scorecard, HR professionals can assess the relationship between experience and competencies to help them understand how turnover among RMs with different experience levels affects competencies and, in turn, customer satisfaction and revenues. They can evaluate the relationship between a range of HR decisions and strategic outcomes. Elaborating on our earlier example of measuring the ROI for development programs, an obvious relationship of interest is how development programs at BankCo affect RM competencies. But as we've emphasized, it doesn't end there. Competencies are only of strategic interest to the extent that they lead to some strategic outcome, in this case, an improved customer assessment of the banking relationship. Another opportunity is to assess the value of some elements of the workforce strategy. For example, we argue for the importance of alignment between the elements of the HR system and employee strategic performance. A simple analysis at BankCo is to evaluate the relationship between RM perceptions of HR system alignment (measures of fit) and both their performance rates and turnover rates.

Foundation and Consequences of Good Workforce Measurement

Upgrading the quality of your workforce measures is not an isolated exercise. It is not just about finding a mid-level measurement guru to take on the assignment and periodically reviewing the new product of these efforts. Better workforce measurement is part of a new approach to strategy management and a new level of personal accountability in executing your organization's strategy. Next we highlight two ancillary changes that also need to occur if new investments in measurement are going to produce valuable dividends.

A New Emphasis on Analytical Literacy

A recent ad for a senior HR position at Google might surprise many HR professionals and line managers. The opening had the job title of "Director of HR Analytics." In addition to building and leading an HR Analytics team of ten to fifteen people, the director is expected to provide senior business leaders with talent solutions to business problems based on metrics and analytics. Is there something unique about Google's talent strategy that requires this kind of role? Or should metrics and analytics have this central role in managing talent strategy in every organization? We think Google is unique only in that it is actually incorporating this role into the workforce strategy. Whether it takes the form of a specific role or not, senior HR professionals generally need to improve their overall analytical literacy.

A good example of the potential influence of analytical literacy is described in *Moneyball*, by Michael Lewis. Lewis describes how one organization, the Oakland Athletics, achieved a performance advantage by incorporating analytical literacy into its strategic decision making. The A's replaced the intuition and gut feel of traditional baseball decision making with objective evidence-based analysis of player performance. By doing so, it redefined *what matters* and *how to measure* it. Most important, *Moneyball* is about senior executives understanding the kind of management guidance that can be drawn from the right measures, analyzed in the right way. Senior leaders obviously aren't doing the sophisticated analyses themselves, but they should be analytically literate enough to "use their conclusions."[4]

Even if you are only superficially familiar with the sport of baseball, you can understand the meaning of "workforce performance" in the game. Several core lessons about analytical literacy are highlighted in a relatively transparent and understandable strategic decision-making model. You can see a clear relationship between the approach to measurement described earlier in this chapter and the attributes of analytical literacy.

Business Logic. Begin with a strategy map that articulates your organization's view of what drives strategy success. Similarly, the Oakland A's formulated a clear business logic that articulates success on the field and developed measures of success drivers. The A's realized that while scoring runs and winning games are the ultimate goals, the strategic driver in a particular game is minimizing the chances of making an out in each inning. Therefore on-base percentage (the probability of not making an out) is a more important measure of player performance than batting average. In short, strategic logic drives measurement decisions. Next the A's identified the workforce (i.e., player) characteristics that increased the chances that the team would achieve those strategic outcomes. This close fit between player attributes and strategic goals led the A's to sign players with a mix of skills and competencies that were different than the skills and competencies their competitors used. The A's developed a strategically based, differentiated workforce.

Causal Relationships. As the team worked back through the causal logic driving the outcome of scoring runs and winning games, the A's realized that the best pitchers were the starting pitchers. If your team could remove the other team's starter, you increased your chances of winning. How to do this? By increasing the starting pitchers' pitch count. The most valuable batters were not only those who eventually got on base (didn't make an out), but also those who were able to create a high pitch count with each at bat. Once again, the workforce attributes were defined by their strategic analysis.

New Modes of Analysis. Analytical literacy is about making decisions based on evidence. Often this means choosing a course of action that your business logic indicates is the best choice, but then collecting evidence (measurement) of performance to determine whether that course of action should continue. The general manager of the A's "concluded that everything from on-field strategies to player evaluation was better conducted by scientific investigation—hypotheses tested by analysis of historical statistical baseball data—than by reference to the collective wisdom of old baseball men."[5] Just as the A's had to move from conventional wisdoms, senior HR professionals need to become more analytically literate. As Sandy Alderson, former general manager of the Oakland A's, recalls, "I couldn't do a regression analysis, but I knew what one was. And the results . . . made sense to me."[6]

Improved analytical literacy has a direct impact on the decision making at several levels in a typical HR organization. Take, for example, what might be called program analysis. Is a particular program a good idea? How do we know? Is it strategic? We return to the example of development programs at BankCo to illustrate. BankCo has an expensive development program specifically targeted at the RM position. The costs are clear, but the benefits are not so obvious. Improved analytical literacy means using a different approach to thinking about the ROI of this program. Thinking strategically, the return is enhanced customer satisfaction with the banking relationship and even improved financial performance. In other words, when the program is analyzed with a strategic logic, both benefits and costs are clear. Perhaps most important, BankCo now sees spending on the development program as an investment rather than an expense. It tracks strategic returns to evaluate whether that investment should be continued or those resources reallocated to higher-performing alternatives.

At the highest level, improved analytical literacy changes the perspective on the financial resources committed to HR. Senior HR professionals usually focus on the overall HR budget in any conversation about HR's financial performance. The tone of the conversation is that the HR budget is an expense and HR could do more with less. But from a more analytical perspective, based on the strategic logic we've described, HR professionals see that, while they appropriately consider part of the HR budget an operational expense, they consider a significant portion an investment. From that perspective, the annual HR budget looks a little different.

Consider the situation at BankCo. What about the costs of the development program for RMs? What about the cost of specialized sourcing practices for RMs and other strategic jobs? Or the higher salary costs associated with the disproportionately higher pay for strategic jobs? All these are expected to pay disproportionate dividends in terms of customer satisfaction, market share, and ultimately profitability. If the programs are genuine investments, rather than just increased expenses, they will produce current and future returns that exceed their cost. With improved analytical literacy and an appropriate strategic framework, both HR professionals and line managers are in a better position to measure these returns and separate the investment portion of the workforce budget from the expense portion. The organization is then in a position to have two different conversations. One focuses on the appropriate expense for HR's administrative activities and the other focuses on how HR and the benefiting business units can share the investment costs of the workforce strategy.

Personal Accountability

Both HR professionals and line managers have to share responsibility for managing strategic talent, which comes with a new accountability for delivering strategic workforce performance. Developing additional personal performance criteria for line managers and HR professionals is not particularly difficult, *once the logic of your workforce strategy is clear.* Goal setting and performance assessment are standard management practices for most organizations. What is new is the *focus* of the goals and performance assessments. Next we bring together some of the measures discussed earlier into a personal scorecard framework.

Senior Line Managers. Without a clearly defined workforce strategy, line managers likely have little responsibility for workforce outcomes. Perhaps there are general assessments of employee development or some mention of employee survey results. There may also be assessments on broad-based leadership skills, but not with respect to how they bear directly on managing strategic talent. These, however, probably have little significant influence on the results of a line manager's annual review. Why should they? It's not likely that there is any clear line of sight between these assessments and business success. However, think about the organization that has a well-developed workforce strategy and a clear understanding of how talent drives strategic success. There are several talent dimensions that a line manager can regularly manage with great care because the business impact of talent is clear.

Once again, take the case of BankCo. What does the personal scorecard look like for senior-level line managers in the commercial credit unit? These are the leaders whose direct reports include a number of BankCo's "A" jobs—the RMs. Is the focus on employee satisfaction from employee surveys? Keith Holmes, director of human resources—IT delivery, observed "At IBM, we measure employee satisfaction and believe that it is important in the context of executing strategy. But there is no freestanding 'maintain a cheery disposition metric' at IBM—our measures are tied directly to our business results."[7]

Figure 6-1 shows the three levels of scorecards and the way they fit together to provide a comprehensive assessment of how talent drives strategic success. Those scorecards, however, are for a strategic capability and are managed at a unit or functional level. Creating a personal scorecard to hold managers and HR professionals accountable for results cuts across several of those scorecards, depending on their respective strategic role.

Table 6-1 shows a personal scorecard for a senior line manager role at BankCo. Developing this kind of scorecard is not difficult, once you have the right perspective. You organize it along the relevant dimensions from figure 6-1 and include the particulars from BankCo's strategy map. For example, begin with the three scorecard dimensions. Where do you expect the senior line managers in the commercial credit unit to have significant influence? There might be exceptions, but normally they are not held accountable for the outcomes in the HR Scorecard. They are, however, accountable for workforce and business outcomes.

Let's begin with the workforce scorecard. Given that BankCo has identified relationship management as a strategic capability and designated the job of RMS as an "A" job for its central role in that capability, the focus of the workforce scorecard measures is relatively clear (first three columns). On the leadership dimension, senior line managers are expected to communicate, reward, and develop strategic talent in a way that is consistent with BankCo's strategic logic. They are also expected to give priority to strategic considerations in their decision making and not be fully consumed by operational issues. The measures on this dimension are based on feedback from the RMs.

TABLE 6-1

Personal scorecard:
Senior line manager at BankCo

WORKFORCE COMPONENT			BUSINESS COMPONENT
LEADERSHIP	**STRATEGIC TALENT**	**STRATEGIC MIND-SET**	
• My performance expectations reflect my strategic role: 50%	• % of "A" players in RM position: 60%	**Employee strategic focus**	**Financial**
• Progress toward strategic goals is regularly communicated: 80%	• RM vacancy rate: 20%	**Relationship managers**	• Unit revenue growth: 6%
• I have the skills to deliver strategic performance: 70%	• RM turnover rate for "A" players: 10%	• Knows the meaning of strategic success at BankCo: 62%	• Unit profitability growth: 9%
• I have the team support to deliver strategic performance: 60%		• Knows how the RM position drives strategic success: 42%	**Market**
• I am recognized when I deliver superior performance: 80%		• Understands the importance of all four dimensions of the customer relationship: 47%	• Wallet share growth 6%
• My rewards are appropriate when I deliver superior performance: 50%		**RM support team**	• Customer relationship index: 85 out of 100
		• Knows the meaning of strategic success at BankCo: 32%	
		• Knows how the RM position drives strategic success: 22%	
		• Understands how my role affects each dimension of the customer relationship: 17%	

The second column, strategic talent, focuses on several dimensions of the strategic jobs, in this case, the RMs. These attributes are not so much the causes of workforce success, but rather explain the nature of strategic workforce performance. This follows our earlier analysis that, in the RM job, the ultimate strategic contribution is a function of both the quality of talent in those jobs (percentage of "A" players) and the vacancy rate. Both are influenced by the turnover rate of "A" players.

Senior line managers are expected to keep the percentage of "A" players high, and both the vacancy rate and the turnover of "A" players low.

The third column, strategic mind-set, captures the strategic focus of the workforce. In the commercial credit unit at BankCo, the workforce is divided into two groups—the RMs and the support team. If the leadership dimension focuses on whether leaders' behaviors are aligned with BankCo's strategy, the strategic mind-set measures capture whether the workforce reporting to this leadership is strategically aligned as well. These measures are drawn from an employee survey. Finally, the last column is the most straightforward because it includes the business measures that BankCo is probably already tracking. The advantage of repeating them on the personal scorecard is to reinforce the idea that the value-creation process moves from left to right.

Senior HR Professionals. Typical performance assessments for senior HR professionals focus on activities within the HR function. Mounting and delivering programs on time and on budget and contributing to the overall operating efficiency of the HR function are the broad assessment themes. As in the case of the senior line managers, we are not arguing that current assessments be eliminated, but rather that they should be extended to include an individual's strategic contribution. Perhaps the most desirable change, however, is to restructure responsibilities so that at least one member of the senior HR leadership team has strategy execution as his or her primary role.

Table 6-2 shows the personal scorecard for a senior vice president for HR whose primary responsibility is executing workforce strategy at BankCo. As in the case of the line manager's personal scorecard, this senior HR leader is expected to influence the outcomes in figure 6-1. Perhaps surprisingly, the senior HR leader has a broader influence on workforce strategy execution than the senior line manager. The HR leader is responsible for delivering not only the HR element of the workforce strategy, but workforce and business outcomes as well. The weight given to these latter two outcomes in the HR personal scorecard is not as high as those in the line manager's scorecard, but they should be present nevertheless. It reinforces the message that the strategic purpose for managing the HR deliverables is ultimately those higher-level results.

TABLE 6-2

Personal scorecard:
Senior Vice President for HR at BankCo

HR Scorecard			Workforce Scorecard			Business Scorecard
HR strategic competencies and mind-set	**HR practices**	**HR systems**	**Leadership**	**Strategic mind-set**	**Strategic talent**	**Business component**
Employee strategic focus index	**Strategic focus index:**	**Strategic alignment index**	**Strategic leadership index**	**Employee strategic focus**	• % of "A" players in RM position	**Financial**
• Compensation	• Compensation	• Relationship managers		Relationship managers	• RM vacancy rate	• Unit revenue growth
• Sourcing	• Sourcing	• RM support		• ESF index	• RM turnover rate for "A" players	• Unit profitability growth
• Selection	• Selection			**RM support team**		**Market**
• Development	• Development			• ESF index		• Wallet share growth
• Performance management	• Performance management					• Customer relationship index
Analytical literacy index						
• Compensation						
• Sourcing						
• Selection						
• Development						
• Performance management						

The first three columns in table 6-2 focus on the HR Scorecard (figure 6-1). The measures are designed to capture the bottom-line deliverables within the HR function that contribute to execution of the workforce strategy. The first column focuses on key mind-set and competency measures for each HR functional unit. This requires BankCo to assess key professionals within each functional unit on their strategic focus and their analytical literacy. These measures are rolled up into two aggregate indices that the senior HR leader tracks. The second column focuses on individual HR practices and how well they are aligned with strategic performance requirements of "A" jobs within this capability. In this example, there is only one "A" job. While the second column measures how each functional practice is aligned with the workforce strategy from the perspective of HR, the third column measures how well the whole system of HR practices is strategically aligned. BankCo collects these measures from the perspective of the RMs and their support team. The next three columns track some of the same workforce scorecard measures found in the line manager's personal scorecard, reflecting the shared responsibility for BankCo's workforce strategy. Finally, the column of business outcomes in the HR leader's personal scorecard highlights the clear line of sight between the strategic decisions in HR and the strategic impact of those decisions.

Summary

Our previous two books are devoted to the broad topic of HR and workforce strategic measurement. Many of the particulars can't be covered here. We are, however, increasingly convinced that for many organizations, one measurement challenge is to have the correct perspective. Once senior line managers and senior HR professionals have the right perspective on workforce strategy and, in particular, the elements of a differentiated workforce strategy, the measurement process will be more straightforward.

CHAPTER 7

Make It Happen in Practice

Creating a Differentiated Workforce at the American Heart Association

FOR MANY OF US who are sports fans, every season is an exercise in frustration. Often before the season is even over, we talk of "next year." Where do we need to make a change? Who should go? Who should we add? Should we focus on the draft or free agency? As sports fans, we think we know what changes our team should make because we all think we know the game. When it comes to workforce strategy, most line managers and HR professionals understand that the game has probably changed, but they aren't quite clear about the new rules. As a result, change is slow and often in the wrong direction. In this book, we have revealed the new rules of the game and presented a new strategy for winning with talent.

In this chapter, we summarize several key points that show exactly how you can avoid "waiting until next year." We organized this chapter around our key themes, using the example of a comprehensive effort at the American Heart Association (AHA) to develop a differentiated workforce. We focus on the AHA for at least two reasons. First, it provides a world-class example of effective workforce strategy design and execution and illustrates the decisions and common challenges you might face at each decision point. Second, we hope to persuade you that our approach is equally effective in nonprofit organizations, such as the AHA, as it is in global multinationals, such as IBM. This book is not about strategy development, but about the role of the workforce in strategy execution. We assume that an organization already has a well-developed strategy, but needs to do a better job driving that strategy with talent. However, if your organization is moving in a new strategic direction or has yet to clearly articulate a strategy, you have work to do before moving on to the workforce strategy.

Once you determine that strategy, our approach is designed to bring that same discipline to the design of your workforce strategy. You need to differentiate your workforce in its management, evaluation, and metrics, just like any other asset. And you need to provide differentiated consequences as well. The process involves developing the right strategy, the right work ("A" positions), the right workforce ("A" players), and the right HR management practices (a uniquely tailored, high-performance HR architecture). In short, you need to design workforce management systems from the top down and execute them from the bottom up.

Clarifying Strategic Choice and Objectives at the American Heart Association (AHA)

The mission statement of the AHA is "Building healthier lives, free of cardiovascular diseases and stroke." The AHA's thirty-five hundred employees are organized into eight affiliates across the United States and Puerto Rico, with a corporate headquarters located in Dallas.[1] AHA measures its progress toward the achievement of its goals against the following strategic objectives:

- Reduce the death rate from coronary heart disease and stroke by 25 percent by 2010.

- Reduce the prevalence of smoking, high blood cholesterol, and physical inactivity by 25 percent by 2010.

- Reduce the rate of uncontrolled high blood pressure by 25 percent by 2010.

- Eliminate the rate of growth of physical inactivity and obesity.

The AHA has been highly successful over the years in raising funds, in sponsoring research, and in raising public awareness of the causes and consequences of heart disease and stroke. The "Go Red for Women" program is one example of a highly successful initiative that incorporated all three of these elements, in this case, focused specifically on heart disease among women. AHA's CEO, Cass Wheeler, summarizes AHA's strategic intent succinctly, "We're going to save more lives, and change more lives." As a result, everything that AHA does is intended to drive this outcome.

In 2006, it announced an ambitious goal, to go from $600 million in 2006 to $1 billion in total revenue by 2010. For AHA, achieving this revenue goal is simply a means to an end—reducing the number of deaths from heart disease by 25 percent.

Over time and after experience with a number of significant business challenges, the AHA management team concluded that both the key challenge *and* the primary solution to achieving the "25 percent by 2010" and $1 billion revenue goal was directly related to attracting, selecting, developing, and retaining top talent. However, AHA had lost many high-potential employees (especially in fund-raising) to firms paying more money and offering more opportunities—often in the for-profit sector. Attracting, selecting, and retaining high-performing talent was a significant challenge for the association, and in some cases, budgetary constraints limited the extent to which it was able to invest in the workforce. The senior management team members knew that strategic investments in talent were the only way that they were going to reach their billion-dollar goal. The war-for-talent metaphor made good sense to them, but they had neither the time nor resources to place "A" players in all positions. What they needed was a model and a process that moved them beyond the metaphor to a place whether they made strategic investments in the workforce, much like any other key organizational asset.

AHA initiated its change effort with two important decisions. First, it established an organizationwide task force to develop the framework for change and guide the process (which was called the Winning With Talent taskforce [WWT]). Most important, the CEO, Cass Wheeler, gave the taskforce full support and encouragement. Second, AHA developed a workforce philosophy that communicated the new role of talent in AHA's strategic success and the expectations and responsibilities required to implement that new role.

Operationally, Wheeler asked the WWT taskforce to design and implement an effective solution to these problems. Working with an external consultant (Mark Huselid), the WWT team concluded that to be successful, they would need to accomplish the following tasks:[2]

- Identify the key capabilities needed to deliver on the AHA strategic plan.

- Develop an association-wide workforce strategy.

- Implement workforce differentiation and the strategic position concepts to ensure that talent is used effectively to execute strategy.

- Develop a new approach to goal setting, performance management, and incentives, and a methodology for rating and ranking staff in key positions.

- Develop and market an AHA employment brand.

- Identify opportunities to simplify routine HR functions.

- Identify ways to better integrate HR staff at senior levels, permitting HR to better understand and contribute to the association's business strategy.

- Identify future HR skill sets necessary in the workforce.

Developing a Workforce Philosophy at the AHA

A key threshold decision for achieving these objectives was the adoption of an organizationwide perspective on workforce strategy. Because the AHA operates with regional affiliates, it had, in effect, eight separate and sometimes conflicting workforce strategies. AHA recognized that talent was an organizational asset; the structural changes that accompanied that recognition were an important change marker.

Chief Operating Officer Nancy Brown chaired the WWT taskforce, partnering with Senior Vice President of HR Bill Achenbach, and eleven executives from AHA's regional affiliates and corporate office. One of the first and most significant accomplishments for the taskforce was the development of a workforce philosophy that would not only guide the design and execution of the strategy, but also provide a road map for interactions with the workforce. The executive team agreed in principle that more differentiation and strategic investment in the workforce was necessary, but there was considerable tension about what form that differentiation might take. With the help of external consultant Huselid, the AHA team had a wide-ranging discussion about the differences between an *equality* model of workforce management—in which all employees are treated pretty much the same and developed in equal measure—and an *equity* model of workforce management—in which jobs are differentiated for investment, based on their ability to have an impact on AHA's strategy. One group asked, Is it really fair to invest in employees in different ways just because they hold different jobs at AHA? A second group asked, If our goal is to reduce heart disease, and we know that some jobs make a greater contribution to achieving this goal than others, don't we have a moral responsibility to be sure that we place the best possible employees in the most important roles? This was a rich and important discussion for the team, as embracing the differentiated approach to workforce management (as they overwhelmingly did) represented a significant philosophical shift for the AHA.

AHA had embraced the Topgrading concept used by GE and other firms and had by all accounts a high-performance, goal-oriented culture.[3] Still, the idea of differentiating by position (and by performance within position) was a new way of managing. After much discussion, the AHA management team concluded that the Topgrading approach was a good start—necessary but not sufficient—but that AHA needed additional differentiation by position for it to reach its strategic objectives.

The conclusion of the WWT taskforce was that AHA would continue to invest in all employees, but would place significantly more developmental resources and opportunities for high-potential employees in key positions. In our experience, many organizations reach the same conclusion over time. The AHA workforce philosophy was the result of a careful discussion of AHA's culture, strategic objectives, and what it thought needed to happen to reach the strategic objectives. In particular, AHA developed very specific ground rules in the domains of *leadership, employee accountability, workforce change,* and the *responsibility of the HR function.* (See figure 7-1.)

FIGURE 7-1

Workforce management strategic focus guidelines
AHA's *ground rules for workforce leadership*

AHA workforce philosophy

1. **Leadership:** Leaders are expected to communicate and mentor the workforce on their role in effectively executing the AHA strategy. Leaders will be evaluated and rewarded based on how well their employees enhance and execute the strategy. Leaders are held accountable for their own behavior and results including acquisition, retention, and development of their staff. They are expected to provide and receive timely and candid feedback to employees. Leaders will also build a shared understanding of the value and impact of the mission of the AHA. Leaders will model volunteer relationship skills to build volunteer management skills associationwide.

2. **Employee accountability:** Employees are expected to understand their role in effectively executing and enhancing AHA strategy. Staff is required to take responsibility for continuing to develop and refine their capabilities to meet the ever-changing business demands. Rewards and career progression are directly linked to performing at a high level, generating ideas, and sharing best practices.

3. **Workforce change:** It is essential for our best talent to be placed in critical strategic positions. Although we will invest in the ongoing development of all staff, the AHA will invest disproportionately in the development and compensation of key talent. Our future success requires us to maintain a laser-sharp focus on developing and retaining our top talent.

4. **Responsibility of the HR function:** HR is required to fully understand the AHA strategic direction. HR must be capable of facilitating the process to identify the capability required to execute the AHA strategy. HR and AHA managers are responsible for delivering the top talent to flawlessly and effectively execute the association's strategy.

Source: AHA internal documents. Used with permission.

Identify Your Strategic Capabilities

Differentiation is about making choices, and those choices have strategic consequences. By now, it should be clear why a differentiated workforce strategy is not only essential to the successful execution of your larger organizational strategy, but also the most effective way to increase the contribution of both the workforce and the HR function.

Beginning with the business logic of your overall firm strategy, you choose which capabilities are the focus of your workforce strategy. Those choices mean more differentiation. Next, you align the execution of workforce strategy with that focus. Finally, you manage and evaluate the workforce strategy with the appropriate measures.

The basis of this differentiation is the firm's strategic capabilities. As we have described, strategic capabilities are an important part of your firm's value proposition, are relatively unique, and ones in which your firm outperforms the competition. The capabilities that really matter might not be immediately obvious, and are rarely as simple as "speed," "focus," or "customer responsiveness." Uncovering and supporting these capabilities requires a more thoughtful, analytic approach. Ensuring that the firm can execute its strategies means that all employees must be managed well, but the firm must place priority on putting "A" players in "A" positions for "A" customers.

Identifying Strategic Capabilities at the
American Heart Association

As we've described, identifying a firm's strategic capabilities is a relatively straightforward process that involves the following steps:

- Review strategic capability criteria.

- List possible strategic capabilities.

- Assess each for present and future wealth-creation impact.

- Determine the most important three to five strategic capabilities for the business.

Identifying strategic capabilities at AHA began with a review of the firm's strategic plan and its 156-page strategy document (by external consultant Steve Kirn). Group discussions on strategy often involved philosophical differences about the nature of workforce strategy, so it was useful to focus the conversation on how the workforce strategy might drive those capabilities. Based on a comprehensive analysis of the strategy document, fourteen initial themes were identified.[4] A survey of one hundred high-potential employees subsequently evaluated these themes and reduced them to three, based on the following criteria:

- How important is this capability in terms of the AHA achieving its goals?

- To what extent would this capability represent a distinctive difference or advantage compared to other nonprofit organizations?

- What impact would this capability have on AHA customers' perception of the value of our programs, products, or services?

- What is the current level of performance of the AHA on this capability?

- If this capability is underperforming, to what extent would a significant upgrade of strategic talent in this area affect its impact?

- Imagine that you have one hundred "investment points" to distribute across each of these capabilities. Where would you invest to yield the highest return?

The results of these analyses are shown in the box, "AHA's Strategic Capabilities." Fund-raising, volunteer acquisition and management, and strategic talent development were ranked as the most important strategic capabilities, by a significant margin. Moreover, strategic talent development was rated as having the greatest gap between the current and needed future states. The finding that one of the most important strategic capabilities for the association was one in which it was the weakest was an unwelcome surprise to the executive team. It generated much discussion and concern, and as we will see, considerable action subsequently.

AHA made an interesting decision. It chose to include several workforce capabilities among its strategic capabilities. This makes sense in a comprehensive process that includes both the articulation of enterprise strategy and a workforce strategy. Nevertheless, it's clear that at AHA, the talent capabilities drive fund-raising and are not ends in themselves.

In order to both clarify the key strategy drivers and achieve consensus on those drivers, the WWT taskforce next developed a strategy map for the most important strategic capability—fund-raising. They viewed the development of a strategy map as a transition step to get the group to the end-point of how to differentiate management practices in support of strategic positions. The strategy map also had an important role in revealing the drivers that guided selection of the "A" positions (see figure 7-2).

AHA raises funds through corporations, individuals, and foundations. Each of these sources is influenced to a greater or lesser degree by *public fund-raising events* (e.g., AHA's annual galas, which occur in each major market), *direct giving* (e.g., direct mail campaigns), *causes* (e.g., the Go Red for Women campaign), *employee giving* (e.g., gifts in the workplace, often linked to a corporate match), and *major gifts* (e.g., planned giving through individual wills and trusts and large current gifts from individuals or from foundations).

Both environmental scanning (where are the opportunities?) and prioritizing high-potential opportunities (how should we rate these opportunities?) drive success in each domain. Successful scanning and prioritization are largely a function of the extent to which the metro directors (which subsequent analyses would show to be an "A" position) are able to effectively manage relationships among donors, AHA staff, and the substantial numbers of AHA volunteers. AHA's analyses indicated that high-performing metro directors were much more likely to exhibit adaptability, low turnover among their own high-potential staff, and significantly higher personal commitment to their success and to achieving their goals. These factors, in turn, were driven by the existence of an integrated system for developing high-performing metro directors, including recruiting, developing, information sharing, performance management and feedback, incentive compensation, patience for results, and finally, the willingness to deal effectively with poor performance.

AHA's Strategic Capabilities

Top Three AHA Capabilities

1. **Fund-Raising and Revenue Generation.** Identify and cultivate or develop potential donors; deliver consistent successful results against challenging goals; develop new and/or innovative methods for increasing revenue; demonstrate success in a variety of approaches for increasing revenue (e.g., direct solicitation, corporate or foundation funding, special events, planned giving).

2. **Volunteer Acquisition and Management.** Recruit and retain skilled, effective volunteers, especially "high-level or corporate" volunteers; effectively manage volunteer activity and effort.

3. **Strategic Talent Development.** Distinctive ability to attract, grow, and retain superior staff via recruiting, training or learning tools, work and workplace design, management and leadership.

Other Strategic Capabilities

Advocate or Influence. Develop and deliver consistent, powerful messages, programs, products, and initiatives. Regarding AHA strategic, science, and policy positions and priorities, translate these AHA positions and priorities into effective practice by influencing healthcare systems, providers, patients, and government and regulatory agencies.

Public or Media Relations and Positioning. Develop productive relationships with media channels to create positive perception of AHA mission and organization, plus the value of providing financial support; collaborate with media to communicate shared agenda.

Partnerships and Alliances. Build productive relationships, create influential coalitions, and create shared goals and mutual actions for multiple constituent groups (employers, providers, foundations, professional associations, and so on).

Consensus Building. Proactive role to build common understanding and action agenda (science, policy, practice) among subject matter experts, organizations, agencies; create shared efforts for measurement and evidence standards, priority research, efficient means to move knowledge into practice.

Cross-function Collaboration. Build partnerships and leverage resources by building cooperation and shared effort among volunteers, staff, departments or functions, and organizational initiatives.

Multichannel Communication and Education. Efficient and effective use of both "traditional" and emerging communication tools and approaches to address different audiences; build literacy or awareness and understanding—especially among underserved groups—to aid prevention, educated health choices, etc.

Customer Relationship Management and Engagement. Customer segmentation and marketing analysis; customer "value" analysis and predictive modeling; assessment of marketing channel cost and effectiveness; measurement of customer satisfaction and engagement, loyalty, and use of these measurement tools to identify ways to improve performance and engage customers more fully.

Issue Scanning, Forecasting, Anticipation. Early and anticipatory (versus "reactive") identification of emerging issues or challenges, policy matters; creating relationships with agencies, payors, etc., to provide information and intelligence on these matters.

Multicultural and Language Skill. Provide effective programs, products, and services to address needs of a variety of racial and ethnic populations; communicate in multiple languages; focus advocacy and action on needs of diverse groups; encourage diversity in research and researchers.

Training and Development. Capitalize on knowledge assets inside AHA (e.g., in various functional areas, affiliates) through active knowledge sharing and management; deliver consistent, powerful message to support AHA mission in all training and development (including orientation, skill development, management or leadership, etc.); build broad and deep cultural, business literacy and collaboration competencies throughout AHA.

Organizational Agility. Rapid learning and application of new ideas; quick "time to market" with programs, products, and services; flexibility and adaptability in responding to issues, challenges and unanticipated obstacles or opportunities.

Source: AHA internal document. Used with permission.

FIGURE 7-2

Fund-raising strategy map

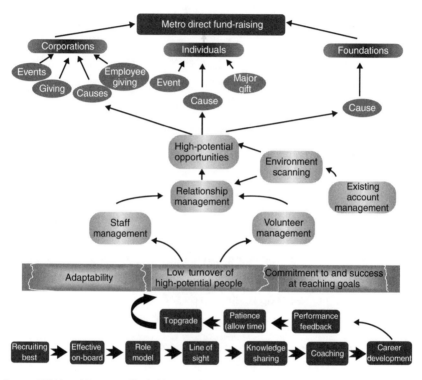

Source: AHA internal documents. Used with permission.

Identify Strategic Positions

Once strategic capabilities have been identified, the next step in the process is to determine which positions have the greatest impact on those capabilities—the "A" positions. As we've described, "A" positions have a significant impact on the firm's strategic capabilities and by wide variations in employee performance in those roles. Part of what makes "A" positions so important is that an improvement in employee performance in those roles has a significant impact on the firm's performance. The steps in the process are as follows:

- List positions within each strategic capability.

- Assess each position on present and future wealth-creation potential.

- Identify strategic positions' performance variability.

- Finalize strategic positions.

- Review other positions (those not in the strategic capability for wealth-creation potential).

Identifying Strategic Positions at the American Heart Association (AHA)

The process of identifying strategic positions at the AHA started with the development of a clear set of ground rules for selecting and managing those positions (summarized in the box, "AHA Key Positions' Guiding Principles"). The discussion of the key position "philosophy" was guided by the workforce philosophy, which helped the AHA leadership team develop specific criteria for strategic-position determination. This essential step in the process set the rules for moving forward. The AHA management team repeatedly returned to this document during subsequent deliberations.

Next, the WWT taskforce appointed a subgroup to evaluate all of AHA's jobs and to propose an initial set of key positions. Using the framework provided in the box, "AHA Strategic Position Criteria," a team of six executives and Huselid met to rate and evaluate AHA's jobs. The result was a hierarchy of positions ranked by importance to the execution of AHA's strategy. The position rated as most influential, the metro director, was a mid-level managerial role that was important not only because of the scope of its influence, but also because of the considerable variability in performance among the metro directors. This job had a direct impact on AHA's ability to raise funds and recruit and

AHA Key Positions' Guiding Principles

1. Key positions are recognized associationwide. With this philosophy, no individual component (affiliate or National Center) will identify separate key positions.

2. Having the right people in the identified key positions is a priority before triggering areas of differentiation such as differential pay.

3. We will disproportionately invest in key positions in recruitment, training, management coaching, and, in some cases, compensation (placement in range and incentive pay).

4. Staff in key positions will be reviewed during an annual national talent review process. We will also discuss staff in feeder positions for key positions.

5. The list of key positions evolves over time. We will roll out the implementation of differentiation for staff in key positions based on our ability to execute.

6. The list of key positions is reviewed annually with an expectation that the list will change.

Source: AHA internal document. Used with permission.

manage volunteers (key strategic capabilities). An improvement in employee performance in these roles would have a significant impact on AHA's performance.

Assess Players in Positions

The next step is to perform a talent inventory. If the overall goal is to place "A" players in "A" positions for "A" customers, then forming a

AHA Strategic Position Criteria

The criteria for strategic positions at AHA are as follows; a position must meet the strategic impact and performance variability criteria if it is to qualify as strategic:

1. **Strategic Impact.** A disproportionate impact on the AHA's ability to execute some part of our business strategy through the strategic capabilities we've identified.

2. **Performance Variability.** The gap between low and high performers in this role is substantial.

3. **Top-Talent Impact.** A position where top talent would significantly enhance the success of achieving AHA's business strategy.

4. **Hard to Get.** Top talent in this role is difficult to attract and retain.

Please keep in mind the following examples and concepts when thinking about what makes a position strategic:

- Strategic positions feature a high degree of variability in performance, even if there is only one incumbent in the role.

- Strategic positions often require a high level of expertise.

- Strategic positions aren't determined by hierarchy.

- Strategic positions aren't defined by how hard they are to fill—workforce scarcity doesn't equate workforce value.

- Not all positions in a job category have to be considered strategic positions for some of the positions in a job category to be considered strategic (for example, all metro director positions may not be strategic positions if they don't meet the criteria above).

- Strategic positions typically represent less than 15 percent of the workforce.

Source: AHA internal documents. Used with permission.

clear understanding of the firm's inventory of talent is essential. The steps are as follows:

- Develop "A," "B," and "C" criteria for each position. "A" positions have already been identified. However, the characteristics of "B" and "C" positions should also be articulated.

- Apply "A," "B," and "C" criteria to all positions.

- List all positions by "A," "B," and "C" designation.

- Assess all employees in positions.

- Determine percentage of "A," "B," and "C" players in all positions.

- Remove "C" positions.

- Remove "C" players from "A" positions.

- Put "A" players in "A" positions.

- Develop "B" players in "A" positions into "As."

At this point, you know which positions are more strategically valuable and which are not. You also know which employees are "A" players and which are not. The top priority of this strategic human capital planning process is getting the "A" players into the "A" positions and the "C" players out of the "A" positions.

Assessing Strategic Players at the AHA

The AHA has had a well-developed performance management and feedback system in place for several years. This system, in many ways similar to the Topgrading process used at General Electric, was considered a valid and reliable basis for differentiating "A," "B," and "C" players. Since high-quality performance measures are the foundation of the strategic human capital planning process, an organization that lacks such measures at this point has to develop them before moving ahead.

Following the process described, the AHA team began with a discussion of the factors that differentiated the high- and low-performing employees in their strategic positions. (See the box, "Understanding 'A' Performance at the AHA.")

Understanding "A" Performance at the AHA

- What does it mean to be successful as a metro director? In terms of advocacy, fund-raising, and mission, what are the kinds of things that we expect them to accomplish?

- What are the *key behaviors* that differentiate successful and unsuccessful metro directors?

- What are the *key skills and competencies* that differentiate successful and unsuccessful metro directors?

- What type of culture and mind-set in the workforce will we expect successful metro directors to develop?

- Where do our most successful (and least successful) metro directors come from?

- How do they learn their roles, and what are the elements of their roles that cause us the biggest challenge?

- What are our expectations in terms of talent development for the metro directors? That is, how will we hold the metro directors accountable for the talent that reports to them?

- Have we gotten the "scope" of the metro director position roughly right? How much time do the metro directors spend on truly value-creating activities vs. things that could be done by a more junior person (or not at all)?

- Are there key elements of the metro directors' role that are routinely not being performed? If so, is this because of a skill gap, time gap, or resource gap?

- What does our current "bench" look like for the metro director position, and what are the implications (if any) for how the job is designed?

- What do we see as the key challenges or problems with how the current metro director role is structured, and where are our opportunities to improve?

Source: AHA internal documents. Used with permission.

The group then engaged in a brainstorming exercise to identify the factors that differentiate average metro directors from high-performers (see table 7-1).

As part of this analysis, the WWT discovered fourteen of the top twenty-five metro director positions had been vacant sometime during the past twelve months. The team also discovered that only four or five of

TABLE 7-1

Comparison of low- and high-performing metro directors at the AHA

Low-performing metro directors	High-performing metro directors
• "Drone-like"	• People-skills
• "On-the-playbook"	• Hire and develop "A" players
• Don't understand individual strengths and weaknesses	• Vision and execution skills
• Don't "work smart"	• Account management
• Take pride in effort instead of outcomes	• Action-oriented
• Poor volunteer management skills	• Superior volunteer management relationship skills
• Don't manage talent well	• Corporate-savvy
• Not strong role model	• Priority management
• Low sense of urgency	• Unbiased peripheral vision, systems thinking
• Don't want to change or evolve	• Strategic thinking skills
• Reactive versus proactive	• Translating worth to constituencies
• Poor conflict resolution skills	• Strategy execution skills
• Don't deal effectively with problems	• Judgment—vision—business acumen
	• Understanding AHA's complexity and translating to local level
	• Create culture of ownership
	• Attract "followership"
	• Can lead without authority
	• Execution—remove barriers rapidly
	• Find a way to make it work within the system
	• Can build shared purpose with volunteers
	• Can build a long-term vision
	• Big donor finesse and engagement skills
	• Smart
	• Can challenge current practices in the spirit of improvement (straight talk)
	• Connected with community and networked
	• Institutionalize thoughtful innovation

Source: AHA internal documents. Used with permission.

the twenty-five metro directors could be considered high-performing; a third, average; and another third to one-half, low performers who would need to be moved out of this role soon. These findings were startling and greatly concerned the executive team, which had a general sense that there was a problem with the metro director role, but were surprised by its magnitude. The group agreed on the goal of 100 percent "A" players in the metro director role, but wondered if it was realistic. The group concluded that the significance of these metro leader positions to AHA's success had been underestimated for years. It wanted to ensure that these positions would be perceived as the most desirable for a thriving career with the AHA. One senior executive noted, "We fully realize some of our recommendations require a significant paradigm shift, and that there will be hurdles to overcome as we roll this new concept out . . . but, we feel this investment will pay off tremendously. It will generate more revenue for the mission, and help with the overall growth of the metro areas, including volunteer growth and programmatic growth, and it will position senior staff such as metro directors to be the next affiliate executive vice presidents in the AHA."

Align the Workforce Management System with Your Strategy

You should design workforce strategies from the top down or from the outside in (from strategic intent to strategic capabilities to "A" positions to "A" behaviors to HR management systems and practices). Developing a workforce strategy requires a clear understanding of (1) how your firm's strategic capabilities drive business success, and (2) how the workforce and HR management systems affect the creation of strategic capabilities.

We've noted that a key element of workforce differentiation is that it helps you discover how and when to change HR management practices to support your workforce strategy. Developing such a system requires that managers address specific questions: How does the HR system need to be differentiated in order to fit the workforce strategy? How do we develop a workforce philosophy and a culture of strategy execution?

What does a differentiated workforce strategy mean for the organization structure of the HR function? We describe how the AHA addressed each question in the next sections.

Aligning Workforce Management Systems at the AHA

AHA's focus on strategic capabilities and positions made the process of HR system change management much easier. The Human Resource Leadership Team (HRLT, led by the senior vice president for HR, Bill Achenbach) systematically examined six areas it thought needed change. For each, a subteam developed a position paper that provided a clearly articulated issue statement, an evaluation of the impact and opportunity on the AHA, the current situation, desired outcome, actions required, accountabilities and resources, and next steps.

The development of these position papers became both resource and action plans for the next phase in the implementation process. The WWT taskforce referred to them frequently, and they became part of the communication with the workforce as the implementation plan was rolled out. The first and broadest of the position papers focused on managing talent across the organization. This internal discussion document marked the first time in the AHA's history that the management team agreed to work together to grow talent and to shift emphasis (and accountabilities) from optimizing talent within a region to optimizing talent across the association (see the box, "AHA Guiding Principles: Managing Talent"). This shift required changes in operating policies, HR management systems, and the AHA's culture, but the executive team was convinced that it was the only way that it would be able to effectively grow and retain the talent to execute the strategy.

Recruiting and Selection at the AHA

The next element that the WWT explored was recruiting and selection. The team discussed the relative importance of all the HR management practices in improving the performance of the metro directors, agreeing that all these elements were important, but recruitment and selection provided the greatest opportunity to increase the average levels of performance in these roles. Because there was so much variance in the pool of candidates (both internal and external) for the metro director role, reducing the probability of hiring low performers and increasing the probability of hiring high performers could have a substantial impact on AHA's ability to execute its strategy. AHA needed a common process to recruitment, selection, movement, and relocation.

Improving the association's acumen in recruiting and selection required a multifaceted approach. The executive team agreed that the goal was to significantly improve bench strength for key positions. First, it needed to directly address the "talent hoarding" that currently occurred in each of the affiliates and at the National Center. The association's leaders were rewarded for meeting their financial goals, and if one of their high-potential employees left an affiliate, for example, for an opportunity elsewhere in the association, the affiliate leader often suffered lower fund-raising results.

AHA also had to work on branding for metro director positions, so that internal and external candidates clearly understood the expectations for the role. The WWT wanted to know more about the sources of their highest- and lowest-performing metro directors; to share information more widely on the quality of the talent pool; to develop better, more consistent training for hiring managers (e.g., advanced interview skills training for managers hiring for strategic positions) and to give them time to do it right; to mechanize the recruiting process wherever necessary; to target recruiting efforts and provide more recruitment resources for strategic positions; to develop incentive-based pay for recruiters, for example, base incentives on lifetime success of strategic hires. Finally, the team felt that it was important to track managers' hiring track record, outcomes, turnover, and promotions and to watch for patterns of poor hirers and poor developers.

Taken as a whole, the magnitude of these changes was significant; however, the WWT felt that its commitment and level of investment in change was consistent with the importance of the problem. See the box, "AHA Guiding Principles: Recruiting and Selection," for a summary of the principles and action items.

AHA Guiding Principles: Managing Talent

Issue Statement

Develop a process and supporting policies and procedures to deliberately move talent across the organization. This is a key component of an effective workforce strategy. The strategic integration team and national strategic team agreed that in order to effectively grow and develop talent and build and manage bench strength, the AHA must manage job movement for strategic positions throughout the association.

AHA Impact/Opportunity

- Develop career paths and move top talent into developmental positions—opportunities to grow and develop are a key retention mechanism.

- Translate existing high-potential lists into practical movement or actions.

- Focus on strategic positions and feeder pools for strategic positions.

Current Situation

- Talent-review meetings, TRIO (three top AHA executives) visits identify top talent.

- Too much focus on "C" players, not enough on "As."

- No standard definition of "high potential."

- Difficult to move talent, affiliates/National Center "hoarding talent" because of fear of loss or nonreplacement.

- Relocation policies not supportive.

- Career paths not fully defined.

- Mobility of high potentials not clearly understood.

Desired Situation

- Leadership model supports current capabilities.

- Focus energy on strategic positions.

- More fully developed TRIO visit process.

- Better specification and follow through on development plans.

- More consistent use of language.

- The AHA's two primary governance bodies, the Strategic Integration Team (SIT) and the National Strategic Team (NST), own and manage strategic positions.

- Associationwide relocation policy in place.

Actions Required

- SIT/NST agree to "own" strategic positions, all job movement recommendations.

- Complete the identification of strategic positions.

- Establish mechanism for SIT/NST to review staff in strategic positions, annual/quarterly review process.

- Develop an associationwide relocation policy.

- Reexamine associationwide employee assessment and review process.

Accountabilities and Resources

- Assessment, review, and movement of talent, SIT/NST accountability.

- Design and administration of the process, HR advisory team accountability.

Next Steps

- Complete the process of identifying balance of AHA strategic positions.

- Define positions "owned" by the SIT/NST.

- Establish a process for SIT and NST to review and assess staff in strategic positions as well as identify high-potential staff as successors for those jobs.

- Develop an associationwide relocation policy or procedure.

Source: AHA internal document. Used with permission.

AHA Guiding Principles: Recruiting and Selection

Issue Statement

To further the mission of the AHA, we need to attract and retain strategic talent in an increasingly competitive environment. We have to proactively source the best talent possible on a continuous basis, using technology to enhance our efforts. Greater growth and opportunity for the entire organization will result from attracting the best talent possible. World-class recruitment and selection strategies are essential for AHA to achieve its goals for 2010 and beyond.

AHA Impact/Opportunity (include "risk of inaction")

In order for AHA to be a world-class employer and develop the bench strength necessary to meet the mission of the organization, it needs to deal with the current excessive turnover rate and develop the strategies and actions necessary to attract and retain the talent we require in an increasingly competitive job market. The organization must address these issues and invest the time, talent, and technology necessary for this organization to be the place that perspective employees see challenge, opportunity, and career growth.

Without immediate action organizational performance will most likely suffer and our strategic goals will be in jeopardy for 2010 and beyond.

Current Situation

There is no current associationwide recruitment strategy. We in effect have thirteen different approaches that affect effectiveness, efficiency, and cost. Associationwide turnover of 23 percent, with the majority of separations occurring during the first three years of service, affects our ability to achieve our goals and lessens the effectiveness of our managers. AHA is not recognized in the job market for career opportunities. We lack an AHA brand and need a strong and effective Web presence. Additional issues include:

- Inadequate pool of ready candidates for strategic positions

- Inconsistent titles, pay, and relocation practices

- Varied effectiveness in recruiting diverse employees

- Inconsistent utilization of CIDS (structured interview)/Topgrading

- Ineffective and nonautomated applicant tracking

- Lack of career paths

- Nonprofit perception affects ability to attract top talent

Desired Situation

To become an employer of choice and attract, select, develop, and retain the passionate and compelling talent necessary to support our vital mission. In order to do this we need the following:

- Powerful, engaging, world-class Web presence

- Strong AHA employer brand

- Defined, proactive, strategic recruitment plan

- Automated tool to sort, screen, track, share, and manage applicants

- Managers proactive and engaged in sourcing and recruitment

- Effective attraction and retention of diversity candidates

- Articulated and developed career path

- Consistently competitive salary and benefits and exceptional total compensation for strategic positions

- Development and implementation of effective interviewing techniques and appropriate testing and selection processes

Actions Required

- Develop an AHA employment brand

- Construct world-class AHA job site

- Consistent training for hiring managers

- Mechanize the hiring process (e-recruit)

- Targeted recruiting for strategic positions

- Advance interview skills training for strategic positions

- Identify optimum recruitment and selection practices for use nationwide

- Identify optimum selection process and implement associationwide
  - Review CIDS/Topgrading and make recommendations
  - Review assessment processes, especially for strategic positions
  - Management assessment, sales assessment, personality inventory, skill check
  - Reference/background checks
  - Application/self-disclosure, data/storage of résumés
  - Design and communicate career paths
- Standardize job titles for implementation July 1, 2007

Source: AHA internal document. Used with permission.

"On-Boarding" at the AHA

The AHA uses the term *on-boarding* to describe the process of bringing new employees into the organization. The WWT taskforce concluded that the AHA culture is difficult to explain to new staff, but something they have to experience firsthand. The AHA work cycle for fund-raising staff is largely event-driven, so recruiting and selection occurs on an ongoing basis. A new hire starting in the middle of preparations for a gala event might never understand the entire process, because she is immediately placed in a demanding job. Because one event invariably follows on the heels of the next one, many new hires never fully grasp their jobs, which, the leadership team found, was a factor in the undesirable turnover of high-potential hires. The AHA executive team needed to interrupt this process and ensure that new hires were ready before they were placed in roles where they were expected to deliver significant results. As one manager put it, "The problem comes from when we have expectations for them before we've given them time to learn."

The WWT agreed that for key positions, an associationwide curriculum for new-staff orientation and supervisors' accountability for training new staff were central elements of the new strategy for on-boarding. This meant that the association needed to effectively train and prepare managers for their role in subordinates' on-boarding success. Supervisors needed to transfer knowledge and information throughout the association, as well as train, coach, and mentor their staff. The WWT also decided to continue using a boot camp for new hires, focusing on staff and volunteer management, and environment scanning of the key elements of workforce success identified in the strategy map. (See the box, "AHA Guiding Principles: On-Boarding.")

Training and Education at the AHA

The WWT taskforce knew from the outset that an effective workforce strategy required significantly enhanced training and education procedures, especially for key positions. The group decided that the process should begin with a careful needs assessment of the knowledge, skills, and abilities for successful performance in each position. It also made clear the expectation that managers be held accountable for the development of their own staff, and that each employee have an individualized training plan that includes core training (received by all employees) and specialized training based on his or her needs. The WWT concluded that specialized leadership training would likely be required for strategic positions. See the box, "AHA Guiding Principles: Learning and Development," for a summary of the key elements in AHA's position paper.

Perhaps the most significant AHA innovation to support its "A" positions was the creation of the AHA University. We believe that AHA University is the first corporate university focused specifically on strategic capabilities and strategic positions in addition to the conventional course offerings offered to all employees. AHA's investment in the AHA University to date has been both substantial and highly successful (see figure 7-3).

AHA Guiding Principles: On-Boarding

Desired Situation

Structured on-boarding process

- Identify the types of activities that drive more interaction between the newly appointed staff person and his or her immediate manager, peers, and mentor.

Mentor/buddy relationship

- Develop key elements of a successful program by examining best practice.

- Introduce as part of the staffing of strategic positions.

Modify goal-setting process for new staff

- Provide time for new staff to effectively transition into the organization. Provide more specific direction to supervisors on the goal-setting process for new staff.
  - Specifics for fund-raising staff previously approved by SIT/NST as part of revised development goal-setting process.

Hold supervisors accountable for on-boarding new staff. Supervisors need to be heavily involved in on-boarding process during the first ninety days of staff's time with the organization. Review current requirements and develop training mechanism through AHA University. Include as consideration within the performance management process.

Actions Required

- New staff orientation, associationwide core curriculum

- Training managers' role in on-boarding

- Hold supervisors accountable for on-boarding new staff

- Modify goals during on-boarding

- Structured process for strategic positions, mentor/buddy relationship

- Structured process for those in strategic positions, on-boarding commitment

- Inventory of all new staff orientation training
  - Determine time and topic requirements

- Conduct needs assessment/gap analysis for core curriculum
  - What staff need to "understand, do, and deliver"

- Identify components of core curriculum

- Establish delivery mechanisms
  - Best methods for timely delivery

- Develop implementation plan/schedule

Resource Requirements

- Managed by HR advisory team subgroup utilizing both National Center and affiliate resources

- Estimated cost for developing training modules, $60,000

Source: AHA internal document. Used with permission.

Managing Performance at the AHA

The organizationwide talent management process at the AHA is designed to provide a consistent framework for discussion, review, and decision making on employment life-cycle events for those in key positions. The senior leaders share accountability for managing the integrity of the process, which is designed to deliver the following attributes:

- A culture of open feedback is fostered.

- Careers of top talent in key positions and feeder pools for those positions are actively managed.

- High-potential staff targeted for top-level key positions are provided with the required development experience and job opportunities.

AHA Guiding Principles: Learning and Development

Issue Statement

A system is needed to identify and address learning needs within the AHA that are essential to creating the strategic capabilities and competencies required to achieve the 2010 goals. The necessity for training and development is linked to the need to maintain superiority in the nonprofit marketplace, the demand for more skilled employees, and the benefits of increasing the productivity of AHA employees.

Research indicates a positive effect of organizational training on learning and specifically training has been found to have a positive effect on salesforce performance when targeted methods and content are used.

The AHA system, supported by current research, needs to be strategically aligned with associationwide goals, effective at delivering core learning, and integrated across the AHA. It should provide a systematic way of identifying learning needs and then provide staff access to the learning. Finally, we must have a way to measure and report the success of training and its effect on organizational performance.

Vision Statement: Deliver comprehensive curriculum of learning and development capabilities and resources focused on enhancing our key strategic capabilities within the AHA.

AHA Impact/Opportunity (including risk of inaction)

In addition to the research cited above, additional studies provide further insight into the approaches and design of effective training programs.

There is ample evidence that organizational training has better organizational results when the training is designed and delivered to meet the needs of the AHA and the learners and when the post-training environment supports the application of the learned material or skills. Our approach to training and education should be based on this wide body of science available.

We cannot deliver on the organization's goals without a means to systematically create and develop the strategic knowledge and capabilities required by the goals.

This system is an opportunity for the AHA to create distinctive market or competitive advantage (set us apart from other nonprofits).

Without an updated, high-impact training and education program, AHA will not grow the bench strength needed to sustain high-level success in fund-raising and knowledge delivery. The current system, while meeting some needs of the organization, is fragmented and cannot, in its current form, focus on meeting the strategic requirements of AHA.

Current Situation

- Decentralized function—all affiliates provide training that creates duplication and a lower return on investment.

- Resources vary widely across the organization (AHA).

- Very little resource devoted toward leadership development.

- Some centralized resource at National Center, but lacks customer input on offerings and desired curriculum as well as desired outcomes to address associationwide needs/strategies.

- Online tracking tool—People Soft—doesn't function well, is very difficult, and is not available online to employees and managers.

- Lack best practices toward external leadership training resources.

- Lack talent development strategy for AHA.

- Lack a blended learning approach.

- Measurements and tracking nonexistent.

- Ownership of staff development not seen as a responsibility of managers.

- Individual development plans lacking or inconsistent.

- Lack identification of core learning that staff need.

- Needs assessment nonexistent.

- Timing of training needs to happen when it will most benefit staff.

Desired Situation

- All training should be under one vision or umbrella, such as an AHA University.

- Senior management role is to articulate strategy, identify "A" positions, and determine priorities, competencies, etc.

- Needs assessment, develop strategy.

- Managers own the development of their staff members; need clear priorities and allow them time, reward managers for doing so.

- Each employee should have an individual learning plan.

- Delivery methods should be offered in a variety of methods including classroom training, e-learning, net meetings, etc., each method guided by the research about the success of various approaches.

- Training plan needs to include core things that everyone needs as well as individual needs.

- We sometimes over-train and overwhelm: need to balance training with one-on-one coaching, on-going application of learning and skills, and regular, specific feedback about success.

- Measurement of results should be research-driven and based on sound measurement methodology.

Actions Required

- Create an AHA University charged with delivering an integrated system of learning experiences at all levels of the organization; "Heart U" should be led by a content expert with experience in line management as well as in education and training.

- Implement a Learning Management System (LMS).

- Strategic guidance or oversight system to ensure linkage to AHA priorities.

- Inventory of current resources: staff, budget, tools, external resources, etc.

Accountabilities and Resources

- Need to assess existing training resources and align those toward achieving critical strategies.

- Evaluate the competencies and skills within training.

- Need cost information.

Next Steps (how do we get started?)

- Inventory of existing training resources, programs, licenses, external, etc.

- Assess skills of existing training staff, what are their current capabilities, future, and gaps.

- Identification of content experts and working AHA managers who can teach classes.

- Identify gaps by mapping existing resources to strategic capabilities.

- Research options and solutions, AHA University.

- Adopt a costing methodology and apply it to determine current associationwide training expenditures and costs.

- Determine organizational value of trained compared to untrained employees; track over time.

- Adopt a standard methodology for assessing employee productivity.

Source: Winfred Arthur, Jr., et al., "Effectiveness of Training in Organizations: A Meta-Analysis of Design and Evaluation Features," *Journal of Applied Psychology* 88 (2003): 234–245; Winfred Arthur, Jr., and Sergio Román, et al., "The Effects of Sales Training on Sales Force Activity," *European Journal of Marketing* 36 (2002): 1344–1366.

- Active cross-sharing of top talent is taking place.

- Development plans are clearly defined and executed.

- Objectives are tailored to strategic capabilities.

FIGURE 7-3

AHA University

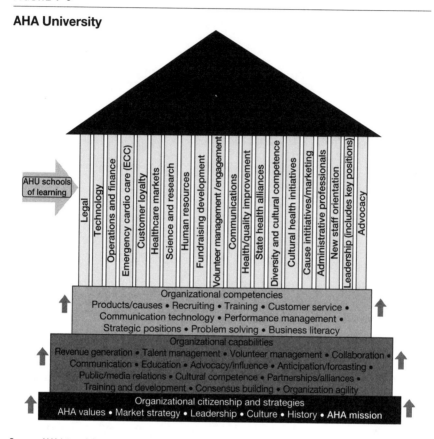

Source: AHA internal documents. Used with permission.

The WWT taskforce decided to model its talent review after the GE Session C process. The executive team would own and manage key positions (e.g., metro directors) centrally and jointly. It would be responsible for the assessment and development of incumbents, as well as movement and overall levels of bench strength. The process consists of:

- *Local talent review.* Annual meetings of the CEO, the chief operations officer of field operations, National Center vice president of human resources, and affiliate executive vice president continues to be the cornerstone for review and collection of data of staff in affiliates.

- *National talent review.* A similar process for National Center staff is chaired annually by the COO, National Center. Data collected becomes part of associationwide review.

- *Associationwide talent review.* SIT/NST meets formally twice a year to discuss status of incumbents in top-level key positions and review readiness of those in feeder-pool positions to those jobs.

AHA developed an integrated strategic human capital planning process. The process culminated in a two-day associationwide talent management summit, with the leaders and senior HR management teams in one large conference room. All the strategic positions and their feeder positions were listed on the wall by region, and each manager provided an assessment of each candidate. Next, discussion among the executive team focused on where the candidate might move and who might be ready now to move into a position, and what the developmental needs might be. This process, which had the look and feel of an NFL draft, has been highly successful. Three meetings are held each year, and each of the two hundred employees in key positions is reviewed once per year. Managers think that the discipline required to prepare for the quality of the discussions has been important for keeping them focused on talent development throughout the year. Expectations of the senior team are very high, and managers know that they have to be ready to discuss their talent development. See the box, "AHA Guiding Principles: Performance Management."

Establishing a Compensation Philosophy at the AHA

Both the level and the structure of compensation were clearly significant issues for the WWT as it considered its options for improving the performance in key positions, in particular the metro directors. First, the WWT taskforce developed a specific compensation philosophy to help managers in their decision making on compensation (see the box, "AHA Compensation Philosophy").

The WWT agreed that the level of pay for metro directors (relative to the external market) needed to be examined and, in some cases,

AHA Guiding Principles: Performance Management

Issue Statement

Based on the key strategic capabilities, the performance management system of the AHA should define, recognize, develop, and reward key strategic behaviors that enable the organization's success.

AHA Impact/Opportunity

The AHA has the opportunity to:

- Provide consistent training to managers so that they can be held accountable for the behavior and development of the workforce.

- Train managers to create a culture of open and regular feedback to employees.

- Ensure that performance standards are focused on the outcomes, not the activities.

- Include strategic positions in the goal-setting process, so there is buy-in to the goals.

Current Situation

- No consistent or formalized training in performance management is provided to managers.

- Managers are not giving regular quality feedback.

- Performance standards focus too much on a list of activities, not enough on outcome.

- There are no consequences for managers not doing reviews.

- Goals are established with no employee buy-in.

Desired Situation

- Consistent performance management training for managers.

- Managers spend more time mentoring, coaching, and managing.

- Managers own workforce development and are rewarded for success.

- Create an AHA culture of open, ongoing, honest feedback.

- Performance standards are simplified and focused on outcomes.

- Use of up-to-date HR information systems (HRIS) technology to support and streamline processes.

Actions Required

- Create an AHA University. Initial curriculum designed would be performance management focusing on managers. Managers' training would include coaching, diversity, hiring/recruitment, leadership, how to give effective feedback, and conflict management. The AHA University could also develop other training courses on selling skills, volunteer management, etc.

- From the time an employee is hired, a training plan should be put in place, based on time in position and succession planning.

- Develop a rewards system if a manager has a member of the workforce able to move up in the organization. Also look at rewarding manager and/or employee for being mobile to other affiliates.

- Develop performance standards that are focused on the outcomes, recognizing the strengths that an individual brings to the position. Managers' performance standards should also reflect points for diversity, hiring/recruiting, coaching, and developing the workforce. In addition, performance standards should reflect consequences for managers who do not provide appropriate workforce development.

- HRIS system updated. Additional modules developed and implemented such as recruitment, succession planning, time and attendance, smoother online performance management, and self-service enhanced for employees and managers to have employee information accessible.

Accountabilities and Resources

- Human resources staff along with the guidance of outside consultants should provide the development and support the implementation of the strategic efforts to ensure the success of performance management.

- HRIS technology is a key to streamlining processes and having a consistent approach across the organization.

Next Steps

- Creation of AHA University. University could have campuses in various locations based on the skills of the training directors and geography of participants. Major cost would be developing the modules of the training program. Currently each affiliate does have dollars allocated for staff training that could be used to send staff to AHA University.

- Develop a rewards system for managers who are effective in developing their workforce. The cost of this would be covered by the reduction of overall turnover within the organization.

- Performance standards revised to reflect enhanced skill set for managers. Timeline: Modifications made at midyear. Update HRIS system. This would be the most costly of the implementation strategies. Timeline: ongoing.

Source: AHA internal documents. Used with permission.

---

increased as along with the level of pay "at risk," which varies directly with performance. The group agreed that incentives at the senior or executive level weren't large enough to warrant the risks involved with being innovative.

The team concluded that a number of changes were required to successfully execute the new compensation objectives. AHA needed a consistent approach to base pay and incentive across the association. AHA had to pay higher for strategic positions, increase frequency of payouts for incentives or other rewards, give managers incentives for development and retention of people, and provide managers more discretion on merit-pay decisions. Finally, salary and title transparency were important to effectively moving and growing talent across the association. See these principles and action items in the box, "AHA Guiding Principles: Compensation."

Changing HR Management Systems at the AHA

The changes the WWT taskforce enacted were significant and comprehensive. Two facets of the process were especially important. First, each of the recommendations and initiatives was based on a careful analysis of the strategic objectives needed to deliver AHA's goals of reducing the incidence of stroke and heart disease by 25 percent by 2010. Second, as a result of the analyses, the WWT taskforce concluded that it would need to increase investment in all employees, but that the proportionate increase for key positions would be greater. Thus, rather than shifting resources from nonstrategic to strategic positions, the net result of the process was to increase investments in all employees, because these investments would provide an economic benefit to the AHA. Table 7-2 summarizes the workforce management practices needed to change for everyone and the additional changes for the strategic positions.

Communication and Candor Are Crucial

Workforce differentiation is most effective when you are completely transparent about how and why you are making differentiation decisions. Being honest and open about the process is central to a successful rollout. All these elements must be consistently (and relentlessly) communicated to the workforce. Employees already understand more about differentiation than we give them credit for. Our experience has been that this process generates real excitement and only a small amount of anguish. We have run many seminars and small groups on the topic of differentiation by position, where managers (especially HR managers) have been more resistant than the employees. Employees are very aware that 20 percent of the jobs create 80 percent of the value in most organizations. If you are

AHA Compensation Philosophy

Statement: Key positions are those specific jobs identified within the organization that have the potential to provide significant leverage to achieving the strategic objectives and mission of the organization. In order to attract, hire, retain, and recognize the contribution of the talent in these roles, it is necessary for us to differentiate key positions in our approach to their total cash compensation—base pay and where applicable incentive.

Key Positions Total Cash Compensation Guidelines

Base Pay. Adjustments to staff currently assigned or moved into key positions will vary greatly depending on their current rate of pay. Under most circumstances, base pay for individuals in key positions will be positioned between the midpoint and the maximum of the salary range. Their level of compensation will be influenced a great deal by the employee's experience and current pay rate prior to being placed in the job. In some cases, individuals may be positioned within a key position at a pay level that exceeds the maximum of the salary range for the new job, base pay adjustments of up to 15 percent are permitted in these instances. In situations where an individual is accepting a lateral or a demotion to assume a key position, a lump sum or base pay adjustment of up to 15 percent in salary may be considered, even if the individual is over the new salary range maximum of the range.

Incentive Pay. Staff assigned to incentive-eligible key positions may be eligible for a target incentive equal to X percent to Y percent of their new base pay. The payout opportunity will range from X percent to Y percent of the targeted payout opportunity. Some senior-level key positions, for example, the senior vice president executive director job, may also be eligible to participate in a long-term incentive program with a target payout opportunity equal to X percent to Y percent of the midpoint of the salary range for the particular position. Details such as the criteria and payout levels of these plans would be outlined in separate documents.

Other Considerations. The significance of the key position's impact on the organization's performance should be considered as part of all pay decisions. Each individual's circumstances will be unique, requiring some discretion on the part of the executive vice presidents and hiring managers. HR will provide guidance. Executive vice presidents or affiliate executive vice presidents will approve any pay levels/changes for those in key positions.

Source: AHA internal document. Used with permission.

---

honest and transparent with employees, they will appreciate the organization's honesty, and some of the best and brightest, who are currently holding less strategic roles, will find their way into these positions.

Some resistance to increased workforce accountability is expected, and that is not irrational from the perspective of the people affected. Expect resistance from the bottom-third performers in your current workforce.[5] Likewise, expect (often enthusiastic) support from your highest-performing employees.

Communication and Candor at the AHA

The AHA devoted considerable effort to socialization and the communication of these goals, and managers credit these efforts as an important component of the WWT taskforce's success. Specifically, the AHA emphasized the following key points in its communications with the workforce:

- Only the very best, most highly qualified candidates can be placed in these key positions.

- These positions will be key training and development positions for future AHA executive vice presidents, affiliates, and National Center.

- Compensation must be reviewed and adjusted according to the importance of the position *and* each individual's performance with their job.

AHA Guiding Principles: Compensation

Issue Statement

The AHA will use a competitive, fixed and variable compensation plan to reward staff in strategic positions as well as use a comprehensive total rewards model designed to attract, retain, and motivate all staff within the organization.

AHA Impact/Opportunity

A standardized and competitive approach to total compensation across the entire organization; make a fundamental shift from an equality- to an equity-based compensation strategy.

Current Situation

In the organization's current environment, we utilize different salary grades, compensation levels, incentive models, job titles, and benefits. This lack of consistency undermines any attempt toward successful implementation of pay-for-performance plans, succession-planning strategies and the implementation of a total rewards model. As a result, the AHA continues to experience an unacceptably high employee turnover rate, a depleted bench necessary to fill key strategic positions, and the utilization of significant resources (time and money) replacing staff.

Desired Situation

- We want employees and applicants to recognize that we are one organization with a strong nationwide employment brand.

- We want employees and applicants to understand that the compensation, benefits, incentive (short and long term), merit, and relocation plans have a global design across the organization (global indicates the framework is consistent; it doesn't mean we treat each position the same. This supports our need to treat key strategic positions differently).

- We want to be able to effectively and efficiently retain, develop, and share top talent across the organization.

- In order to accomplish the above, we need top-down buy-in to implement a consistent total compensation and total rewards plan throughout the organization.

Accountabilities and Resources

Human resources, with input from identified staff responsible for managing strategic positions and the utilization of human resource consultants.

Next Steps

- Continue to work with compensation consultants for *salary range, grade, geographic assessors, cost-of-living* recommendations for all positions; initial focus will be on key strategic positions.

- Work with a taskforce made up of experts in the field and HR to determine acceptable titles that can be used nationwide.

- Work with consultants, experts in the field, and HR to recommend acceptable incentive plans (short and multiyear).

- Develop a relocation policy and procedure that has a global impact.

- Evaluate the current staffing model within HR to determine if additional staffing resources are needed to support the compensation project plan and timeline.

Source: AHA internal document. Used with permission.

- The AHA must position these leadership positions in a way that clearly communicates the importance and value they bring to the organization.

To emphasize these points, CEO Cass Wheeler sent a memo to all the managers and executives at AHA, which kicked off the communication process (see figure 7.4).

The WWT also developed some frequently asked questions (FAQs) for the entire workforce (see the box, "Winning With Talent FAQs").

TABLE 7-2

Management practices of the Winning With Talent taskforce

	All AHA employees	Additional recommendations for strategic positions
Recruiting	1. Develop AHA employment brand 2. Construct world-class AHA job site 3. Develop better, more consistent, training for hiring managers; need time to do it right 4. Mechanize the process	1. Targeted recruiting efforts 2. Advanced interview skills training
On-boarding	1. Hold supervisors accountable for training new staff 2. Managers prepared/trained on their role in subordinates' on-boarding success 3. Modify goals during on-boarding process 4. Core associationwide curriculum 5. Balance learning classroom/field	1. More structured commitment to on-boarding process 2. Mentor/buddy relationship with senior manager
Training and education	1. AHA University: leverage a common approach 2. Develop strategy for needs assessment 3. Managers need to own development of their staff 4. Each employee should have an individualized training plan that includes core training and individual needs	1. Specialized leadership training
Compensation	1. Salary transparency 2. Increase frequency of payouts; incentives/other rewards 3. Need more recognition 4. More manager discretion on merit pay decisions 5. Consistent approach associationwide on base pay and incentive 6. Motivate managers for people development/retention	1. Pay higher in range 2. Long-term incentive
Performance management	1. Consistent training for managers 2. Need culture of open feedback 3. Develop link to tailored objectives to strategic capabilities 4. More focused standards; not meant to include requirements for entire job	1. Include input of staff in strategic positions in the goal setting process

Source: AHA internal documents. Used with permission.

FIGURE 7-4

CEO's Memo to the Executive Team

Memo

DATE:	May 21, 2007
TO:	Top 50 Metro Market Executives
FROM:	M. Cass Wheeler, Chief Executive Officer
SUBJECT:	**Invitation to attend AHA Key Positions Conference**

Earlier this year I announced several new initiatives for AHA focusing on "winning with talent." By now you're aware of what is one of the most critical of our new initiatives—our increased focus on and investment in our organization's "key" positions. As Metro Executives for the top 50 markets, your positions were identified as "Phase One" key positions due to the impact each of you have on AHA's ability to raise money to fund our life-saving work, and your impact on people development—both staff and volunteers—for the organization. *(Please see the attached for a complete list of the top 50 market Metro Executives)*

Because you hold a key position, the organization will provide you with additional training and development opportunities to strengthen your leadership capability and prepare you for future executive roles within the AHA. Keeping this commitment in mind, it is with great excitement that I invite you to attend AHA's first Key Positions Conference to be held on Wednesday September 26, 2007, in Dallas, Texas.

The conference will kick off with a special dinner that I will host on Tuesday September 25. Additional logistical details will be provided in the next several weeks. For now I ask that you hold the evening of September 25 and all day September 26 for our inaugural Key Positions conference.

I look forward to sharing time with each of you in September as we work together in furthering our mission.

Thank you.

Winning With Talent FAQs

General

Why is AHA putting all these new initiatives in place now? As an organization, we realize that our future success requires that we have innovative, talented, motivated employees who are dedicated to our mission. The talent we have determines how successful we can be. The changes we are making will help us retain the great employees we currently have and will also help us to attract the best candidates for open positions within the organization.

How will the changes affect me? First, we are committed to helping you more clearly define your career path and to provide greater training and development opportunities to help you develop the skills you need to move forward. Second, our fund-raising and health initiatives staff will see some changes to their performance goals to ensure that there is both a base goal that's very realistic and a plan goal that challenges staff to stretch their capabilities. Finally, if you're a supervisor, you'll play a more active role in the recruiting and hiring process through our new e-Recruit tool. There will be less paper to sift through, and you'll have more direct access to candidates you wish to interview.

Are these changes designed mostly to attract new talent to the AHA? No. While some of the changes are focused on attracting new talent, the majority of the changes are focused on our current talent within the organization. We want to do everything we can to keep our current employees engaged in their jobs and encourage them to continue growing professionally throughout their career with the AHA.

When do these changes take effect? The programs will be rolling out throughout 2007.

How can I learn more about the status of the rollout? Visit our special section of HeartSmarts at www.heartsmarts.org/talent for the latest details on the implementation of these programs.

Key Positions

Why are we identifying some positions as "key positions"? Since certain positions have the greatest impact on revenue generation and mission-related activities, it's critical that we have top performers in these positions. We also need to invest disproportionately in strengthening the capabilities of the employees in these positions to help them develop further and be better able to contribute to our success in reaching our 2010 goals and beyond.

If I'm in a key position, what will be required of me? If you're currently in a key position, you'll be receiving additional coaching and training to both help you excel in your current role and prepare you for future executive roles with the AHA.

What is the role of the foundational positions? All positions play a role in AHA's ability to reach our goals. The positions that are not defined as key positions are foundational positions, because they help lay the foundation for our success.

If I'm not in a "key" position, will I still have a career path at the AHA? Absolutely. We will be conducting talent reviews in which we sit down with employees to determine their skills and aspirations along with potential areas for training and development. We want all of our employees to understand their career path and what they need to do to move ahead. Many of our foundational positions are "feeder" positions to key positions. In addition, our business is constantly changing, and positions that are currently foundational may become key positions in the future, based on our business needs and drivers.

How are key positions determined? We use four main criteria to define key positions:

- Strategic impact—a disproportionate impact on the AHA's ability to execute some part of our business strategy

- Performance variability—the gap between low and high performers in this role is substantial

- Top-talent impact—a position in which top talent would significantly enhance the success of achieving AHA's business strategy

- Hard to get—top talent in this role is difficult to attract and retain

Why are only the top fifty metro directors considered key positions? This is only the first phase of key positions. More positions will be identified by the end of 2007. However, we chose to focus on these positions as our first phase because they clearly meet the criteria for key positions, and we believe the metro director role has the greatest opportunity to impact the future revenue success of the association. **Are all key positions related to fund-raising?** No. Although the first key positions we have identified are related to fund-raising, there will be key positions throughout the organization representing many different functions.

Source: AHA internal document. Used with permission.

Communicating Workforce Strategy at the AHA

In addition to CEO Wheeler's memo and the FAQs, the AHA communication team developed a comprehensive communication plan to ensure that everyone understood the outcomes of the WWT project and the resulting implications for their jobs. The important point was that the communication rollout was thoughtful, integrative, and carefully staged. The AHA management team was forthcoming about each element of the process, and as a result, the workforce developed more understanding and trust about the process. AHA executives credit this process as a key element in the overall understanding and acceptance of the entire WWT process (see table 7-3).

Although we have provided many examples of workforce differentiation from a wide variety of firms, the AHA case is an unusually comprehensive, highly successful effort. In the following interview, Cass Wheeler, Nancy Brown, chief operating officer, and Bill Achenbach, senior vice president of HR, provide some personal reflections and observations on the Winning With Talent project at the AHA.[6]

Executive Interview: AHA's Winning With Talent taskforce

What were some of the factors that led you to initiate the Winning With Talent taskforce in late 2005?

CASS WHEELER: A lot of it had to do with frustration associated with high turnover, recruiting top talent, and recognizing that we

TABLE 7-3

Developing a differentiated workforce at AHA
Phase 1—Program announcement

Communication vehicle	Description	Key messages	Audience
Graphic e-mail invitation	Flash e-mail that creates excitement and anticipation of upcoming Webcast (1/5) and encourages employees to attend.	• We're changing the way we attract, recruit, and retain new talent for the American Heart Association. • We want to share these important changes with all of you.	All employees
Meeting request	Outlook calendar announcement including date (1/5), time, and link to where Webcast will appear.	• Be sure to watch the Webcast to learn how AHA is Winning the War for Talent. • Here's how to access the Webcast.	All employees
Cass voice-mail	Brief voice-mail from Cass that encourages employees to attend Webcast on 1/5.	• Be sure to watch the Webcast to learn how AHA is Winning the War for Talent. • Here's how to access the Webcast.	All employees
Executive vice president (EVP) toolkit	Deck, Q&A, key messages, handouts, timeline; EVP presents information to managers either in-person or via conference call/Net-meeting.	• The metro director role is critical to our success at AHA because it directly affects our ability to raise money to fund our mission. • We've identified the top 50 metro directors as the first phase of key positions. It is essential that our top talent be placed in key positions. Additional key positions will be identified over the next year. • We have also created a group that includes the top-ten metros based on population along with three of the next largest metros (to ensure every affiliate had a large metro market in the group). This group will work together to leverage best practices and focus on accelerating our growth in large metro markets. Additionally, for the next year, we will provide specialized training and development programs that will strengthen their leadership abilities and prepare them for even more senior executive positions in the AHA.	Affiliate and National Center EVPs

TABLE 7-3 (CONTINUED)

Communication vehicle	Description	Key messages	Audience
		• The new initiatives we are introducing include: a new employment brand, a revamped employee referral program, changes to our goal-setting process, enhancements to our on-boarding/orientation processes, and a new AHA University devoted to providing consistent training and development opportunities across the organization. • Although we are investing more in the ongoing development of all employees at AHA, we are investing disproportionately in our key positions because our future success depends on our ability to develop and retain talent in these positions.	
Managers' meetings with employees	Face-to-face overview of programs that make up the Winning the War for Talent initiative, with opportunity for employees to ask questions. Each EVP should decide how information should be presented at their affiliate. Options: 1. EVP presents to full staff at All-Affiliate Meeting. 2. EVP presents via conference call/Net-meeting to direct reports, who then present to their staff.	• Our future success depends on our ability to develop and retain the most talented employees. • We are introducing a new employment brand that will help us attract and recruit employees that are a good fit for AHA and will help set us apart from other employers competing for the same talent. • All employees will have additional training and development opportunities available to them through the new AHA University. • There will also be changes to our goal-setting process to ensure that all employees have a clear career path and are receiving the development they need to move along that path. • We are making enhancements to our on-boarding/orientation processes to make it more consistent across the organization and ensure new employees get off to a good start. • Everyone at AHA can have a clear career path and can develop the competencies they need to move ahead.	All employees

TABLE 7-3

- Certain positions that most directly affect our business strategy will be identified as key positions.
- Those in key positions may have additional training and development opportunities that strengthen their leadership skills and prepare them for future executive positions with the AHA.

Source: AHA internal documents. Used with permission.

---

wouldn't be able to meet our strategic goals if we didn't have the right talent in place. We took the management team to the World Business Forum in New York in 2005, and one of the common themes we heard was the difficulty of achieving your goals if you don't have the top talent that you need in place. So, as a result of the exposure to these "outside eyes" as well as our own experiences, we concluded that we've just got to do a better job in the whole talent-development area. So, we appointed a taskforce of senior executives with Nancy Brown as chair to address these issues and gave them the authority and the resources to solve them.

NANCY BROWN: Our executive vice presidents were also expressing concern about entry-level turnover and attracting and retaining the younger workforce. So we combined what we learned from you [interviewer Mark Huselid] and from others into the formation of the Winning With Talent taskforce. The taskforce includes eleven of our most senior executives and representatives from our National Center (corporate) as well as each of our regional affiliates. Two-and-a-half years later, all of the initial taskforce members (except for two people who left the organization) are still actively involved with the taskforce.

The scope of the WWT team was unusually broad—the mandate from Cass was to reconsider virtually all aspects of how the workforce contributes to AHA's success. At the outset, did you think that the project was as large as it turned out to be?

NANCY: We didn't realize how much work was involved until we got into it. We thought it might be a twelve- to eighteen-month process.

But once we recognized all of the pieces and the importance of doing them in sequence, we realized that it was going to take us longer to get there. But we also recognized the importance of generating some early wins and not feeling as though we were dragging out the process.

CASS: The important difference about the WWT was that it was responsible for both strategy development as well as execution. This has provided a lot of continuity and increased the quality of the execution.

NANCY: Reporting the WWT's progress to the executive team on a regular basis, instead of waiting until there was a final outcome, was also an important part of the process. This helped to keep everyone engaged and helped keep those not on the taskforce to remain involved in the process and to make a contribution to the outcomes. There have been many times when we have taken feedback back to the taskforce and incorporated it into the process.

What were some of the key factors that helped drive the success of the WWT taskforce?

NANCY: I think that the key issue is to get the workforce philosophy right at the outset. For us, it was critical to have a conversation and build consensus on our expectations for both employees and for managers. What is it that we expect managers to do? What is it we expect employees to do? What is it we expect HR to do? For example, as a result of this process, we've been clear that we expect HR to support these new strategies, so they will need to figure out what they will stop doing to ensure that this will happen. So, they'll need to talk about the work that they will need to stop doing.

Another key issue was to have open and honest conversations about how we were going to implement our workforce strategy. We have had a lot of robust dialogue over decisions that we have made, but we spent the time at the outset to reach consensus. So, once we reached the decision, we have been very good about executing and not going back and rehashing old ground. We've had excruciating two-day meetings in windowless rooms where we've worked to reach consensus, but once we've done that, the leaders have become advocates for our workforce strategy.

BILL ACHENBACH: I think that a key driver of our success is that all the work we have been doing and will continue to do is centered on our strategy document. This is a tremendous resource—156 pages—that describes what we want to accomplish and what we want to be known for, as well as all the tactics we should pursue to get there. It really helps us understand what we need to be good at, right now and going forward. This was a big difference for us, everything we have developed within our workforce strategy, as well as all of the HR initiatives, ties back to a focus on building muscle around the capabilities that drive toward the mission of the organization. So we hope we have avoided the often typical HR disconnect—appearing to be like mad scientists, out there doing HR stuff just for the sake of doing HR stuff. To the contrary, we've been able to demonstrate what we need to do within our HR initiatives to accelerate performance. As we build toward becoming an even more compelling place to work, HR must stay connected to the strategy in all of its deliverables. I think that this has been a revelation to me as we have gone through this entire process. We've been very diligent in connecting the dots so that everyone understands the measure of our success. Everything we do, whether it is a long-term incentive plan to drive performance, a performance management plan, or AHA University—all are being developed and executed to move the strategy forward. And the strategy—in my opinion, having seen strategies in many other organizations—is one of the most comprehensive, evolving documents that I have ever seen. We'll continue to pay attention to the inevitable changes in direction. As being a "compelling place to work" changes, we'll continue to adjust and adapt our workforce strategy as well. Reality today dictates that we examine our strategy much more frequently than in the past, and HR needs to react accordingly, asking ourselves: how might our management practices need to change?

CASS: I think that people will read this book and jump right in and start changing things. And I think the strong point is that if they don't have a good strategic plan in place, they've put the cart before the horse.

NANCY: A real strength of the organization is planning and that we are constantly in touch with the external environment. We're very good at taking advantage of new opportunities for growth that we might not have anticipated. We're able to do this because we have focused on execution of our workforce strategy; this is not just a bunch of ideas written on a piece of paper. This process has been executed, not perfectly, but it has been executed very well.

CASS: A lot of that has been due to the fact that the WWT has assumed responsibility not only for design but for execution and implementation as well. Almost like a submarine that would submerge and then come up for air and work with broader groups, and then submerge again and work some more. And more often than not the decisions would improve as a result of this process. The process has really elevated the HR function at the level of the affiliates so that the HR staff is focused on being a strategic partner instead of just executing transactions. And that's my goal for the HR staff. I want them to be strategic partners to the affiliate executives and not let the "tyranny of the urgent" crowd out the important.

How has the thinking of the executive team changed during the course of this project?

NANCY: Their eyes have been opened to a more structured approach to the end game. This is a group of people who consider themselves pretty well-read and up to date on contemporary management practices, but they have really embraced all of the new principles that you have helped us see and understand. They have been much more open to a unified approach and to what would be best for the association as a whole and not just for their territory.

And while no one has left the taskforce, many people have been asking how they can get *on* it. So, the taskforce is seen in an extremely positive light throughout the organization. Two of the taskforce members have said that this has been the best-executed project that they have ever worked on in their professional careers. Going forward, I want to keep everything together; I don't want to interrupt the flow of what we are doing.

What has not worked well? What would you do differently if you had it to do over?

NANCY: We haven't yet moved people around the organization as effectively as we will need to. The art of helping to facilitate the movement of people into open positions is something that we're still fine-tuning. Every day, we've got to be looking at which one of the key positions is open, how do I help to get these positions filled, and how do I get the people on the high-potential list moved into these positions? This is our biggest area of opportunity moving forward.

What was the reaction of the workforce to this process?

NANCY: There was a mild hum throughout the organization when we published the list of key positions. Some employees asked: Why isn't my position here? What does it all mean? We began by putting the process in perspective—240 of 3,600 employees are in key positions—and by reinforcing the point that we invest in all employees and positions, but there are a few key positions that drive our success and they have to be managed differently. But on a day-in, day-out basis, people aren't sitting around concerned about whether or not they are in a key position. But when there is some activity or announcement for the key positions, questions may arise.

BILL: I think that the reaction of the workforce has created a healthy curiosity about things that are important to the AHA. The questions we hear are mostly, how do I move into a key position? In fact, one of the interesting outcomes is that employees are now interested in working for people who hold key positions. This was an additional positive impact that we hadn't expected.

Any special reaction to particular changes in how you are managing the workforce?

NANCY: No negative reactions, but some have asked: how can we execute faster? For example, everyone is excited about the AHA University; they just want to see it available right now. We actually expected more resistance than we've gotten. People were ready for this.

BILL: I expected some resistance, but overall we really have gotten a great deal of support for all of the initiatives we've put in place. We want our best people to want to be in key positions, and we're starting to see this happening.

NANCY: We're putting a lot more into the development of key positions, and the expectations are going up as well. We're starting to get the general acceptance that the bar has been raised.

Are you beginning to see any tangible benefits of the differentiation process yet?

NANCY: All of the attention that we have paid to attracting, moving, paying, training, on-boarding, and talking about people, all of this effort is really paying off. The turnover rate of employees with less than three years of AHA experience has gone down eight or ten points in the past two years, while our employee engagement scores have gone up dramatically. Look at the behavior of executive vice presidents with their staff. They are doing a lot of things because they know that the spotlight is on them to reduce turnover of top talent and to have a more engaged workforce. A lot of those things wouldn't have happened if we hadn't begun to focus on key positions. We're really starting to focus on how managers are spending their time.

Executive management is engaged and involved in worrying every day about their people and how good they are. They don't want to lose them. That focus is significant.

AHA's HR team has been able to show that highly engaged employees demonstrate 23.4 percent less turnover, 15.5 percent higher campaign revenue per employee, and 147 percent higher revenue growth. Moreover, engagement scores have increased substantially over the past two years as a direct result, we believe, of the work of the WWT taskforce and AHA's new emphasis on talent development. So we're seeing tangible economic success.

BILL: The key position discussion made us think very differently about how we apply our resources. For example, the top thirteen metro directors are clearly in much better places than if we had not gone through this process. The things that we are doing to support their growth and development, the attention they are getting, and their new position in the organization are clearly having a positive impact on performance. The key position initiative in and of itself is a huge part of the foundation of our workforce strategy, and it is already having a significant impact. Differentiation around key positions was really a rallying point for everyone. It was something that everyone agreed was a good approach to drive results. The work we did together with the executive team really brought us together. The conversations that I hear today are much more about what we are doing together than what we are doing differently.

What do you have planned next for the WWT taskforce?

NANCY: We will continue to strengthen the execution around key positions, differentiating activities for them. We've identified leads for each of the key position groups, and those leads are accountable. We have meetings once every other month to talk about what they are doing to strengthen the sense of community of their key position group. The launch of the AHA University is another big initiative that we will see in the coming months.

Our new HR process-improvement initiative is a huge focus for us right now. How are we most efficiently and effectively delivering HR services and using the time of our talented HR executives the right way?

BILL: The continuing work of the HR Leadership Team supporting the execution of our workforce strategy is very important. HR also needs to keep in close contact with the evolution of our management practices and systems to ensure that they are fine-tuned to effectively support the execution of the strategy. We'll also establish new practices; for example, career banding [providing broad instead of career paths for employees] as part of our workforce strategy may ultimately be where we need to go. Whatever we need to do to ensure that we're ahead of the curve creating a compelling place to work is where we'll focus our efforts. The days when the HR team could meet once a year to decide how much to move benefits or compensation up or down are gone forever. Given the scarcity of the available workforce now and in the future, we've just got to always be on top of our game. We need to innovate and execute.

What additional advice would you have for other organizations starting on a similar path?

NANCY: We could have quietly tried at the National Center to do some of this work, but I think that creating an associationwide group of people who feel ownership and both design and implement the process was a key element of our success. We also made sure to include a wide variety of perspectives on this taskforce. And it is important to make sure that this is a management initiative, not just an HR function initiative. If we hadn't done that, my guess is that it would not be where it is today.

BILL: Select a senior team that creates a healthy tension among the members (the right mix of field and corporate executives) to ensure all the issues get on the table. Create a compelling case for change and have the group own the process and outcomes.

CASS: Engaging the senior team *and* making it a collaborative process were critical. Even if you are in a centralized environment, you get a lot further by building ownership into the process.

Conclusion

The key lesson of this book has been that most organizations need to embrace what we have described as a *differentiated workforce strategy* to ensure successful strategy execution in the current economic environment. An undifferentiated or one-size-fits-all approach, even if couched in the latest jargon, does not deliver the strategic success you know is possible. You've enlisted in the war for talent, but it isn't all that clear what victory might look like. We've offered an alternative: our emphasis is on winning the war *with* talent. Our approach links your organization's strategic success directly to your workforce strategy and outlines a systematic approach to implementing that strategy. As shown by the experience at the American Heart Association, this approach delivers on all the promise of competing on talent. You don't have to wait until "next year."

NOTES

Chapter 1

1. Eric Bonabeau, "The Perils of the Imitation Age," *Harvard Business Review*, June 2004, 46.

2. See Robert S. Kaplan and David P. Norton, *The Execution Premium* (Boston: Harvard Business School Press, 2008); and Larry Bossidy and Ram Charan, *Execution* (New York: Crown Business, 2002).

3. See Brian Becker and Mark Huselid, "Measuring HR? Benchmarking Is Not the Answer," *HR Magazine*, December 2003, 56–62.

4. Jeffrey Pfeffer and Robert I. Sutton, *The Knowing-Doing Gap* (Boston: Harvard Business School Press, 2000).

5. David Adler, "Trickle Down Investment Advice," *Barron's Online*, March 26, 2007.

6. See R. W. Beatty and Craig Schneier, "New HR Roles to Impact Organizational Performance: From Partners to Players," *Human Resource Management* 36, no. 1 (1997): 29–37; Dave Ulrich and Dick Beatty, "From Partners to Players: Extending the HR Playing Field," *Human Resource Management* 40, no. 4 (2001): 293–307.

Chapter 2

1. Michael Porter, "What Is Strategy?" *Harvard Business Review*, November–December 1996, 61–78.

2. Ibid.

3. Ibid.

4. See Robert S. Kaplan and David P. Norton, "Having Trouble with Your Strategy? Then Map It," *Harvard Business Review*, September 2000, 167–176; and Robert S. Kaplan and David P. Norton, *Strategy Maps: Converting Intangible Assets into Tangible Outcomes* (Boston: Harvard Business School Press, 2003).

Chapter 3

1. Quoted in Stephen Covey, *The 8th Habit: From Effectiveness to Greatness* (New York: Free Press, 2005), 14.

2. Glen Phelps, "The Fundamentals of Performance Management," *Gallup Management Journal* (February 10, 2005): 1–4.

Chapter 5

1. We typically use response scales from 1 "Strongly Disagree" to 5 "Strongly Agree" for each item. In addition, questions are asked separately for the "Now" and "Future" categories.

2. R. S. Schuler, "Strategic Human Resources Management: Linking the People with the Strategic Needs of the Business," *Organizational Dynamics* 21 (1992), 18–32.

3. R. S. Schuler, "Personnel and Human Resource Management Choices and Organizational Strategy," *Human Resource Planning* 10 (1987), 1–17.

4. For an introduction and overview of strategic human resource management in practice, see S. E. Jackson and R. S. Schuler, *Managing Human Resource Through Strategic Partnerships* (New York: Thompson/South-Western, 2006).

Chapter 6

1. S. Kerr, "On the Folly of Rewarding A, While Hoping for B," *Academy of Management Journal* 18 (1975): 769–783.

2. See Anthony J. Rucci, Steven P. Kirn, and Richard T. Quinn, "The Employee-Customer-Profit Chain at Sears," *Harvard Business Review*, January–February 1998, 91.

3. Mark A. Huselid, Brian E. Becker, and Richard W. Beatty, *The Workforce Scorecard: Managing Human Capital to Execute Strategy* (Boston: Harvard Business School Press, 2005), 243.

4. Michael Lewis, *Moneyball* (New York: Norton, 2003), 57. See also M. A. Huselid and B. E. Becker, "Improving HR's Analytical Literacy: Lessons from *Moneyball*," in *The Future of HR: 50 Thought Leaders Call for Change*, eds. Dave Ulrich, Mike Losey, and Sue Meisinger (New York: John Wiley and Sons, 2005), 278–284.

5. Lewis, *Moneyball*, 56–57.

6. Ibid., 57.

7. Personal conversation with Mark Huselid, October 2006.

Chapter 7

1. At the beginning of this WWT project, the AHA had twelve affiliates plus the corporate center. During the process, these twelve affiliates were consolidated into eight.

2. Mark Huselid was the lead external consultant on the AHA WWT project, working closely with the management team from December 2005 through 2008. Members of the WWT included Bill Achenbach, senior vice president, human resources; John Brennan, executive vice president, Greater Southeast Affiliate; Nancy Brown, chief operating officer, National Center; Midge La Porte Epstein, executive vice president, South Central Affiliate; Meighan Girgus, executive vice president, Healthcare Markets; Sunder Joshi, executive vice president and CFO; David Markiewicz, executive vice president, Mid-Atlantic Affiliate; Gordon McCullough, chief operating officer, field operations; Sara Robertson, chief operating officer, business operations, Western States Affiliate; Suzie Upton, executive vice president, development; Michael Weamer, executive vice president, Founders Affiliate. Tim Bateman provided world-class project management and logistical support.

3. Bradford D. Smart, *Topgrading: How Leading Companies Win by Hiring, Coaching, and Keeping the Best People* (New York: Prentice Hall Press, 1999).

4. This work was performed by consultant Steve Kirn, who was subsequently involved in all phases of the WWT taskforce project.

5. M. A. Huselid and B. E. Becker, "An Interview with Mike Losey, Tony Rucci, and Dave Ulrich: Three Experts Respond to HRMJ's Special Issue in Five Leading Firms," *Human Resource Management* 38 (1999): 353–365.

6. Mark Huselid conducted this interview in Dallas on April 8, 2008.

INDEX

ABOUT THE AUTHORS

BRIAN E. BECKER is Professor of Human Resources and Senior Associate Dean in the School of Management at the State University of New York at Buffalo. Professor Becker has published widely on the financial effects of employment systems in both union and nonunion organizations. His current research and consulting interests focus on the relationship between human resources systems, strategy implementation, and firm performance. He is coauthor, along with Mark Huselid and Dave Ulrich, of *The HR Scorecard: Linking People, Strategy, and Performance* (Harvard Business Press, 2001) and, with Mark Huselid and Dick Beatty, of *The Workforce Scorecard: Managing Human Capital to Execute Strategy* (Harvard Business Press, 2005). Both *The HR Scorecard* and *The Workforce Scorecard* have been translated into more than ten languages and are international bestsellers.

MARK A. HUSELID is Professor of Human Resource Strategy in the School of Management and Labor Relations (SMLR) at Rutgers University. Professor Huselid has published and consulted widely on the linkages between workforce management and measurement systems, strategy execution, and firm performance. He was the editor of *Human Resource Management Journal* from 2000 to 2004 and is a current or former member of numerous editorial boards. He is coauthor, along with Brian Becker and Dave Ulrich, of *The HR Scorecard: Linking People, Strategy, and Performance* (Harvard Business Press, 2001) and, with Brian Becker and Dick Beatty, of *The Workforce Scorecard: Managing Human Capital to Execute Strategy* (Harvard Business Press, 2005). Both *The HR Scorecard* and *The Workforce Scorecard* have been translated into more than ten languages and are international bestsellers. Dr. Huselid is a frequent speaker to professional and academic audiences, having delivered more than five hundred presentations throughout the United

States, Europe, Asia, and Africa. He is among the most frequently cited scholars in the field of management.

RICHARD W. (DICK) BEATTY is Professor of Human Resource Management at Rutgers University and a member of the Core Faculty of the University of Michigan's Executive Education Center. Professor Beatty was an associate editor of *Human Resource Management Journal*, was president of the Society for Human Resource Management Foundation and a recipient of the Society's Book Award, and twice received the Research Award from the Human Resource Planning Society. His research interests are in human resource strategy and measuring all aspects of workforce performance.

He is the coauthor, with H. John Bernardin, of *Performance Appraisal: Assessing Human Behavior at Work* (Kent Publishing Company, 1984), and, with Craig E. Schneier, of *Personnel Administration: An Experiential Skill-Building Approach* (Addison-Wesley). Professor Beatty is also a coauthor, with Mark Huselid and Brian Becker, of *The Workforce Scorecard: Managing Human Capital to Execute Strategy* (Harvard Business Press, 2005).

Brian, Mark, and Dick can be reached at www.bhbassociates.com.

DATE DUE

#47-0108 Peel Off Pressure Sensitive